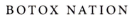

BOTOX NATION

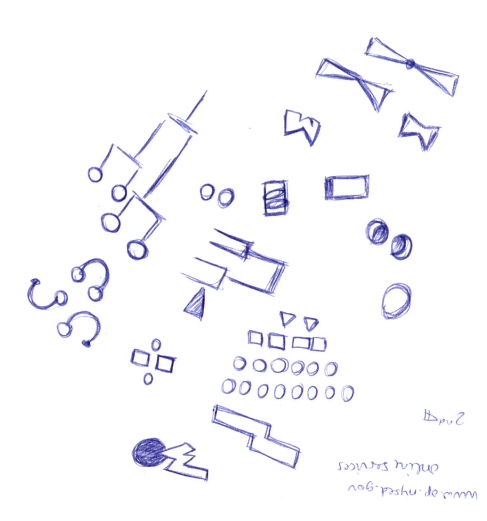

INTERSECTIONS

Transdisciplinary Perspectives on Genders and Sexualities

General Editors: Michael Kimmel and Suzanna Walters

Botox Nation

Changing the Face of America

Dana Berkowitz

NEW YORK UNIVERSITY PRESS

New York

NEW YORK UNIVERSITY PRESS
New York
www.nyupress.org

References to Internet websites (URLs) were accurate at the time of writing. Neither the author nor New York University Press is responsible for URLs that may have expired or changed since the manuscript was prepared.

Library of Congress Cataloging-in-Publication Data
Names: Berkowitz, Dana, author.
Title: Botox nation : changing the face of america / Dana Berkowitz.
Description: New York : New York University Press, [2017] | Includes bibliographical references and index.
Identifiers: LCCN 2016023915| ISBN 9781479847945 (cl : alk. paper) | ISBN 9781479825264 (pb : alk. paper)
Subjects: LCSH: Beauty, Personal. | Skin—Care and hygiene. | Botulinum toxin—Therapeutic use. | Surgery, Plastic—Social aspects.
Classification: LCC RL87 .B465 2017 | DDC 646.7/2—dc23
LC record available at https://lccn.loc.gov/2016023915

New York University Press books are printed on acid-free paper, and their binding materials are chosen for strength and durability. We strive to use environmentally responsible suppliers and materials to the greatest extent possible in publishing our books.

Manufactured in the United States of America

10 9 8 7 6 5 4 3 2 1

Also available as an ebook

CONTENTS

ACKNOWLEDGMENTS

A great many people have dedicated their time, energy, support, generosity, and advice to me during the five years I spent researching and writing this book. There would be no book without the generosity of my participants. I am profoundly grateful to the women and men who so generously shared their stories with me. To all of those people who willingly sacrificed their time to speak with me, I owe you an inordinate amount of gratitude. Thank you for trusting me to represent your views fairly and honestly.

All of the research and writing that went into this book took place while I was at Louisiana State University where the Department of Sociology and the Program for Women's Studies and Gender Research enthusiastically supported my work. Many of my colleagues at LSU read and commented on multiple drafts of this work, and countless others provided me thoughtful feedback and suggestions along the way. I am especially thankful to Justine Tinkler, Sarah Becker, Susan Dumais, Katherine Stamps-Mitchell, Benjamin Kahan, Debbie Goldgaber, Rachel Hall, Bryan McCann, and Ashley Mack.

I have been tremendously lucky to be mentored by excellent sociologists over the years. I am particularly grateful to Peter and Patti Adler, who adopted me as their student, friend, and surrogate niece. I am eternally thankful for their expertise, honesty, and patience and for their extensive constructive criticism, which nudged this book into new and exciting directions.

My sincere appreciation goes to Linda Belgrave, whose passion for critical scholarship made me the sociologist I am today. I am also especially indebted to William Marsiglio, who instilled in me his tireless work ethic and ethnographic curiosity, without which this book would not be possible. Linda and Bill, your fingerprints will always be found on anything I write. I am also grateful to Michael Kimmel for taking me under his wing and for always providing me insightful and candid wisdom.

So many others have helped me along the way, reading drafts of chapters, allowing me to bounce ideas off of them, and providing me thoughtful feedback at all stages of the game. For this I am grateful to Lisa Wade, D'Lane Compton, Danielle Dirks, Meggan Jordan, Emily Mann, and Patrick Grzanka. My research assistants were instrumental in helping me complete this project. Crystal Paul, you are an absolute gem. Your organizational skills and attention to detail are unparalleled. Thank you also to Leah Drakeford, Emily Blosser, Inga Kastrone, and Tasia Kazi.

My research was made possible by several different grants. The LSU College of Social Sciences and Humanities awarded me summer funding in 2011 and 2012 that provided me the monies to collect data for this project. The Louisiana State Board of Regents generously awarded me an Awards to Louisiana Artists and Scholars (ATLAS) Grant, which provided me a year off from teaching in 2015–2016 to finish writing this book.

Many thanks to Ilene Kalish, my editor at NYU Press, who was excited about this project from the beginning and who never gave up on me or this book. I am also grateful to her assistant editor, Caelyn Cobb, and the series editors, Michael Kimmel (yet again) and Suzanna Walters. I also thank the anonymous peer reviewers for NYUP who gave me valuable feedback on earlier drafts of this book.

Personal life feeds intellectual life, and I am indebted to my friends and family for the various ways they have supported me personally and emotionally. A close group of old friends deserves my deepest gratitude: Rena, Gina, Nikki, and Jordana, I am so lucky to have had over twenty years of friendship with such powerful and fearless women. My sister Daryl has been my sidekick since birth, and I am so lucky to have her. I am grateful to my parents for their help and encouragement and for their steadfast support of my work. Mom, I owe a special debt to you for having me interview homeless families for my social studies project in sixth grade, an experience that I am certain was responsible for planting the seeds of the budding ethnographer and sociologist in me. Finally, to Casey, who is unwavering in his support of me: Thank you for making my personal life so fulfilling and for always telling me I am beautiful with or without Botox.

Introduction

We have seen the face of the future and it is wrinkle-free.
—Kendall Hamilton and Julie Weingarden[1]

The holiday season in Miami Beach is always a lively and bustling occasion—while the rest of the country is covered in snow and enduring blizzard-like conditions, Miami is a temperate 70 degrees. During my early postcollege years, every late December all of my high school girlfriends and myself, regardless of where we were living at the time, would make our annual return home to Miami to visit our families, reconnect with old friends, and enjoy a subtropical time-out from our busy work (or in my case, graduate school) schedules. On one such balmy Miami winter night in 2006, a large group of us reunited at a casual holiday cocktail party. In the midst of catching up over some cocktails and light party snacks, Mara Siffman,[2] an old friend, who at that time was enjoying a blossoming career as a fine art dealer and had just relocated with her husband from their posh apartment in the West Village to a high rise in South Beach, pulled three of us aside. Once she was out of earshot of the other partygoers, she exclaimed, "Guess what I did today?" When the three of us ran out of guesses, she screeched, "I got Botox!" We were flabbergasted. We all seemed to share the same sentiment—Botox? But we were only twenty-eight. That was supposed to be something older women did. Shocked that we knew someone (and, at our age, no less), who had tried Botox, the three of us began to bombard her with questions: What does it feel like? How much was it? Where did you go? With whom did you go? And, Why in the world would you get Botox at twenty-eight?

Feverishly recounting her morning, Mara told us how a new girlfriend she had recently become acquainted with told her about a special offer that her dermatologist was having. The two of them went together, and it cost them each three hundred dollars. She described how, after the dermatologist told her to scrunch her forehead a few times, she injected her with a needle at three different points on her forehead. With each shot, she felt a pinching sensation between her eyebrows for just a few short seconds. And then, Mara brazenly declared, "You should all do it, too. If you start doing it now, before the wrinkles in your forehead even form, you will never get that ugly line between your eyebrows." Now I was even more dumbfounded. Did my friend just tell me that I was supposed to begin using Botox before I even had any perceptible creases on my brow? I wasn't even thirty yet! Armed with a concoction of contempt, outrage, perplexity, and curiosity, I returned home that night to my childhood bedroom wondering whether my friend was being ludicrous, inordinately vain—or forward-thinking and on to something.

To a growing number of young women, Botox is seen as a type of insurance against future facial wrinkles, a preemptive strike that might guarantee that they won't develop deep crevices in their face in the future. To many others, it is akin to a fountain of youth—just a few pricks in their brow, and in less than a week, their face would be returned to a younger-looking self, untouched and unfurrowed by the responsibilities and anxieties of adulthood. For the majority of Americans, Botox stirs up images of vanity-obsessed, narcissistic women, and for some critics, it symbolizes everything that is wrong with our oppressive contemporary beauty culture.

Regardless of how we might each think and feel about Botox, known by the brand name Botox Cosmetic (drug name onabotulinumtoxinA), the fact is that it has forever transformed the primordial battleground against aging. A cultural force, Botox has been celebrated as "the miracle drug for Boomers"[3] and "youth in a syringe."[4] Praised for its reliability, relative affordability, and convenience, Botox promises a quick fix, with no surgery or downtime, and can even be "administered over a lunch break."[5] Since the early 2000s, we have witnessed unprecedented numbers of users paying big money to inject the drug into their facial muscles and paralyze their wrinkles into smoothness and invisibility.

Botox is marketed as appealing to the American Everywoman, not just the economically prosperous and the socially ambitious. Even though a small proportion of the population in relative terms currently uses Botox, its cultural significance is widespread. These days Botox is so firmly entrenched in our cultural consciousness it has become common vernacular. It is even used as an adjective, as in "she's so Botoxed."[6]

According to the product's website, eleven million women and men have experienced "the proven results of Botox."[7] In 2014 alone, the American Society for Aesthetic Plastic Surgery estimated that there were over six million Botox procedures.[8] The simplicity and popularity of Botox has sparked a wave of in-home Botox parties, where a doctor (or other certified injector) performs the procedure on a dozen or so eager patients, sometimes over a cheese platter and a few bottles of Chardonnay. Medical spas are sprouting up in strip malls across the nation, from Manhattan to Miami, Orange County to Omaha, selling Americans Botox injections in a nonclinical spa-like setting. Daily-deals websites like Groupon regularly e-mail subscribers bargain deals on Botox injections. Allergan, the pharmaceutical company that manufactures Botox, recently launched "Brilliant Distinctions," a new program (complete with its own app) that works like a punch card that consumers can use to earn savings on Botox and other select Allergan treatments and products every time they make a purchase.

Considered the preeminent remedy for expression lines on the upper part of the face, Botox is widely marketed as a quick, easy, safe, and reliable way to temporarily improve the look of moderate to severe frown lines. Even before the U.S. Food and Drug Administration (FDA) approved it for cosmetic use in 2002, Botox was known among Hollywood celebrities and New York City's Upper East Siders as the anti-aging wonder drug. In fact, without any marketing whatsoever, Botox became the most popular cosmetic medical procedure in the country, with more than one million people using it in 2000.[9] Since then, Botox use has increased almost 750 percent between 2000 and 2014, making it the most widely used cosmetic procedure to date.[10]

Here's how Botox application works: In a typical cosmetic treatment, a licensed provider injects an extremely diluted form of the drug into a user's facial muscles. Results are not immediate, as many believe. In fact, it is a myth that Botox provides instant gratification. Rather, over the next three to ten days, the toxin (more on that, later) paralyzes the muscles that control facial movement, smoothing individuals' dynamic wrinkles (also known as their expression lines). Because the treatment is so diluted, there is no significant risk of becoming infected with botulism (this is actually quite important, given that botulism can cause respiratory failure and even death in severe cases).[11] Over these next few days, people experience a change in their ability to make certain expressions, specifically in their ability to scowl or furrow their brow.

The rising popularity of Botox Cosmetic's use is due in part to the fact that it is a cash cow for physicians and other licensed injectors. Because it is billed as a cosmetic procedure, there are no health insurance costs with which to deal. A vial can cost a licensed provider approximately $500, and that single vial can potentially generate revenue of up to $3,000.[12] Botox is extremely time efficient, with each procedure taking approximately fifteen minutes. There are very few other medical-cosmetic procedures that are as profitable as Botox.

Botox is widely marketed to middle-aged women "whose faces tend to be more animated than men's, and whose skin is typically more delicate" causing the wrinkles and crinkles that result from expression to appear exaggerated and more permanent.[13] Because women make up the vast majority of Botox users, in this book I pay particular attention the experiences of women Botox users and the marketing of Botox to women. In 2014 approximately 94 percent of all Botox users were women, and almost 60 percent of these procedures were performed on women between the ages of forty and fifty-four.[14] What sets Botox apart from other anti-aging interventions is that Allergan seduces its young consumer base with claims that Botox does not simply eradicate wrinkles but can actually prevent them from forming by forbidding the face to muster wrinkle-producing scowls. Consequently, it is not only middle-aged women who are using Botox but also women in their thirties and even their twenties who are also taking the plunge. In 2014 close to 1.2 million Botox procedures were performed on people aged nineteen to thirty-nine, constituting about 20 percent of the total.[15]

In this book I examine the growing trend of women in their twenties and thirties who use Botox as a means to prevent and thwart the appearance of aging. It is this growing trend that distinguishes Botox from every other cosmetic intervention in the anti-aging armamentarium. Unique from the plethora of cosmetic nonsurgical procedures on the market, Botox is passed off as a medical procedure with curative and preventive powers. Because of Botox's ability to paralyze facial muscles and prohibit facial movement, proponents of the drug argue that regular injections can stop the appearance of dynamic wrinkles from forming, in that no facial movement ultimately means no facial wrinkles. Thus small but notable growing populations of young women are using Botox prophylactically in the hopes that they won't develop future facial creases.

In her book, *Beauty Junkies: Inside Our $15 Million Obsession with Cosmetic Surgery*, the *New York Times* "Style" section contributor Alex Kuczynski wrote that, as the magic wrinkle eraser grows increasingly popular with aging baby boomers and their daughters, the rise of a Botoxed nation means that "we are fast becoming a culture where we look at wrinkles as a remnant of the unhealthy, imperfect past, something to be fixed, like a broken tooth or bad vision, something that can be addressed in one office visit."[16] But herein lies the dilemma: Botox's ability to freeze the youthful face is ephemeral, since it only lasts four to six months. So, because Botox injections are temporary, they only really prevent wrinkles if one continues to get injections every two to three times a year. That Botox needs to be continually topped off to maintain a wrinkle-free ageless appearance means that we are seeing a growing population of relatively young women potentially enlisting in a lifetime of Botox maintenance.[17]

For these reasons I argue that Botox is changing the face of America. Slightly over a decade after its debut, the impact of Botox on American society is evident—not just on people's faces, in the media, and in the massive advertising and marketing campaigns but also in the ways it runs through our cultural commentary. In a literal sense, Botox is changing the face of America in its reduction and erasure of forehead wrinkles among a growing percentage of the population. In a more metaphorical sense, Botox is changing the face of America in the way that it has transformed people's expectations about aging faces, especially about women's aging faces.

A Sociological Approach

The recent proliferation of Botox procedures and the rise of numbers of relatively young women injecting the drug pose multiple sociological questions about the medicalization of aging and the incessant marketing of youth. In the pages that follow, I show how a sociological analysis of Botox can tell us a great deal about cultural norms related to aging, gender, embodiment, and medical consumerism. I take up the increased popularity of Botox as a case study that provides a unique glimpse into American culture and reveals some potentially troubling social truths about the society in which we live. Botox can have multiple, sometimes competing meanings: It can be an anti-aging wonder drug, the fountain of youth in a syringe, a fleshly symbol of patriarchal oppression, a routinized component of body maintenance, or a financially lucrative biomedical technology.

The cultural explosion of Botox use is a result of large constellations of people and institutions acting within social, cultural, and historical shifts. In *Botox Nation: Changing the Face of America*, I focus on the people who construct and perpetuate both the demands and anxieties for Botox—those at Allergan Pharmaceuticals, dermatologists, plastic surgeons, medical spa entrepreneurs, journalists, and other participants in the beauty and anti-aging industries. I also explore how individual Botox users make decisions about Botox and how they make sense of their Botoxed bodies. By investigating how different individuals and groups construct, manipulate, and invest Botox with multiple meanings,

I examine how social norms about gender, aging, bodies, and medicine are constructed, negotiated, and reproduced on institutional, cultural, and individual levels.

Whenever I tell someone that I am writing a book about Botox, inevitably the first question they ask me is, "So are you for it or against it?" Before you read on, let me be clear, my intent is not to examine whether Botox as a technology is good or bad. Rather, in the pages that follow, I interrogate how Botox makes visible the ways that cultural norms and social inequalities are mapped onto bodies, how gender is significant in the production of bodies, and how bodies become the object and subject of consumption.

Bodies, Selves, and Society

In this book, I want to think about what sociological theories can offer to our understanding of Botox. First and foremost, a sociological analysis of Botox makes visible questions of embodied selves and identities, specifically how contemporary selves and identities are constructed in and through the body. Scholars from varying disciplines disagree about whether to view the body as a subject or an object—where some see the body as an object regulated by social and cultural norms, others conceptualize the body as an active subject, one that is purposeful, reflexive, and negotiated. In my analysis of Botox, I resolve this subject/object tension and employ the plurality of a both/and approach to understanding bodies. Drawing on symbolic interactionism, a sociological theory that focuses on meaning making and social interactions, I emphasize how the body is a subject that individuals experience, create, and negotiate. Seeing bodies as subjects illuminates the extent to which people do not merely have bodies but, rather, *do* bodies. Bodies are always being performed, and "the theatre of the body are the raw materials by which the drama of our everyday embodied life are produced."[18] Focusing on the reflexivity of selves and bodies, symbolic interactionism accentuates the processes by which humans cultivate their bodies in ways that meaningfully construct and demonstrate their selves and social identities. Such a lens is also useful for understanding ways that social relationships shape bodies and how imagined appraisals reflect onto the self and body in an interpretive process.

However, larger structural forces and social discourses also influence our decisions about how we modify, shape, and present our bodies. Thus, in addition to a symbolic interactionist approach, I integrate structural and critical sociological theories to consider how bodies are produced, regulated, and disciplined by power relations. Throughout this book, I interrogate the ways that social institutions such as medicine, the pharmaceutical lobby, and the beauty industry discipline and govern human bodies. Related to that, I consider how cultural discourses such as biomedicine, neoliberalism, and postfeminism operate pedagogically, that is, how they teach us how to talk about our bodies and our experiences of embodiment.

Biomedicalization, Neoliberalism, and Consumer Bodies

Biomedicalization is one process by which the body as an object is actively constructed, experienced, and transformed into a subjective body. "Medicalization," a term first used by sociologists in the 1970s, was introduced to describe the expansion of medical authority into a wide range of areas not previously under its jurisdiction.[19] In light of the collectivity of technoscientific interventions in our postmodern global world, the medical sociologist Adele Clarke and her colleagues have argued that the term "biomedicalization" more aptly captures the new and complicated ways that medicalization is intensifying and is "ubiquitously webbed throughout mass culture."[20] Emphasizing the "increasingly complex, multisited, multidirectional processes of medicalization," the concept of biomedicalization allows sociologists to push medicalization around the postmodern turn.[21] In other words, the focus is on thinking about how humans can remake and reconstitute their bodies and the extent to which the transformation of bodies and selves and the production of new bodily properties and identities are central to our contemporary era. For example, being able to walk with prosthetic limbs, hear with cochlear ear implants, see with laser eye surgery, and appear wrinkle-free with Botox injections are just some of the many biomedically engineered bodily transformations currently available to humans.

Where once medicine only had jurisdiction over sick, diseased, and injured bodies, now medical authority is extended over healthy bodies. Perhaps the biggest paradigmatic shift with biomedicalization is the commodification of health and healthy bodies. As Clarke and colleagues have noted, in our current era, health has become a "commodity and the biomedically (re)engineered body" has become a sought-after possession.[22] The consumer quest for healthy, young, and attractive bodies is accompanied by another trend, known as "lifestyle medicine." Lifestyle medicine now regularly corrects, cultivates, and improves healthy bodies. Lifestyle drugs engineered to treat the visible signs of aging, such as Viagra, human growth hormone, and Botox epitomize the desire for bodily enhancement.[23]

We now have a highly lucrative industry dedicated solely to the treatment and renovation of aging bodies—an industry opportunely dubbed "the anti-aging industry." A multibillion-dollar enterprise, the anti-aging industry is a commercial and clinical industry that designs and markets products to stall, prevent, or reverse aging. Redefining aging as a target for biomedical intervention, the anti-aging industry reflects a shift from seeing aging as a natural and normal process to a process that should be remedied by all means possible. Highly profitable and growing at an astronomical rate, the anti-aging industry's 2015 earnings, as estimated by the American Academy of Anti-Aging Medicine, were approximately $291 billion.[24]

Anti-aging medicine is one of the many biomedical changes that expand health care from sick bodies to aging but otherwise healthy bodies. Anti-aging is part of a widespread shift toward "cosmetic wellness," a strand of lifestyle medicine that shifts the medical gaze from the health of the inner body to that of the external aesthetic body.[25] Because we assume that our health is written on our bodies and that looking old means looking sick, it is the appearance of being young, rather than the actual reality of being young, that matters. To look old is morally, physically, and aesthetically lacking. Aging bodies are constructed as ugly bodies and as the product of poor and irresponsible consumption. However, it is vital to keep in mind that appearances often tell us very little about actual health, or as the sociologist Toni Calasanti aptly noted, "Wrinkles tell us nothing of one's heart function."[26] Moreover, while health and youth are correlated with attractiveness, our cultural preoccupation with beauty often comes at the expense of minding our actual health status. For example, many extreme body projects—such as strict calorie restriction, excessive exercise, and cosmetic surgery—can potentially harm our bodies in more ways than help them. Yet we do them anyway because we assume that our outward appearance reflects our internal health and because of the exceedingly high value we place on appearance and others' perceptions of us.

Although the human desire to beat the clock is not a recent phenomenon,[27] the rise of anti-aging consumer culture has profoundly magnified and intensified the moral imperative to fight aging. Aggressive phrases like "fighting aging" the "battleground of aging" and the "war against aging" are pervasive in anti-aging discourses. As the Canadian sociologist Laura Hurd Clarke pointed out, the very idea that we should be against growing old is a taken-for-granted assumption and that "we are rather proudly and openly hostile toward, or 'anti' aging."[28] The underlying messages in anti-aging advertisements is that youthfulness is a commodity that is not restricted by one's actual chronological age and now, with scientific advances, everyone has the tools to halt, reverse, and stall the aging process. Reigning discourses construct aging as a deviant and diseased physical state, projecting the idea that individuals have a moral responsibility to participate in the battle against (the appearance of) aging. The message is not that one can control aging but that one must control aging; we can and should do everything in our power to resist looking old.

This singular focus on personal responsibility within anti-aging discourses promotes neoliberal ideologies of individualism and autonomy.

No longer confined solely to the political economic sphere, neoliberal principles of individualism, consumerism, and free-market competition now penetrate the ways we interpret and interact with the noneconomic world.[29] The neoliberal panacea of autonomy and free choice encourages subjects to take control over their health, wellness, and appearance through responsible and conspicuous consumption. Held accountable for their own individual fate, neoliberal citizens are responsible for their own self-care and structurally accorded the responsibility for the governance of their own bodies. Obligated for making their own conscientious "lifestyle" choices and for managing the risks associated with these choices, "neoliberalism calls upon the individual to enter into the process of his or her own self-governance through processes of endless self-examination, self-care, and self-improvement."[30]

In our postindustrial economy, contemporary Western identities and bodies cannot be separated from consumer culture. So much of what modern citizens know about their selves these days, they know through daily visits to the marketplace.[31] In consumer culture, the self is circuitously bound up with the body. The human body is the ultimate medium between consumption and identity and is conceivably our most precious commodity.[32] Just as with biomedicine, "consumer culture is constructed out of the interplay between disciplined/objectified bodies and governed/subjective bodies."[33] Some scholars, like the British sociologist Anthony Giddens, believe that consumer culture contributes to an increasing awareness that our bodies, selves, and identities are chosen and constructed.[34] For Giddens, the self in late modernity is a reflexive project that is created and re-created through a variety of consumer choices and lifestyle decisions. Suggesting that the decline of religious and political authority means that people are no longer provided with a clear worldview from which to construct their sense of self, Giddens argues that, in the era of late modernity in which we live, humans place more importance on the body as constitutive of the self. The body has emerged as the foundational material for constructing a reliable sense of self, and in our current age of increasing political and economic uncertainty, the body becomes one of the few things we can control and use to express our identities.

Whereas bodies have always been used to express social and cultural meanings, consumer capitalism speeds up the ways people can reinvent their bodies, augmenting the body's role in identity production. The production of the self is now wrapped up in the continual transformation of the body, and investing in bodies provides people a means of self-expression and a way of increasing the control they have over their bodies and their selves.[35] Projects to be worked on as part of an individual's identity, bodies are now "malleable entities, which can be shaped and honed by the vigilance and hard work of their owners."[36]

Giddens calls attention to the ways by which modernity fuels the project of the self and body "under conditions strongly influenced by standardizing effects of commodity capitalism."[37] Bodies are part of an endless process of marketplace definition, and consumerism puts acute pressure on individuals to transform and improve every aspect of their bodies and selves. In consumer culture nothing satisfies our desires to be better, healthier, and more attractive. The success of the marketplace depends on inducing sufferings of personal inadequacy that create a culture of lack, rendering consumer behavior and consumer bodies essential to their continuation.

It is vital to mention that the ubiquity of biomedicalization and consumption in the production of twenty-first-century bodies and selves means that the bodies we inhabit, as well as those that we see and appraise and with whom we interact, are never wholly natural but, rather, are the cumulative effect of a lifetime of purchases, cultural norms, and social practices. Although a lingering debate about the reality of a natural body still persists among some scholars, most feminist and postmodern theorists deny any existence of a natural body unmarked by collective norms, cultural discourses, and other social pressures external to them.[38] In the tradition of these scholars, I argue that any idea of a natural body is illusory and, even more, that the very concept of nature itself is temporal, shifting, and socially constructed by biomedical discourses and consumer practices. We live in a reality of prosthetics, pacemakers, and cosmetic surgery that exposes the fictitious distinction between nature and culture. However, it is vital to keep in mind the extent to which technology is always embedded in power relations and the ways in which bodies and selves are always subject to gender, race, class, and a host of other inequalities.

A Gendered Lens

Perhaps no subject matter in body scholarship has been as thoroughly considered as gender. To say that a body is gendered refers to the ways that hierarchical norms and ideals of masculinity and femininity are written on and performed by bodies. Because bodies are gendered, or encouraged to participate in gender conformity, the bodies that we see and interact with on an everyday basis are not natural or innate but, rather, are a product of a lifetime of gendered practices, relations, and ideologies. The dominant image of a feminine body is a youthful, thin, toned frame with flawless wrinkle-free skin. Unattainable and elusive, the feminine beauty ideal is such that very few women can meet these norms, and no woman can do so across her life span. However, despite breaking through unprecedented legal, political, and cultural obstacles, women's beauty and their bodies continue to be presented as their most important possessions, and women are afforded more social and economic value the closer they come to attaining this elusive beauty ideal.

Gaining weight and aging are perhaps the most dangerous enemies of the beauty ideal. Whereas many women can exercise and diet to prevent gaining weight, aging is inevitable and is thus the most restrictive aspect of the ever-tenuous beauty ideal. The visible signs of aging, like sagging skin, wrinkles, and graying hair, can pose a profound threat to women's sense of self, identity, and heterosexual desirability and are significantly more problematic for women than for men, and at considerably younger ages. The experience of aging is thus an explicitly gendered phenomenon, and the ways that bodies and faces are marked and experienced as old occur within a larger system of gender inequality in which aging female bodies are increasingly devalued. In the early 1970s, the feminist cultural critic Susan Sontag used the phrase "the double standard of aging" to describe the long-standing adage that women get old and men get distinguished. In a poignant essay, Sontag wrote that "one of the attitudes that punish women most severely is the visceral horror felt at aging female flesh . . . that old women are repulsive is one of the most profound esthetic and erotic feelings in our culture."[39] We have a narrow and elusive standard of beauty that marginalizes and excludes older women, and women are shamed when their aging bodies and faces no longer display qualities of youthfulness and sexual attractiveness. In our culture, older women become irrelevant and invisible.[40] Even more, since what we perceive to be feminine and beautiful is an unlined, smooth, soft, and fair face, and since there are actually only a few short years in their early twenties when this look is physiologically natural, a woman hardly has to be anything that would be considered old to start agonizing about her age. Describing aging as a "movable doom," Sontag bemoaned that women are old "as soon as they are no longer very young,"[41] and even women in their early thirties can feel like they are racing against the calendar.

A wide range of scholarly research has confirmed that the double standard of aging produces meaningful social inequalities that profoundly contribute to women's cultural and economic inequality. Media images of aging men are far more diverse and prominent than those of aging women. Older women are significantly underrepresented in and negatively portrayed by popular culture—both in films and in television commercials.[42] In our culture, because men are more visually diverse they are privy to a sense of security in their aging bodies that women do not have. Similarly, a celebrity woman's worth and talent is measured by her attractiveness in a way that a man's is not. Female celebrity status is often concentrated on the body, and the figure of the aging woman celebrity is a heavily contested site. Madonna recently underwent scrutiny from *New York* magazine as critics speculated on her use of dermal fillers, eyebrow lifts, and facial reconstruction.[43] A 2014 *Daily Mail* article about Renée Zellweger declared her "unrecognisable with her super line-free forehead, altered brow and suspiciously puffy face."[44] Yet aging does little to impair the careers of male film stars like George Clooney or Robert Redford, and Mick Jagger is commended for strutting onstage before sold-out arenas with a tattered, leathery face.

Moreover, employment-based ageism disadvantages women more so than men, and women are more likely to cite appearance-based age discrimination in the workplace.[45] Women achieve peak earnings at a younger age than men, resulting in economic disadvantage over their life course.[46] Employers frequently perceive women as being older than their same-aged male counterparts.[47] Because of the penalties that ensue with the visible signs of aging, women are encouraged to engage in various kinds of beauty work in order to look younger and more attractive.

From makeup and hair dye to cosmetic surgery, the gamut of products and services available to women is endless. While gray hair can be easily concealed with hair dye and body fat can be strategically camouflaged with clothing, facial wrinkles have long been a physical marker of aging that is challenging, if not impossible, to hide—that is, until now. Until recently, a face-lift was the only option available to individuals who wanted to rid their faces of creases. But now, with the development of nonsurgical interventions like Botox, we have an abundance of products designed to "fix" facial wrinkles. An issue of cultural wattage, Botox plays on the sociocultural need for women's bodies and faces to remain young, thin, and beautiful and is one of countless feminized practices marketed to women with the goal of appropriately and effectively doing femininity.

Feminist Frameworks

Feminist scholars have made substantial contributions to debates about bodies and gender, particularly in trying to make sense of women's participation in beauty culture. The problem of cosmetic surgery, with its severe and extreme bodily transformation, has been at the forefront of this conversation. Intellectually rich and theoretically complex, the body of feminist scholarship on the subject of cosmetic surgery has long tried to understand what motivates women to have a cosmetic procedure and how this decision is informed by a larger social structural context pervaded by gender inequality.[48]

Historically, much of this scholarship was characterized by disputes about whether cosmetic surgery was oppressive or empowering, and there has been considerable debate among feminist scholars around questions of how we should theorize and research cosmetic surgery. Consistent with the feminist tradition of "giving voice" to women's experiences,[49] the approach that dominated much of the earliest scholarship was marked by an interest in understanding the reasons women gave for their cosmetic surgeries and their experiences within cosmetic surgical culture. Centered heavily on questions of women's subjectivity, this body of scholarship has been critiqued for constructing a theoretical debate that positioned the surgical patient as either a victim of internalized oppression or as an active and rational agent. On the one hand, some feminist critics saw women's participation in cosmetic surgery as an attempt to achieve impossible standards of beauty produced within a capitalist, heteropatriarchal, and ageist society and characterized it as an exclusively repressive regime.[50] On the other hand, a separate camp of scholars argued that women were hardly "cultural dupes" and saw women's decision to undergo cosmetic surgery as an opportunity to increase their social and embodied currency in their own terms—albeit in a patriarchal and ageist culture.[51]

Critics of the victim-agent debate argued that these "voice-centered" projects prioritizing individuals' surgical stories obscured "how gendered sociocultural and sociopolitical contexts shaped the choices women make, and the kinds of stories women can tell about these choices."[52] For example, the feminist cultural critic Susan Bordo calls for conceptualizing women's decisions about cosmetic surgery beyond the binary of self-determination or self-deception. Specifically, Bordo challenges feminist discourses about agency for creating "a diversionary din that drowns out the orchestra that is always playing in the background, the consumer culture we live in and need to take responsibility for. More than an individual choice, cosmetic surgery is a burgeoning industry and an increasingly normative cultural practice."[53]

Whereas the victim-agent debate is based on Marxist understandings of power, in which power is held by only one person or group at a time, I am more interested in using a feminist poststructuralist lens that redefines power in terms of Foucault's more dynamic and mutually constitutive view. Feminist theorists influenced by Foucault have been instrumental in complicating the victim-agent debate by revealing how power is not something that acts on subjects through domination or force; rather, power is enacted through subjects, producing explicitly gendered selves, identities, and bodies.[54] For example, accentuating how power is not "overbearing and obvious,"[55] the British feminist cultural theorist Rosalind Gill argues that women do not make decisions about their body modification because of the power of an external patriarchal gaze. Rather, women's choices about whether and how to cultivate their bodies are shaped by socially constructed, mass-mediated ideals of beauty that are internalized and made their own. Thus women make decisions about body modification through conscious self-surveillance and assessments about how to increase their power and status. Recent research on women cosmetic surgery subjects revealed how they were competent actors who carefully thought about "how to position themselves in relation to social and cultural imperatives and opportunities."[56] Thus, when viewed through this lens, cosmetic surgery recipients have agency, but this agency is constituted within circumstances in which pharmaceutical and medical experts and fashion and beauty authorities dictate and interpret what is acceptable and appropriate body modification.

In this book I interrogate women's agency around cosmetic enhancements against a cultural and medical backdrop in which the vast and far-reaching tentacles of the cosmetic surgical industry affect everyone, not only those who choose to go under the knife, needle, or laser. I conceptualize women's agency as a fluid and shifting construct, produced through machineries of knowledge that create the very possibilities for the production of selves and subjects.[57] I am influenced heavily by the work of the sociologist Victoria Pitts-Taylor, who draws upon interviews with surgeons and psychiatrists; analysis of newspaper articles, legal documents, television shows; and ultimately her own experience having a nose job to show how the agency of cosmetic surgical subjects was shaped in and through their engagement with social and medical discourses and through "the process of becoming and being a cosmetic surgery patient."[58] I am similarly influenced by Suzanne Fraser, who, in an analysis of cultural, medical, and feminist texts about cosmetic surgery, suggests that it is theoretically productive to think about women's agency as emerging through their encounters with cultural repertoires and material phenomena.[59]

In this book, I consider how women's agency is constructed throughout the process of objectification and the ways that women can experience subjecthood and pleasure while concomitantly encountering bodily objectification. In a society that encourages women to derive their worth from their physical appeal, pursuing and achieving beauty will feel pleasurable because successfully packaging oneself as an appealing commodity is socially rewarded. For many women, their participation in beauty culture makes them temporarily satisfied with their ability to fulfill a patriarchal projection of an attractive, desired, and worthwhile subject. In the pages that follow I do not seek to challenge the notion that some women feel their quality of life has been improved by using Botox; rather, I want to consider the structures that encourage women to use Botox and other cosmetic procedures in the pursuit of achieving physical perfection.

I also want to think about why participating in an oppressive beauty culture makes so many women feel good about themselves. In addition to internalizing patriarchal and capitalist ideals of beauty, many women are now convinced that conforming to these standards can be a pleasurable and autonomous act. A primary reason for this is that young women are coming of age in a distinctive culture that scholars have referred to as "postfeminist." A "messy suturing" of feminist and antifeminist ideas, postfeminism projects the impression that the goals of feminism have been attained and activism around gender is no longer needed.[60] Predi-cated on the belief that feminism has accomplished its goals of ameliorat-ing structural gender inequality, contemporary postfeminist discourses emphasize women's individual empowerment and agency. Within our contemporary postfeminist era, women's empowerment is complicated and paradoxical, in that women can embrace their liberated status as long as it is not at the expense of their feminine appearance. In fact, one of the most conspicuous components of postfeminist culture is its obsession with the feminine body and the extensive surveillance of women's bodies by the media, by men, and by women themselves. Though women have gained access to occupational fields from which they were once excluded, their bodies continue to be routinely disciplined and policed. Opportuni-ties for women to enter and to thrive in the male-dominated workforce have not been matched by a corresponding freedom to eschew the ex-pensive, demanding, and time-consuming requirements of hegemonic femininity. Thus women's social power still too often resides within their beauty and their bodies. To put it bluntly, in our postfeminist era, being hot is what women's liberation looks like.

Moreover, contemporary culture places intense scrutiny on more and more areas of women's bodies—from their bikini lines to their brow creases. It seems that no part of the feminine body is safe from the beauty industrial complex—we now have cosmetic surgery for women's necks, hands, and feet, and practices like "vaginal rejuvenation" surgery, anal bleaching, and vulva color "correction" are becoming more and more popular. Moreover, these beauty practices that once were a target of second-wave feminism and were criticized for alienating women from their bodies have been reconfigured in the postfeminist era as pleasur-able and as ways of expressing feminine selves.

Recent feminist research has demonstrated that women articulate their participation in beauty culture within postfeminist discourses of choice and empowerment.[61] For example, in an analysis of the reality television program *Extreme Makeover*, Cressida Heyes showed how con-temporary discourses about cosmetic surgery projected fantasies of self-transformation consistent with feminist ideals of agency and autonomy.[62] Used by women to position themselves as unaffected by social regulation, discourses of choice and autonomy allow women to attribute their actions to their own desires, obscuring the social structural influences of gender inequality. What is more, these discourses have a constitutive function, in that they allow women to uphold a view of themselves as autonomous and self-governing agents. Feminist critics have noted that when a woman's actions are considered a result of her own choosing, no further problematization or critical analyses of these choices is warranted.[63] To utterly discount the influence that decades of marketing, media, and cultural messages play on the consciousness of someone who simply feels happier with tighter abs, a wrinkle-free face, and bigger, perkier breasts wrongly presumes that women are able to make choices free from hegemonic beauty norms, gendered constraints, and institutionalized inequality.

Intersections of Gender, Race, Class, and Sexuality

Women's relationships with their bodies and their participation in consumer beauty culture is shaped not only by their gendered identities but also by other intersecting identities, such as race, social class, and sexuality. Research has revealed that racial and ethnic groups hold different beauty ideals. Some scholars have argued that African American women have historically fallen outside of Eurocentric beauty norms and that race is a protective factor against female body satisfaction. However, other scholars have documented that women across race categories are just as vulnerable to body dissatisfaction and engage in similar self-monitoring of their bodies.[64] Studies looking at the experiences of Latinas have produced inconsistent results. Some indicate that Latinas report lower rates of body dissatisfaction than White women, whereas a number of others have suggested no differences. Recent research has found that Latina and African American women are less likely to engage in social comparisons with White thin media images because they do not see themselves reflected in such images. However, when they do engage in these comparisons they are just as vulnerable to negative body image as their White counterparts. The research on Asian women has also produced inconsistent results. Some studies suggested that Asian women have more positive body images than Latina, White, and African American women, whereas other studies found that Asian women endorsed mainstream beauty standards in a similar fashion to White women and experienced greater dissatisfaction with their bodies than did Black women.[65]

Research also indicates that the beauty ideals to which women subscribe and the resulting beauty work that follows is deeply associated with social class. This is because beauty work is about appropriating and communicating social status by cultivating the body in a particular way. For example, women of higher socioeconomic status have been found to be more dissatisfied or concerned about their physical appearance than those in lower social strata, and those with high levels of education are more likely to report dissatisfaction with their bodies.[66] In one study, researchers found that working-class older women saw economic hardship as more of a pressing concern than attractiveness and thus placed less emphasis on appearance than their upper-class counterparts.[67] Although poor people look older earlier than their wealthier counterparts, anxiety and fear about aging is more common among middle-class and rich women. Those who lack the financial wherewithal to purchase cosmetic enhancements are more hopeless (and perhaps more realistic) about aging, as they cannot afford the expensive anti-aging regimes of the wealthy. The irony is that the women who keep their youthful appearance the longest—those who lead the most unstrenuous lives, privileged by balanced organic diets, expensive gym memberships, and regular dermatological and spa appointments on their smart-phone calendars—are the women who feel the defeat of age most severely.

With respect to sexual orientation, the research is divided as to how sexual orientation and identity influence women's body image and perceptions of their aging bodies. Some researchers have found that lesbians are more satisfied with their bodies than are heterosexuals because they are buffered from those standards of beauty perpetuated by heterosexual dating norms;

other studies have found that body image perceptions are similar across sexual orientation lines.[68] However, with respect to men, research has found that gay men have higher rates of body dysmorphia, eating disorders, and cosmetic surgeries than do their heterosexual male counterparts.[69]

Looking at men's experiences with cosmetic surgery and enhancements adds complexity to existing feminist analyses because it disrupts established approaches that foreground patriarchal culture as the determining reason for participation in beauty culture.[70] Although men constitute a very small number of cosmetic surgery and enhancement consumers, the number of men seeking Botox and other aesthetic procedures is on the rise. Integrating men's embodied experiences creates new spaces for questioning the epistemological basis of the structure-agency dualism since such overgeneralized conceptualizations of patriarchal oppression must be discounted. The small but growing numbers of men having cosmetic procedures reveals the "objectifying propensities of consumer culture for all bodies" and the ways that men's bodies are increasingly subject to surveillance and socially regulated.[71]

Although in this book I heavily emphasize the experiences of women subjects, I also attend to the experiences of men, who are already becoming a growing target audience of Allergan's aggressive marketing campaign. I devote significant time to teasing out the ways that discourses about men and Botox and men's experiences with Botox operate relationally with those of women. In our postindustrial social world, men's bodies have joined the ranks of feminine imperfections and insecurities. Yet men's forays into the world of cosmetic enhancements must be understood against a cultural and historical backdrop of shifting gender relations and as part of a broader landscape of changing socioeconomic structures.

Studying Botox

Botox is the star of this book; those who produce it, sell it, use it, and market it are the supporting characters. In the pages that follow, I explore how these different characters construct and negotiate meanings about

Botox. I am interested in understanding why individuals choose to use Botox, how they articulate these decisions, and how media, medicine, and pharmaceutical marketing shape how individuals know what they know about Botox. Attention to Botox as *both* a personal experience and a cultural phenomenon required me to look at individual narratives *and* institutional discourses. Here, I briefly describe my methodology for studying the rise of Botox. For those readers interested in the nuances and minutiae of my recruitment, sampling, interviewing, and analysis, a detailed appendix appears at the end of the book.

My research on Botox spanned over five years and uses several sources of data. Much of what I have to say about Botox is based on my interviews with thirty-five Botox users and twenty Botox providers. I began the process of soliciting interviews by telling everybody I knew about my study; much of my initial recruitment, then, primarily took place through my social networks. Recruitment began in 2010 in Miami, the city where I was born and lived for much of my life. Beginning my research and recruitment in Miami was fruitful, not only because it was my childhood home where I had multiple contacts, but also because Miami has a renowned and well-established reputation as a city where looks determine social status. Miami was the home of Ryan Murphy's edgy, graphic, and often grotesque television series *Nip/Tuck*, which followed the lives and careers of two fictional plastic surgeons. Moreover, Miami was ranked third on *Forbes*'s 2007 list of America's vainest cities, and in 2012 it was ranked eighth by *Men's Health* in its list of vainest cities.[72] According to the *Forbes* report from 2007, there were 218 board-certified plastic surgeons practicing in Miami, or 5.2 surgeons per 100,000 people. However, a more recent report from 2010 claimed that Miami had close to 10 plastic surgeons per 100,000 people.[73] Considered a hub of vanity and cosmetic surgery, Miami was an ideal place to begin my research on Botox.

In addition to speaking with people in Miami, I conducted interviews with Botox users and providers in other parts of the country. I spoke with people from other stereotypically body-conscious cities such as Los

Angeles and Manhattan, but I also spoke with people in southern Louisiana, central Florida, suburban Massachusetts, and coastal Mississippi. Women represented the bulk of my sample of Botox users since they are the overwhelming majority of Botox users. Although the ages of the Botox users with whom I spoke ranged from twenty-seven to sixty-two, most of the women and men I recruited were in their twenties, thirties, and early forties because I was most interested in the phenomenon of relatively young consumers who use Botox "preventively." The vast majority of Botox users with whom I spoke were White. However, four women identified as Latina, and one man was Latino. Every Botox user identified as middle class, except for one who identified as upper class. Every single Botox user with whom I spoke made over $30,000 annually except for one woman, and every user except for three earned under $100,000 annually. All women participants identified as heterosexual, except for one who was bisexual. Among male Botox users, three were gay, and two were heterosexual.

Among my sample of Botox providers, two were cosmetic dermatologists, seven were dermatologists, one was a dermatological resident, one was a practicing dermatologist and a former plastic surgeon, four were plastic surgeons, two were dentists, one was an emergency medicine physician, and two were registered nurse practitioners. It is rather noteworthy that every single practitioner, except for one, was also a Botox user, and most of these practitioners injected their own brows with Botox. Some providers had been practicing in their field for over thirty years, and others had just completed medical school or residency. Fifteen providers were men, and five were women. With respect to their ethnic backgrounds, one was South Asian, one was Middle Eastern, two were Latino, and the remaining sixteen were White.

In addition to speaking with people about their Botox use, I also examined discourses in the marketing of Botox, the mass media, and medicine as a means of taking into account the reach of Botox beyond the experiences of those who use it. Collecting and scrutinizing Allergan's advertisements for Botox allowed me to see how Botox was marketed and sold.

Sampling and reading hundreds of print and digital articles about Botox provided me information about how knowledge about Botox was constructed and disseminated. I also collected press releases and news reports from the American Society for Cosmetic Dermatology and Aesthetic Surgery, the American Society for Aesthetic Plastic Surgery, and the Medical Spa Society to make out how these professional organizations interpret their knowledge and expertise about Botox. In 2013, I attended the American Academy of Dermatology's annual meeting in Miami, where I conducted four days of research, attending panels, speaking with prominent dermatologists, and seeing firsthand the vast exhibit hall where pharmaceutical, cosmeceutical, and beauty companies alike extended bags of free samples to conference attendees, hoping that they would then be marketed prominently in dermatological offices across the globe. Finally, my analysis of Botox is also informed by my own experiences becoming a Botox user and living in a Botoxed body.[74] Using Botox provided me with a perspective different from what I gained from researching texts, speaking to providers, and listening to other Botox users' experiences.

Integrating My Own Experiences

The very foundations of sociology and of social research are dedicated to understanding how historical, cultural, and social forces shape our personal biographies. Turning my analytic gaze inward offers both readers and myself a uniquely grounded opportunity to pursue the connections between biography and social structure that are fundamental to the sociological imagination. Instead of being ashamed of my subjective experience of the world and of my perceptions of my own aging body, I found it more analytically productive to draw upon my experiences as a resource. Thus there are many times throughout this book when I draw upon my own experiences with Botox to illustrate the deeply personal ways we are all constituted by the sociocultural contexts in which we live.[75] As such—as a writer, researcher, and subject—I am always "visible, active, and reflexively engaged" in this text.[76]

I began researching Botox in 2010 when I was thirty-one years old. During the process of working on this book I aged well into my mid-thirties. Watching my skin lose its volume and elasticity and witnessing new wrinkles slowly creep up next to my eyes, around my mouth, and into my brow profoundly affected my sense of self. Reading countless women's fashion and beauty magazines, where I was confronted with hegemonic discourses about femininity, youth, and beauty, made me increasingly sensitive to what these messages communicated about how my body should look. The process of subjecting my face to agonizing, close readings during my interviews with facial cosmetic surgeons, dermatologists, and other Botox providers called my attention to which of my wrinkles could benefit from paralysis, which lines should be filled, and which blotches should be lasered. My otherwise healthy face became defined as faulty as medical and aesthetic "experts" repetitively scrutinized my body.

In my early conversations with Botox users, countless women my age told me how amazing Botox was and how I was a fool for not jumping on the Botox bandwagon. What is more, they expressed serious doubt in my ability to personally understand the benefits of Botox, how it worked, and why it became so important to their beauty regimens. During these five years, I grew closer to my subjects' perspectives, coming to view the world and my body through their lens, approximating the emotional stance of the very people I was initially highly critical of and only intended to study as an uninvolved observer. Yet, as a feminist sociologist acutely aware of sexist and ageist social norms, I was skeptical of the idea of injecting a poison into my forehead that promised only a temporary cure for my wrinkles.

I eventually acquiesced to group and social pressure and decided to try Botox in 2012—an event that marked an immersion in my research that was never intentional. Within a week of the procedure, I was in awe of the results. I was surprised at how refreshed, awake, and yes, a little bit younger I looked. When others began commenting on my appearance, not being able to place the change as maybe a new haircut or perhaps a suntan, I could not help but feel secretly pleased yet still a little bit guilty with my decision. This was a personal decision that I struggled with, and I continued to struggle with it, especially as I began to see the effects of the toxin wearing off and the faint lines reappearing on my face. When debating whether to inject my face again, I was profoundly cognizant of my critical feminist ethics pulling me in one direction and my desire to look more youthful and attractive in a very different direction.

Ultimately, in November 2014, slightly over two years after my first Botox experience, I decided to try the drug again. More aware this time of how the injections changed my face by inhibiting my ability to scowl and by lifting my brow in a way that made me look more awake, I was increasingly self-conscious, even terrified, that my students and colleagues would notice. During an undergraduate class discussion on the regulation of women's bodies and beauty culture I felt like a fraud, a failure to my young women students who were only just sensing their budding feminist consciousness. Then, during a visit to my doctor for the mandatory follow-up appointment a week later, he took pictures of my newly Botoxed face. Comparing the snapshots from only seven days before gave me the opportunity to observe a close-up of my facial transmogrification. My (very magnified) placid forehead now looked better to me than the creased one I had only one week earlier. My membership into the social world of Botox users dramatically shifted my perception of beauty and of normalcy. Just as my study participants did, I began to internalize the ideals of a wrinkle-free face that are unattainable without the use of Botox. These before-and-after photos provided me a sense of self-indulgent pleasure and accomplishment in seeing myself transformed into what I learned to believe was something "better." They became all I needed at the time to temporarily relieve my otherwise guilt-ridden decision.

As I detail throughout this book, the analytic insights I gained throughout the process of becoming a Botox user reveal how moral and cultural pressures can transform our beliefs, our actions, and our sense of self. Yet this is not a book about my story, my narrative, and my meditation. While many of my participants have similar narratives, each of us had a unique story to share.

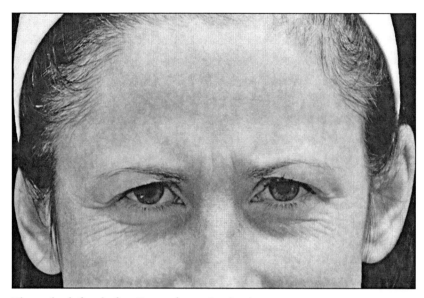

The author's face before Botox, furrowing her brow.

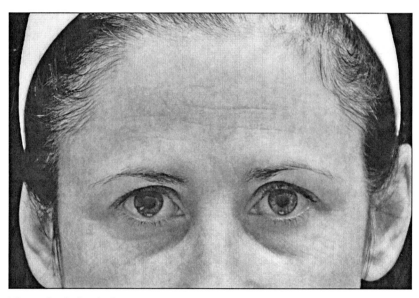

The author's face before Botox, at rest.

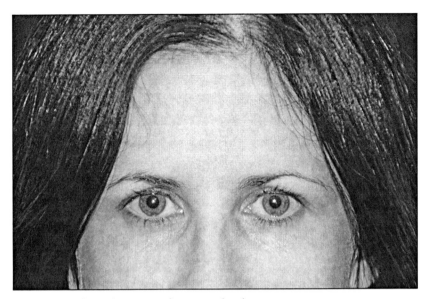

The author's face after Botox, furrowing her brow.

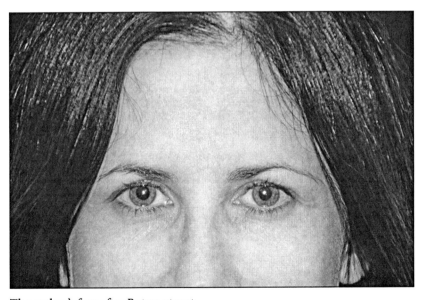

The author's face after Botox, at rest.

The Plan of the Book

This book is structured to show how Botox users construct their selves and their bodies from the cultural resources and institutional discourses available to them. Analysis of these dominant discourses reveals how knowledge about Botox is produced, diffused, and ultimately embodied. Thus, the first two chapters of the book center on the social structural sources, cultural repertoires, and institutional discourses that have given rise to the cultural phenomenon of Botox. In the following three chapters, I move to an investigation of the individual experiences of becoming, negotiating, and being a Botox user.

Chapter 1 begins with the accidental discovery of Botox and the historical and social factors that generated fertile ground for the Botox phenomenon. I then describe the early years of Botox treatment, detailing many of the legal troubles and public relations scandals with which Allergan had to deal. I argue that one of the primary reasons that these calamities did not create a lasting cultural panic about Botox is because of the cultural and medical discourses that project Botox's positive effects. Pharmaceutical marketing, medical organizations, and the media are arguably the most powerful sources from which people formulate their understandings of Botox. Thus the bulk of this chapter focuses on analyzing the marketing and selling of Botox, using my interviews with Botox providers, text from popular magazines published between 2000 and 2013, and Allergan's print and digital marketing materials from the same time period. The magazines articles, marketing material, and the providers I interviewed did not always have consistent and agreed-upon messages about Botox. However, despite these inevitable contradictions and disagreements, the dominant overlapping discourses that repeatedly surfaced were the normalization of Botox and the presentation of Botox as a practice of individual responsible self-care. After I discuss each of these in detail, I then consider how Botox is marketed with specific assumptions about race, class, and gender. Because discourses around Botox primarily assume a White, middle-class female body, I consider how men's magazines and practitioners who market to male Botox users construct and negotiate gendered norms around aesthetic labor.

In Chapter 2, I explore the intraprofessional turf war that has ensued among Botox providers. Changes within medicine, the economy, and the health-care industry have powerfully shaped the supply of practitioners willing and eager to provide Botox injections, and the commercialization of medical products and services have made elective procedures that are paid for out of pocket, such as Botox injections, an attractive area of practice. In this chapter, I draw upon my interviews with Botox providers, analyses of popular media and news releases, and my experiences at the American Academy of Dermatology annual meeting to explore how individual practitioners and professional associations construct and manage messages about the turf war around Botox. Physicians from varying subfields, along with other medical and spa practitioners, actively defend their profitable turf from the threat of open-market competition through institutional control mechanisms, using claims about concerns for public safety and other fearmongering tactics. I argue that, in addition to obfuscating the political and economic interests fueling the turf war, these profit-driven maneuvers further stimulate a supplier-induced demand for Botox and other aesthetic medicine.

In Chapters 3–5, I draw upon my interviews with Botox users and my own experiences to consider the processes through which one becomes a Botox user, negotiates the Botox self, and engages with a Botoxed body. In Chapter 3 I begin with a discussion of participants' first time trying Botox and move backward from there, detailing the personal circumstances and social forces that led them to the moment they found themselves with a needle in their brow. While there was neither a single nor monolithic script that all participants followed, what each of these people had in common was that they turned to Botox as a solution, albeit a temporary one, to remedy their facial wrinkles.

In Chapter 4 I interrogate how Botox users made meaning of their Botoxed selves and consider what these meanings reveal about the construction and maintenance of twenty-first-century bodies and identities. Turning to the ways individuals negotiated the variegated tensions and stigmas that permeated their decisions around Botox, I show how users' strategies of bodily disclosure were shaped by their gendered, sexual, classed identities and by their social locations. After detailing the ways users navigated the taint of inauthenticity, I then analyze the discursive tools that they used to account for their decision to use Botox. Because Botox straddled the realm of acceptability when it came to appropriate bodywork, it always demanded some sort of justification from users. Users fashioned similar justifications for this choice—often the decision to use Botox was constructed as a calculated strategy to preserve youth and beauty privilege and maintain a competitive edge in economic and intimate marketplaces. Locating their accounts about Botox within the postfeminist neoliberal sensibility in which they are situated, I conclude the chapter by exposing how reigning sociopolitical discourses provided Botox users a model for constructing personal narratives of the self.

Chapter 5 is centered on developing a textured analysis of how participants engaged with and interpreted their Botoxed bodies. Providing thick descriptions of Botox users' embodied subjectivities and introducing rich narratives that canvas Botox users' conscious experience, I detail how Botox users articulated the lived experience of being in a Botoxed body. Situating my findings in psychological research on facial feedback and sociological literature on facework and emotion work, I examine how Botox users interpreted and managed their newfound inability to fully express their range of affect. Detailing how Botox, because of its temporality, becomes addictive, I consider how it functioned as a gateway drug into other cosmetic procedures. Finally, because so many users looked to Botox as a means to carefully cultivate the appearance of an ageless body, I interrogate what it means to age "naturally" and "gracefully" in a social world that precludes any such possibility.

Finally, I return to the relevant sociological and feminist literature, summarize my most important findings, and discuss some of the conclusions I reached after spending five years researching and writing about Botox. My findings both expand and complicate prior research on women's body projects, begging scholars to ask new questions about gendered body practices, enhanced bodies, and medical consumerism.

1

Marketing Agelessness

The discovery of Botox—a purified and diluted form of the botulinum toxin, the world's deadliest toxin—followed a series of accidents involving a batch of spoiled sausages, a band of musicians at a Belgian funeral, a pickled ham, and a married pair of Canadian doctors. The toxin is a naturally occurring by-product of the microorganism that causes botulism, a potentially lethal paralytic disease caused by eating contaminated preserved food.[1] Although botulism has likely been around since ancient times, or at least as long as humans have been attempting to preserve and store food, the relationship between spoiled food consumption and the paralytic infection was not scientifically documented until the early nineteenth century.[2]

The first recorded instance of botulism dates back to 1820, when Justinus Kerner, a German poet and medical enthusiast, discovered that a substance in spoiled sausages, which he called *Wurstgift* (German for "sausage poison"), was responsible for a growing number of lethal food poisonings.[3] Kerner, considered by his contemporaries to be an expert on sausage poisoning, published the first scientific descriptions of what physicians now recognize as the symptoms of foodborne botulism. The next important scientific step in the discovery of Botox came in 1885, when Emile Van Ermengem, a Belgian physician and professor of microbiology, was called in to investigate a massive outbreak of botulism that occurred after a band of musicians who had been playing at a funeral in Belgium became ill from eating pickled and smoked ham, many of whom later died. Through performing a clinical, toxicological, and bacteriologic analysis of the food and the victims, Van Ermengem was the first to successfully isolate the anaerobic bacterium causing the illness, which he appropriately named *Bacillus botulinum*, after *botulus*, the Latin word for sausage. Today we recognize the bacterium by the scientific name *Clostridium botulinum*.[4]

Both Kerner and Van Ermengem found that, even in small doses, the botulinum toxin could be lethal. Early symptoms of botulism, such as blurred vision and difficulty speaking and swallowing, typically appear within eighteen to thirty-six hours after eating contaminated food.[5] Without treatment, the mortality rate ranges from 10 percent to 65 percent, and death usually occurs within a week.[6] An excruciatingly painful experience, untreated botulism paralyzes victims' bodies from the inside out: their bowels open, their autonomic nervous system fails, and eventually their lungs stop functioning, resulting in death by suffocation.

Only relatively recently has the medical world applied the botulinum toxin—in highly dilute form—for therapeutic purposes.[7] In the 1970s Dr. Alan Scott, an ophthalmologist in San Francisco, began using a form of the toxin, botulinum toxin A, for the treatment of blepharospasm, a disorder of uncontrollable blinking. He branded the new drug with the less-threatening name "Oculinum."[8] Around the same time, the biochemist Edward Schantz started using the nerve toxin to treat strabismus, the condition more commonly known as "crossed eyes." By the 1980s, the toxin was widely applied by both ophthalmologists and neurologists as a remedy for crossed eyes, uncontrollable blinking, and other facial, eyelid, and limb spasms.[9]

Jean Carruthers, an ophthalmologist who was using Oculinum to treat crossed eyes and optimal spasms, was the first to discover the botulinum toxin's cosmetic potential. During a routine procedure in 1987, one of her patients pointed to her brow and told her, "When you treat me there I get this beautiful, untroubled expression." The next day Jean and her husband Alastair, a dermatological surgeon, decided to inject Oculinum in the forehead of their assistant, Cathy Bickerton Swann. Less than a week later, they observed that the lines on Swann's brow that used to make her look angry and tired had completely vanished. From that day forward, Swann has been famously known as "patient zero" in the Botox trials.[10]

Even though the Carruthers "discovered" what we know now as Botox in 1987, it took another decade before people could be persuaded to use it.[11] The idea that you could use a poison to paralyze and relax muscles to take away lines was foreign and bizarre, even for dermatologists to grasp. Word about the toxin traveled slowly but steadily; doctors would hear about it at a conference or through colleagues, they would try it on a patient, and then the patient would tell their friends about it. In 1991, Allergan bought Oculinum for about $9 million, rebranding it "Botox."[12] During the 1990s, as increasing numbers of dermatologists became convinced that the Carruthers had stumbled upon an extraordinary discovery, they persuaded more and more of their patients to give it a try, and Botox slowly became a beauty secret among insiders, celebrities, and socialites. By 2002, when the FDA finally approved the drug Botox for the cosmetic treatment of glabellar lines, word had already been widely circulated about the revolutionary drug.

By 2015 over eleven million people in the United States had used Botox, a derivative of the deadliest toxin on the planet, to smooth their facial wrinkles.[13] As the journalist Alex Kuczynski notes, seemingly overnight Allergan was "transformed from a relatively small potatoes pharmaceutical company that sold acne products and eye drops to a hugely influential player on a billion-dollar global field."[14] So how did this happen? If we want to understand the roots of Allergan's sudden transformation from a small pharmaceutical company into a multibillion-dollar giant, we have to go back forty years to the beginnings of the deregulation and commercialization of American medicine.[15]

America's recent era of deregulation began in the 1970s when the Federal Trade Commission (FTC) filed an antitrust complaint against the American Medical Association's (AMA) ban on direct advertising and patient solicitation. By 1978 the FTC declared that the AMA ban against soliciting business through advertising and marketing was a violation of the Sherman Antitrust Act, which made it illegal to prohibit certain business activities that reduced competition in the marketplace and restrained trade. In 1982, the Supreme Court upheld the FTC's ruling.

Then in 1992 Congress passed legislation that sanctioned reductions in the testing time of new drugs by the Food and Drug Administration (FDA), reducing drug approval times by close to 50 percent. As a result of the Federal Trade Commission's rulings, the FDA's ability to control the marketing and advertising of drugs has been significantly truncated. This deregulation was further accelerated in 1998, when pharmaceutical companies began to advertise in print media and television and on the Internet, opening the gate for Viagra ads during *Monday Night Football* and Botox commercials in between nightly reality TV programming.[16]

When the FDA approved Botox for cosmetic use in April 2002, Allergan spared no expense and wasted no time. The company began advertising the following month, committing a whopping fifty million dollars to its consumer ad campaign. By May 2002, Botox advertisements ran in twenty-four different magazines, including *People*, the *New Yorker*, *Vogue*, and *In Style*.[17] By 2007, Botox had its first celebrity spokesperson, the actress Virginia Madsen, and in 2009, the actress, singer, and beauty queen Vanessa Williams became the second celebrity spokesperson for the product.[18]

But advertising alone does not account for Botox's sudden rise in popularity. In addition to marketing in traditional ways, Allergan used other creative product placement strategies to ensure that Botox was promoted throughout the editorial pages of magazines. Even before Allergan committed to spending a single dollar on marketing, journalists, a group significantly more trusted by the public than advertising executives, functioned as ghost marketers in the public relations campaign for Botox. Nobody seriously trusts advertisements these days, but many of us still believe what we read in magazines. And it is this credibility on which Allergan's public relations campaign banked.

By 2002, Allergan's strategic marketing campaign was already skillfully woven throughout the editorial pages of national magazines. In 2002, *Newsweek* published a landmark article titled, "The Botox Boom."[19] Pegging it as "the miracle drug for Boomers," *Newsweek* wrote that Botox was "helping to make trophy wives out of ordinary ones, turning character actresses back into ingénues, and erasing the stigma of failure from the brows of laid off technology executives."[20] Similarly, an article in *Time* said Botox was a "facelift in a bottle . . . a true miracle drug."[21] Another 2002 headline from *Harper's Bazaar* read, "Imagine looking younger in an instant, with no surgery and no side effects."[22] Journalists raved that Botox was "easy, reliable and can be administered over a lunch break."[23] Word was out. We had finally found the fountain of youth, and its waters could be harnessed in a syringe.

Trials and Tribulations

When I asked dermatologists to tell me how they felt when they first learned about Botox, every single one emphasized the drug's extraordinary properties and wave-making consequences. I heard phrases like "revolutionary" and "transformational." Ivan Camacho, a Latino dermatologist with a thriving practice in Miami whom I met at the American Academy of Dermatology meeting in 2014, told me, "It is really amazing how a toxin has created a generational change in how we have been able to intervene in the aging process." And it has.

It has also proved useful for a range of other ailments, including cerebral palsy, carpal tunnel, tennis elbow, migraines, facial tics, incontinence, and chronic anal fissures. In fact, its applications are so versatile that medical authorities have begun comparing it to penicillin. Mitchell F. Brin, a neurologist and senior vice president of development at Allergan, pronounced, "Botox will transform the world the way penicillin has transformed infectious disease."[24] One German doctor even likened Botox's significance to that of chemotherapy.[25] If these analogies seem a bit hard to swallow, then how about those studies reporting that Botox could potentially cure depression? In 2013, Dr. Eric Finzi, a dermatologist lauded for his pioneering research on Botox and mental health, made international headlines when he found that more than half the people that he treated for depression with Botox shots showed significant improvement in their mood.[26] A profusion of articles with titles like

"Can You Really Botox the Blues Away?" and "Don't Worry, Be Pretty" littered magazines, newspapers, and digital media that year, shaping a new cultural imaginary about the relationship between aesthetic enhancements and mental health.[27]

Botox has enjoyed some considerable publicity over the last decade and a half. Yet, despite riding high on an unprecedented period of success, there have also been a host of legal problems and public relations scandals with which Allergan has had to deal. Within only one year of Botox's cosmetic approval, Allergan received a scorching letter from the FDA accusing the company of minimizing the drug's side effects, for having advertisements that neglected to disclose facts about the product's use, failing to present all of the serious risks associated with Botox, and omitting the duration and severity of such risks.[28] This initial reprimand generated an outpouring of negative press coverage, stimulating early patient concern about the dangers of the drug.

However, it was not until a year later that the real publicity nightmare started—an acrimonious high-profile Hollywood lawsuit that instantly made media headlines. In a trial that could have easily been the subject of a theatrical melodrama, Irene Medavoy, a former model, actress, and wife of a high-powered Hollywood film executive, sued her dermatologist, Dr. Arnold Klein, after she fell gravely ill when he treated her migraine headaches with over 80 units of Botox.[29] Medavoy had already been going to Klein, a celebrity dermatologist with A-listers like Michael Jackson and Elizabeth Taylor on his client roster, for her Botox Cosmetic injections. When Klein suggested she try Botox to relieve her debilitating migraine headaches, Medavoy saw it as a no-brainer. In addition to injecting her that day for her usual cosmetic routine, Klein injected Medavoy at the base of her skull, behind her neck, and behind each ear. Within one week of the procedure, Medavoy reported being incapacitated by headaches and had fever, blurred vision, ringing ears, respiratory problems, gastric distress, and difficulty swallowing. After her medical problems persisted for months, Medavoy sued Klein for unspecified damages, alleging that Klein committed malpractice by failing to get informed consent from her for use of Botox and its potential side effects, especially those arising from off-label uses such as her migraine treatment. She also sued Allergan for product liability, condemning Botox for being "an inherently dangerous product."[30] Medavoy sought reimbursement for both her medical bills and her lost wages from a proposed talk show. Throughout the trial, Medavoy was painted as a vain and frivolous opportunist and ultimately lost her case when the jury eventually sided with Allergan, nine to three. Despite the win for Allergan, the trial was not "without wrinkles for Botox," and neither Allergan nor Klein left the courtroom looking innocent.[31]

One of the most crippling testimonies against Allergan came from Mitchell Brin, a senior vice president at Allergan and neurologist (the same man who compared Botox to penicillin), who confessed under cross-examination that the risks of Botox were unknown in dosages higher than 20 units and that the drug can spread to other parts of the body, affecting neuromuscular transmission. He also confessed that Allergan's own clinical studies suggested that Botox might be associated with headaches, pain, sinusitis, flu-like symptoms, and respiratory problems. Medavoy's own neurologist told journalists that he had conducted independent research demonstrating how Botox's paralysis of facial muscles could potentially cause changes in other muscles around the body. He found that injecting Botox in a person's forehead could cause changes in muscle function in the hands and the feet—something that Allergan's product literature gives very little attention.[32]

In addition to exposing the potential risks of Botox, particularly with respect to the off-label uses of the drug, the trial turned the spotlight on the larger issue of the dubious relationships between pharmaceutical companies and doctors. As one of the forty doctors who were trained by Allergan's public relations experts to act as media spokespeople for Botox, Klein was paid over $100,000 a year by Allergan for his work as a consultant and media spokesman and had not disclosed this conflict of interest to Medavoy.[33] In addition, Klein also received bonuses of $10,000 a day and travel expenses for his attendance at professional meetings where he promoted Botox, championing the drug's diverse applications.[34] Klein's company, Minimally Invasive Aesthetics, received a total of $499,000 from Allergan between September 2000 and December 2003. When interviewed about the case, Jerome Kassirer, the former editor of the *New England Journal of Medicine*, said Allergan was "turning doctors into sales reps"; about Klein, Kassirer alleged, "It is clear he is being paid to promote the drug."[35]

In his book, *White Coat, Black Hat: Adventures on the Dark Side of Medicine*, the medical bioethicist Carl Elliott observed how one of the ironic consequences of the American Medical Association's increased policing of pharmaceutical salespeople at the turn of the millennium was that doctors rather quickly became the new drug reps; after all, doctors are the best people to market a drug to other doctors and to their patients. Physicians are not only given free samples of drugs and encouraged to promote and prescribe them, they are also urged to use them for off-label purposes, as Klein did with Medavoy to treat her migraines.[36] Although in our current age of commercial medicine, these ethically ambiguous relationships between physicians and pharmaceutical companies are routine, most people typically do not know about them. Only recently have they come under public and governmental scrutiny. Some argue that the landscape has changed somewhat since 2002, after the Office of Inspector General in the U.S. Department of Health and Human Services declared that it would crack down on big pharma's promotional practices. Under the imminent threat of prosecution, the Pharmaceutical Research and Manufacturers of America began to self-regulate more seriously, adopting a "voluntary code of ethics" on their relationships with health-care professionals.[37] However, skeptics have alleged that this new code is nothing but smoke and mirrors. Even with the increasing transparency of payments from pharmaceutical companies to health-care professionals, the vast majority of patients are not aware that their physicians are paid consultants and spokespeople for pharmaceutical companies. To combat this, one consumer advocacy group, ProPublica, has started a website, aptly named "Dollars for Docs," where patients can see if their physicians have received money from a pharmaceutical company. According to this site, Allergan spent over seventeen million dollars on Botox, paying close to sixty thousand doctors across the globe.[38]

Despite the fact that the Medavoy case made media headlines and was a public relations debacle, expenditure of Botox declined only minimally in the months following the trial. Yet it would only be a year before Allergan's next major scandal—and this time the consequences would be even grimmer. In November 2004, Bach McComb, an osteopath with a suspended medical license from Florida, got his hands on some black-market Botox and injected himself, his girlfriend Alma Hall, and another couple, Eric and Bonnie Kaplan, with catastrophic amounts of improperly diluted raw botulinum toxin A—a research-grade botulinum not suitable for human use.[39] The outcome was dire. McComb was on a respirator until February 2005, and his girlfriend Alma Hall was in the hospital for seven months, four of which were spent on a respirator. The Kaplans spent over two months on respirators before they were able to breathe on their own. Eric Kaplan had recovered by 2005, but his wife was not as fortunate. Bonnie's face was still partially paralyzed over a year and a half later, she could still barely walk, and she had lost 50 percent of her hearing. In court, the Kaplans and Hall vividly described their tormenting experience after the poison began to take effect—they were fully conscious, but they were unable to move, speak, or even breathe on their own.[40] At the conclusion of the hearing, McComb's medical license was revoked, and he was sentenced to three years in federal prison for misbranding and trafficking an illegal drug.[41]

During the trial, it came to light that McComb purchased his research-grade botulinum from a California company called List Biological Laboratories, owned by naturopathic physicians Zahra Karim and Chad Livdahl. A report by federal prosecutors revealed that Karim and Livdahl's company bought over three thousand vials of the research-grade botulinum for $30,000, reselling it for $1.5 million to over two hundred doctors across America. After pleading guilty to federal charges of illegal

drug distribution, Livdahl was sentenced to nine years in prison, Karim
to five and a half years, and both were ordered to pay substantial fines.[42]

The case made international headlines, exposing the chilling under-
ground industry of black-market Botox. A subsequent 2004 investigation by the FDA uncovered that bootleg botulinum was being imported
illegally into America from all over the world. The mid-2000s saw the
publication of several magazines articles warning consumers about
crooked providers purchasing impure Botox from China, Afghanistan,
and the former Soviet Union. Take for example, the following excerpt
from *Newsweek*:

> He came for his pinprick like everyone else, lured by the promise of
> wrinkle-free skin. But for 47-year-old Freddy Borges, the price of vanity
> was higher than the $300 per injection he paid to a New York City couple,
> Iris and Eliezer Fernandez. The Fernandezes weren't doctors, according
> to law-enforcement officials who charged them with assault and reckless
> endangerment. (They pleaded innocent.) And the treatments weren't Bo-
> tox, the antiwrinkle wonder drug. Whatever they were, they left Borges
> with ugly purple scars that no injection can fix.[43]

A cultural panic around Botox rapidly ensued, and the editorial pages
of magazines were punctuated with horror stories about black-market
Botox, cautioning consumers that, in a hurting economy, greedy doctors
and other aesthetic practitioners were cutting dangerous corners—they
were buying fake Botox, diluting their Botox, and taking advantage
of consumers who were vain, insecure, and starved for a quick fix.[44]
Magazine articles with titles like "Doctors without Borders" warned
readers about the dangers of getting duped by practitioners using bargain, botched, and black-market Botox.[45] Stories about vanity-obsessed
women falling prey to unscrupulous providers made for entertaining
journalism and were commonly picked up by magazine editors.[46]

Readers were repeatedly advised to choose a physician who was board
certified in dermatology or plastic surgery and who had years of experi-

ence with injectables. Alongside foreboding allegations like "Qualified doctors don't go to parties with syringes of Botox," readers were warned about the risks of going to private residences, Botox parties, hair salons, and medical spas.[47] Yet the arousing concern over bootleg Botox soon subsided. A week after the McComb incident, Allergan's stock dipped slightly but then quickly rebounded. And although consumers were initially alarmed, the overwhelming majority had not stopped using Botox.

Why didn't the Medavoy or McComb case create a lasting cultural panic about Botox? And why didn't a discourse on "Botox as dangerous" ever catch on? One reason for this obviously has to do with the millions of people who have used Botox without any major risks or side effects. Another is that Botox appeals to the kind of people who are willing to modify their bodies in order to look younger, and these are people who tend to overlook risks. Much of the reason Botox did not fail, however, stems less from individual people and their choices than from cultural and medical discourses that project Botox's positive effects. Drawing upon media coverage, advertising, and conversations with Botox providers, I now turn to an analysis of the dominant cultural and medical discourses that have contributed so greatly to Botox's success.

"Everybody's Doing It": The Normalization of Botox

"You are going to have to do it, and not that long from now . . . not because you hate yourself, fear aging, or are vain. You're going to get a cosmetic procedure for the same reason you wear makeup: because every other woman is."[48] These are the provocative opening sentences of Joel Stein's 2015 cover story for *Time* magazine, entitled "Nip. Tuck. Or Else," where he predicts that cosmetic procedures will become even more common than they are today and that those who choose to age without technological intervention will eventually become the minority. Stein shows how the stigma that once accompanied cosmetic procedures has been dramatically reduced and how the notion of "having work done" has lost much of the shame that had accompanied it only a few decades ago. According to Stein, "This is the first generation that thinks about plastic surgery as almost a given. . . . They're the first generation to grow up with the idea that plastic surgery is neither superexpensive nor a weird thing that only the maladjusted would do."[49]

While his argument is problematic and flawed for many reasons—most notably in that many cannot afford such procedures or that some might not even want them—in some respects Stein is not so far off. Survey data have confirmed that Americans have grown increasingly comfortable with the practice of altering their faces and bodies through surgical and nonsurgical procedures. Since 1997, the number of Americans who underwent cosmetic surgical procedures increased from 900,000 to 1.7 million.[50] In 2014, there were over 15 million surgical and nonsurgical cosmetic procedures performed in America.[51] Of these 15 million procedures, 1.7 million were surgical procedures, and nearly 13.9 million were nonsurgical procedures.[52] The growth in cheaper, nonsurgical procedures rose from 700,000 in 1997 to well over 13 million in 2014.[53] In less than two decades, there has been a 500 percent increase in the total number of minimally invasive procedures—such as injectables, skin resurfacing, and laser procedures—and nonsurgical facial rejuvenation procedures have experienced more growth than any other cosmetic procedure.[54] In 2014, Americans spent almost 13 billion dollars on cosmetic procedures. Two billion of these dollars were spent exclusively on Botox.[55]

A 2010 survey revealed that almost half (48 percent) of all Americans, regardless of income, approve of cosmetic surgery, and almost a quarter would consider it for themselves.[56] More striking is that 48 percent of respondents with an income of under $25,000 approve of cosmetic surgery, and 23 percent of these respondents would consider cosmetic surgery for themselves.[57] These statistics suggest that feeling good about the way one looks is important to the majority of Americans—even those who can't easily afford cosmetic surgery without accruing debt. Cutting across gender lines, these ratings show that women's approval rating for cosmetic surgery is only slightly higher (59 percent) than men's (51 percent). Despite this almost gender-neutral approval rating, the actual practice of cosmetic surgery and enhancement is nowhere near gender neutral; in 2014 women accounted for 92 percent of the total number of cosmetic procedures. The numbers for Botox injections are similar, with women constituting 96 percent of the total.[58]

Cosmetic procedures are something that Americans no longer keep secret, as 73 percent of women and 66 percent of men said they would not be embarrassed if others knew they had gone under the knife, needle, or laser.[59] Recent analyses of print media revealed narratives of pride among celebrities as they recounted their cosmetic surgeries with a combination of "graphic realism, enthusiasm, and cheerful exclamation."[60]

Where the normalization of Botox is related to a broader trend in the mainstreaming of aesthetic procedures, the fact that Botox injections are temporary, repetitive, addictive, and marketed as preventive has made it such that these injections are fast becoming regular body upkeep, just like teeth cleaning and haircuts. Rebecca Steinberg, a tall, slim, self-assured Miami dermatologist with enormous brown eyes, told me that Allergan's success in marketing Botox injections means that they are increasingly becoming a normalized, routine, and casual component of female maintenance for its consumer base: "For these women, its now like you get highlighted, [you get a] manicure, you get your teeth bleached, and [you get] your Botox. It's not a big deal. It's one more thing you do." According to an article in *Vogue*, Botox injections had become "an appointment many of us . . . greet every few months with about as much ceremony as a manicure."[61] In an article in *People*, one skin-care expert proclaimed, "I don't know why people want to make a controversy about Botox—it's a basic thing, like getting a manicure or getting your hair dyed. It's on the grooming checklist, its part of the game."[62] Similarly, soap-opera star Lisa Rinna, who famously underwent surgery to drain her botched lip injections, announced that Botox for her is "like changing the oil in your car."[63]

The growing nonchalance and mainstreaming of Botox was nowhere more evident than in the slew of candid celebrity narratives that colored the pages of *People* magazine. One article in this magazine reported that celebrity doctors in New York and Los Angeles estimated that 75 percent of stars over thirty-five get injected with Botox regularly.[64] Declaring that Botox was "not all that different from getting fake tans or teeth whitening," Hollywood starlet Nicole Richie asked, "Why grow old gracefully when you have the technology to prevent it?"[65] Even men were jumping on the Botox bandwagon. Former *Baywatch* star David Hasselhoff admitted, "Of course I have had Botox, everyone has," and TV personality Simon Cowell maintained, "To me Botox is no more unusual than toothpaste."[66]

Extraordinary interest in the lives of celebrities and, in particular, fascination with their beauty secrets, surgeries, and enhancements has been a vital force in fueling the rise of Botox and cosmetic surgical culture more broadly. It is increasingly more common for celebrities (and even more so for manufactured celebrities such as the Kardashians) to document the amount of time, energy, and money they spend on their appearance. In celebrity culture, vanity and superficiality are celebrated, and obsessing about one's physical appearance and tweaking it with cosmetic enhancements is now the "cool" and "hip" thing to do. Moreover, with the rise of new technologies like tablets and smart phones, the quest for feminine youth and beauty is made public; women, particularly celebrity women, no longer become beautiful in private. All the creams, potions, lasers, and needles that go into making bodies beautiful are now public for the entire world to witness, emulate, and scrutinize. We watch as manufactured celebrities from reality TV shows like *Keeping Up with the Kardashians* or *The Real Housewives* franchise get injected with Botox in their own homes. Even when celebrities do not come forward about their aesthetic enhancements, tabloids and gossip blogs subject celebrity skin to close readings in an attempt to discern whether or not these starlets have gone under the needle or the knife.[67]

To see the body through the lens of celebrity culture is to see it in terms of constant nips, tucks, and tweaks—and not just the big stuff, like breast implants and nose jobs. We now scrutinize the most miniscule details of the skin, a practice that has prompted many celebrities to adopt what doctors are calling "red-carpet dermatology," or tiny tweaks that involve scalpel-free procedures that create less detectable changes than a face-lift. Red-carpet dermatology has developed in response to websites and blogs like *TMZ* and *Perez Hilton* and the increased use of camera phones, posting of YouTube videos, and increased prevalence of high-definition television. Our scrutiny of celebrity bodies, though magnified, mirrors the increasing surveillance of the bodies of everyday Americans.

Moreover, our technologically simulated connections with celebrity culture have resulted in the hunger of many of us to participate in lavish celebrity lifestyles, emblematic as they are of unlimited possibility. In celebrity culture, faces and bodies have dismantled the time-honored truth that one looks older as one gets older.[68] Patricia Heaton, television star and leading actress in the popular family sitcom, *Everybody Loves Raymond*, proclaimed, "There's a reverse thing that happens when you move to [Los Angeles], you get younger looking as you get older. It's odd."[69] For a growing number of Americans, celebrity perfection seems attainable, even normal, and for these individuals, bodily self-expression may very well mean celebrity imitation and worship.

In addition to celebrity culture and its obsession with bodily perfection and modification dramatically fueling the normalization of Botox, so, too, does the fact that many Botox injections happen outside of clinical settings. In 2002, the late Joan Rivers predicted, "Botox is nothing. They'll be doing it in malls pretty soon."[70] Less than a decade later, her prophecy turned out to be true. As of 2014, there were approximately 1,750 medical spas operating in the United States—a staggering number, considering the medical spa business model has only been around for slightly over a decade.[71] In addition to medical spas, we can now get Botox at our dentist's office or with our annual pap smear at the gynecologist. Botox is even available at parties. One article in *Marie Claire* reported on an affair called "Botox and Lox" at a trendy South Beach hotel, where packages started at $750 a person.[72] In *Newsweek* another journalist wrote about a "Brows & Botox" promotional event in a Beverly Hills cosmetics store where she witnessed firsthand "more than two dozen women sipping Perrier and nibbling finger sandwiches as they wait[ed] for their brows to be waxed into shape and their free Botox injections."[73]

That Botox is being reconfigured into what some have referred to as a lighthearted "Girls Night Ouch" illuminates both the carefree and, some would argue, careless attitude many seem to have surrounding Botox.[74] Dr. Rebecca Steinberg, the Miami dermatologist with enormous brown eyes, declared that "the stigma is gone. People talk about it with their friends. I mean it is everywhere." When I spoke with Dr. Jacob Steinmann, a lanky South Florida plastic surgeon with an intelligently comedic demeanor, he told me that "Botox is becoming less taboo, and people are more comfortable. It's no longer something that rich people can have. I have housekeepers and I have CEOs, it's the whole gamut. It's accessible to everyone."

Consistent with the diffusion model of deviance that illustrates how the stigma of a particular practice or behavior decreases once middle-class individuals begin to identify with it, Botox's cultural destigmatization is crossing over from the affluent classes to the middle classes.[75] Yet, even as the stigma of Botox is being diffused among some middle-class Americans, it is not yet a procedure that is accessible to the masses, and I have some suspicions about the number of housekeepers that are actually in Dr. Steinmann's client roster. Miami dermatologist Ivan Camacho's response to my question about the social class backgrounds of his Botox clients lends some clarification to Steinmann's point: "Of course maybe not everyone can do it, but you know the majority of my patients are just professional people at different levels—counselors, and teachers or housewives, and lawyers—not necessarily the majority of America but that segment of America who are fortunate enough to have enough disposable income to take care of that part of themselves." Similarly, when I asked the late Frederic Brandt, a celebrity dermatologist whom *W* magazine once called the "Baron of Botox," about what I saw as the increasing normalization of the drug, he answered, "You know, when you look at the numbers of people that do these procedures, be it injections or fillers or both, it's still a very small percentage of the population." Reiterating the significance of Dr. Brandt's point, I want to emphasize that it is not the number of people who are using Botox that makes it normalized. Botox is in no way normal in the statistical sense. In fact, according to my rough estimations, only about 3–5 percent of Americans have used Botox. Rather, the normalization of Botox refers to the rise of discourses that project it as a regulating presence in our cultural landscape.[76]

"You're Being Negligent": The Responsible Neoliberal Subject

In addition to cosmetic surgeries and enhancements becoming increasingly normalized, celebrity tabloids, women's magazines, and news sources suggested that *not* having work done was now the new shame. In the abovementioned 2015 *Time* exposé, the sociologist Abigail Brooks told Joel Stein that "it's becoming harder and harder to say no [to these procedures] without being read as irrational or crazy."[77] Brooks's interviews with middle-aged and older women revealed how, in light of the growing prevalence of aesthetic anti-aging technologies, more and more women were resigning themselves to what she referred to as "the technological imperative."[78] Among those women who did succumb to the technological imperative, many described their "naturally" aging counterparts by using negative expressions like "letting themselves go" and "not taking good care of themselves."

Furthermore, in her analysis of media depictions, Brooks found that consumers of cosmetic procedures were frequently portrayed in magazines as rational, practical, and virtuous,[79] an observation that echoes Elizabeth Haiken's historical analysis documenting the ways that cosmetic surgery has long been associated with ideologies of personal responsibility and practical action.[80] I, too, found that narratives in magazines about Botox were colored with themes of individual responsibility, moral obligation, and at times, feelings of inadequacy and personal failure. For example, in an article in *Vogue*, journalist Julia Reed admitted, "I suddenly felt enormously irresponsible. I may take care of my eyebrows and my perpetually white roots, but the last time anyone took so much as a laser to my increasingly lined and blotchy face it was for my wedding. And I just celebrated my fifth anniversary. In the practice of the proactive department I am clearly failing miserably."[81] Aleksandra Crapanzano, a journalist for *Marie Claire*, similarly lamented, "Was it now uncouth of me to show up at dinner with my fine lines? Was this akin to showing up with mud on my boots and a moth hole in my sweater? Ten years ago, I might have splurged on a manicure and had my hair blown dry before a formal dinner party. Was I now obliged to add Botox and fillers to the routine?"[82] Such confessionary tales emphasize a moral violation in not participating in aesthetic labor. Situated along a continuum of women's beauty practices, Botox, laser treatments, and dermal fillers were presented in media accounts as normalized ways of performing femininity and of neoliberal citizenship. Accentuating a woman's personal responsibility for managing her exterior body, such editorials implied that attending to one's physical appearance through the consumption of an ever-expanding technological toolkit was compulsory for social status and inclusion.

Many Botox providers with whom I spoke also interlaced their narratives with repertoires of responsible self-care. For example, in 2011, when I asked Sonya James, a New Orleans dermatologist with a detached Southern charm, what she would say to someone like me who—thirty-two years old at the time—colored her hair to camouflage gray roots, used topical creams and serums, and was concerned with the onset effects of aging but was not quite ready to begin Botox injections. Her response stunned me: "I would say you are being negligent. Botox is almost a requirement. If you make enough money to afford it, it should be one of those affordable luxuries. . . . It's still a luxury, but certainly it's something that you should have in your budget. For women, I always say you know skin care is first. Sunscreen, Retin-A, antioxidants . . . and the next dollar you should spend should be Botox. Literally." Evoking the mandate that a responsible woman consumer was required to make Botox a priority, no matter how dire her financial situation, Dr. James projected the imperative that even women who are poor and economically struggling should scrimp, save, or use their credit cards and go into further debt to get Botox shots, almost as if Botox were on par with material provisions like food and shelter. Women who refused to go under the needle were presented as failing to follow normative prescriptions of femininity and stigmatized as lazy and irresponsible.

This idea that "letting yourself go" was a personal choice was also reflected in Allergan's marketing strategies. For example, one advertisement for Botox read: "It took forty years to get it. And ten minutes to do something about it."[83] Another asserted: "It is really up to you. You can choose to live with wrinkles. Or you can choose to live without them."[84]

Couched within discourses of autonomy, responsibility, and empowerment, such marketing tactics held individual women accountable for either succeeding in erasing their wrinkles or for failing to do so. Botox's advertisements projected the message that control over our aging faces was putatively in our grasp; if we "choose to live" with our wrinkles, we are complicit in our own aging and thus have consciously chosen to fail to live up to normative standards of femininity. Promoting neoliberal ideologies that govern ideas about healthy, beautiful bodies, this singular focus on personal responsibility renders structural constraints about who can be considered healthy and beautiful invisible. The message that women are supposed to uncritically embrace Botox specifically and anti-aging medicine more broadly obscures the reality that this choice takes place within a context of massive social inequality, where many women do not even have access to basic health care, let alone cosmetic enhancement. Moreover, ageist messages are blatantly interwoven throughout Botox's advertisements. Seeking to convince consumers not only to use the product but also to buy into prevailing ideologies about aging and femininity, these messages reinforce the assumption that the only right appearance for women is a youthful and beautiful one. Veiled

Advertisement promoting Botox as a personal and responsible choice.

within these advertisements is the idea that older women are physically repugnant, that they are the benchmarks against which younger women should resist.

These kinds of media and medical messages regularly advocated early proactive efforts that were supposed to guard against any appearance of aging and reduce the need for more invasive procedures later in life. For instance, one celebrity dermatologist interviewed in *Vogue* warned readers: "Think of yourself as a house. The house ages, the foundation cracks, the internal structure starts falling down. A lot of women wait until their house has collapsed and then they want to fix it."[85] Keeping with the house metaphor, another dermatologist who was quoted in a later issue of *Vogue* said, "I liken it [the face] to a house. I tell my patients, I can spackle the walls, but when the foundation gets weak, the spackle won't hold. So I send them out to get it fixed."[86] It was widely advised that women should begin a lifelong regimen of preventative aesthetics early on, before reaching thirty, in order to gradually "freeze" their youthful look instead of drastically changing it all at once, producing a phenomenon that the feminist cultural theorist Meredith Jones referred to as "stretching middle age." No longer a "transit lounge, passively inhabited between youth and old age," Jones observed how the rise of cosmetic medicine and other biomedical advancements has caused middle age to become an "increasingly significant, actively worked upon" phase of life.[87]

Regularly situated within a broader ethos of preventive aesthetics, Botox has been marketed to prolong the appearance of not only middle age but also youth. In fact, the phrase "preventative Botox" has been circulating for almost as long as the drug itself. Responding to the advice of many dermatologists who preach the gospel of prevention, a growing contingent of young Botox consumers are being advised that the best time to start using Botox is when their wrinkles are minimally visible. Consequently, Botox procedures in the nineteen to thirty-four demographic have more than doubled in the last decade, and more women between the ages of twenty-two and forty use Botox than do women over sixty.[88] Journalistic pages in magazines have been peppered with such claims as "You want to clean up your room before it gets too dirty"[89] and "I do tons of Botox because I believe in holding yourself in place to prevent aging."[90] One twenty-five-year-old doctoral student told *Marie Claire* that she gets Botox injections every four to five months because "a lot of women wait until they are really in bad shape, and that's kind of like saying, 'I'm going to wait until I have a heart attack to go to the cardiologist.' Botox is just like putting on sunscreen for me."[91] Where sunscreen protects against skin cancer and visiting a cardiologist for a routine screening can manage the risk factors of cardiovascular disease, Botox injection, a cosmetic practice designed to stall the appearance of wrinkles, has relatively nothing to do with our actual health.

Nonetheless, several Botox providers with whom I spoke also accentuated Botox's preventive potential. One such physician was Alex Weinstein, a licensed osteopath with a laid-back demeanor and hippy style, who at the time of our interview was shadowing a cosmetic dermatologist in Fort Lauderdale in order to learn the nuances of injectables and lasers. During our conversation, he told me how using Botox not only can "soften wrinkles" but can "actually prevent wrinkles from ever forming" by changing the amount of expression that is made on a person's face. He elaborated, "Now, obviously, if you told someone never smile, never frown, laugh, or do anything with their face, they'd never have any wrinkles, but we can't do that, so with Botox we can specifically design what they can move or not, in order to create the wrinkles or expressions that they want to keep. . . . The biggest thing is it prevents you from making the facial movements that cause the wrinkles, so you can actually use it to ensure that you never make wrinkles and continue to have a young-looking face for the rest of your life."

Even if early Botox injections are capable of preventing the formation of deep lines through the paralysis of facial movement and the reeducation of facial muscles, the theory of preventative Botox use is problematic and flawed for several reasons. First, since Botox's ability to freeze the youthful face is only temporary, it can only prevent wrinkles if a user continues Botox use every for to six months. Because of this stipulation, some providers I interviewed were highly critical of the way that Botox's preventive potential was being marketed. For example, Michael Rosenblum, a young, enthusiastic plastic surgeon I interviewed in Baton Rouge in 2013, told me that "Botox covers up the presentation of wrinkles, but as soon as that person stops using Botox those wrinkles come right back. So, I would argue that it's preventive in the sense that it covers it up, but your physiology of you having wrinkles is still there." Second, some practitioners expressed concern that, because young women were being sold the idea that Botox was preventive, they were being seduced into using the drug before it was necessary. South Florida facial plastic surgeon Jacob Steinmann shared, "I have a lot of young women come to me and say they have had Botox, and I don't understand why they have had it. They say it's because it's preventive; sure it's preventive, but it's only preventive when you start to see a line . . . but otherwise what are you preventing?" The idea that women are freezing their faces in time even before they see a hint of a wrinkle is disconcerting, to say the least, and speaks volumes about the unattainable appearance demands we place on women, our cultural infatuation with youth, and our inability to accept the changing, creasing face that comes with time. These perpetual visits to the Botox doctor can also be quite expensive over the long run. Even though the immediate expense of Botox is between $300 and $400 and, therefore, seems more financially accessible and less burdensome than a face-lift or eye-lift, a woman who starts using Botox in her twenties or thirties will likely end up spending the equivalent of these costs, should she undergo the recommended repeated injections.

Despite these significant caveats, Botox was often cast as an appearance intervention that could yield psychological, social, and economic benefits. Just as Fraser found that women's magazines framed cosmetic surgery as part of a toolkit designed for achieving success, I also found that Botox was frequently construed as a means for improving the enterprising self.[92] Magazine articles were punctuated with stories about women who felt that, because they were in workplaces saturated with so many young people, they needed to do whatever they could to keep up a more youthful appearance—without using surgery. Nonsurgical procedures like Botox injections, even more so than cosmetic surgery, were presented as a résumé boost; they were quick, marketed as more affordable than surgery, and had little to no downtime, so there was no risk of missing any valuable face time at the office.

Practitioners also projected the idea that Botox injections were a strategy for maintaining a competitive edge in today's job market. Jonathon Black, a dermatologist who was born and raised in Miami and somehow still managed to have skin that looked like it had never seen a ray of sunlight, rationalized that "your face is like your handshake, so if somebody has deep etched-in lines, they always look like they're angry even if they're happy. It can be tough socially, in business, you know with this emphasis on youth in our culture, and older people kind of being put to pasture a lot earlier now, like in their fifties. So, for people who are in sales, or for people who are in very social interactive fields, it is very important." Not only does it cost money to pursue societal ideals of attractiveness, it is also financially consequential not to, as researchers have found that those who conform to current cultural standards of beauty receive higher incomes than those who do not.[93] Moreover, our contemporary blurring of health and appearance is such that we assume that people with wrinkles lead socially irresponsible lives and are lazy, negligent, and untrustworthy. Apparently, according to Dr. Black, we also assume that people with wrinkles are perpetually angry.

In the same way bad teeth are a gamble in the professional world, soon having a wrinkled brow might also be a risk. Since the 2008 economic crisis, more and more people are taking steps to ensure that they are not the victims of corporate layoffs, and one way to do so is to pay closer attention to physical image. Fear of job loss, diminished prestige, and shrinking incomes have led increasing numbers of employees to embrace anti-aging medicine, especially Botox. In fact, recent statistics have indicated that Botox injections increase in times of economic downturn.[94] When I spoke with Rumi Acevedo, an exquisitely handsome and seemingly ageless cosmetic dermatologist in Fort Lauderdale, he told me that he has patients coming to him, saying, "You know I'm putting off that face-lift for two years, I can't afford it. So I need my Botox." Similarly, said one woman in *Vogue*: "There is no spa appointment or a sea salt body scrub in my near future, but I'm keeping my Botox, it's preventive."[95] An article in *Marie Claire* reported that "people who were on the fence about big-ticket procedures are essentially buying time with less expensive ones. I have a top ad exec who still gets fillers and Botox despite sweeping layoffs."[96] Thus, even in a failing economy, and especially during economic uncertainty, Botox has been presented as a rational, practical, and necessary upgrade to maintain one's edge in competitive marketplaces.

In addition to being presented as a strategy for success, Botox has also been cast as a practice of self-care, as something a woman does to make herself look and feel better, just like exercise, practicing yoga, and responsible eating. For example, Botox spokeswoman Virginia Madsen told one journalist, "If something about my body bothers me, I go to the gym. Something about my face bothered me-and there was an alternative."[97] Our visually oriented consumer culture mandates that care of the self should be publicly perceptible, as the exterior body is used as a visual marker for our interior health, character, and our morality. However, the catch is that our bodily self-care should not be so perceptible that it disrupts the illusion of ease. The paradox of an attractive body is that it should be earned through merit and hard work—but it should also appear effortless. A Botoxed face that is too tight or frozen is seen as vain, fake, and just plain ridiculous—and this is to be avoided at all costs. Instructions about using Botox "the right way," as to maintain the illusion of naturalness, has punctuated journalistic commentaries. An article in *Redbook* schooled readers that "the best results are undramatic and almost imperceptible. No one should say, 'Hey, did you have something done?'"[98] Using Botox proactively, early, and often was one way that youth and beauty could appear effortless and natural. The risk of waiting until one was too old, after facial lines were already visible, was that the Botox would look obvious and fake, delegitimizing its aesthetic appeal. Beginning Botox injections early on, before the wrinkles even appeared, would result in a youthful and attractive face that seemed to appear out of thin air, thus obscuring any of the expensive and time-consuming labor that went into its creation.

Marketing, media, and medical discourses have regularly projected the message that women should use Botox, but only to the extent that this use goes undetected. Advertisements for Botox that read "Freedom of Expression" have broadcasted the fact that Botox should not make you look like you have had any work done.

Sharing the sentiment that the objective of Botox is to create a face that passes as natural, many of the practitioners with whom I spoke said the goal of Botox was to keep interlopers guessing about a subtle, albeit noticeable, change in appearance. Practitioners were highly articulate vendors who wove in subtle aphorisms like "natural," "like you, only better," and "refreshed" into their conversations about Botox as proxies for notions of acceptability and normalcy. For example, Miami derma-tologist Rebecca Steinberg explicated, "I tell them [my patients] with Botox, you are going to look like yourself, and you are just going to look better. You are going to look relaxed but you still are going to look like yourself." And plastic surgeon Jacob Steinmann explained that "every-thing I do is philosophically based, I try to target aging in a certain way: to make things look very natural and make people look like themselves only younger." Woven throughout narratives was the notion that the good Botoxed body should be visible enough that it gets compliments and approving glances but should not stand out so much that it becomes a spectacle. Implicit in these statements is the notion that "looking like you" is not good enough, but now, with the advent of Botox, you need to look "like you, only better." Seen as preferable to the "natural" body, the Botox body looks more relaxed, awake, and refreshed even if it is exhausted, stressed, or pissed off. In this way, Botox exposes the flawed "natural" body, setting new standards for deficiency and normalcy.[99]

An ad painting Botox use as empowering.

One such "Freedom of Expression" advertisement.

Colloquialisms like "baby Botox," "actress Botox," or "softening" were interposed among practitioners' narratives to refer to techniques that involved injecting lower dosages of Botox that still allowed for facial movement. Detailing his injection philosophy, Alex Weinstein, the South Florida dermatologist with a laid-back demeanor and hippy style, explained that "some people want to be completely frozen, and, you know, and look like a deer in a headlight, . . . but I really advocate against it, I really am more of a proponent of the, 'actress style,' where you have some movement, and it looks natural and people can't tell that you had things done."

In her analysis of media accounts about cosmetic surgery, Fraser observed that the socially constructed repertoire of the natural fulfilled multiple functions.[100] First, it was used to conceal the labor behind its creation, and second, it projected an image that the surgically altered or enhanced body was not inherently wrong or unnatural, as long as it went undetected. Mirroring Fraser's findings, one common way that the repertoire of the natural was woven throughout discourses about Botox was to distinguish between "good" and "bad" Botox—"good" Botox was Botox that could not be detected, and "bad" Botox referred to faces that appeared frozen, or obviously paralyzed. Dr. Weinstein and the overwhelming majority of practitioners with whom I spoke rejected and even ridiculed Botox injections that created the appearance of an expressionless blank slate. Moreover, because their patients were fleshy advertisements for their practice, many dermatologists and plastic surgeons refused to overinject their patients. Fort Lauderdale cosmetic dermatologist Rumi Acevedo proclaimed, "I will never inject someone so that they have zero mobility. I always make sure they have control over their facial movements. If somebody tells me they want to have no movement, I will try my best to persuade them otherwise, or else I will send them elsewhere."

The interviewees revealed that the moralization of aesthetics is a means by which practitioners inscribe their expert knowledge on their patients' bodies. Fashioned within a White, middle-class habitus, their limited view of beauty and normalcy was quite literally etched onto their patients' faces. Nonetheless, the strong individualist tone that permeated Botox's marketing revealed how, at the end of the day, the onus is always on the consumer to use Botox appropriately and responsibly.

The Universal and Invisible White Middle-Class Body

Marketing, media, and medical discourses around Botox regularly implied a generic body that was White, middle-class, and female. Although Botox users are disproportionately White, racial and ethnic minorities do constitute approximately 25 percent of all Botox users, and these numbers are rising.[101] However, the fact that one-fourth of its consumer base was women of color was not something I heard when I asked Botox providers about the racial and ethnic distributions of their consumer base. All practitioners told me that their consumers were over 90 percent White (except for those in Miami, who were more likely to tell me that a larger percentage were Latina), and a few of them even mentioned the off-point truism of "Black don't crack" to reference the common, though not universal, tendency for White skin to show signs of aging earlier than non-White skin. Some practitioners went into great detail with me, explaining how most pigmented people, specifically, darker-skinned Latinas, Asians, and African Africans, get much less sun damage to their skin because of their pigmentation and that their skin does not become thin and lose elasticity in the same way that Caucasian skin does.[102] However, although physicians used medical and scientific rationales to explain racial differences in pigmentation and aging skin, my analysis of media images and discourses suggested that women of color fall outside of the mainstream aging panic not just because of their darker phenotypes and facial muscle makeup, as so many dermatologists and other providers told me, but more so because the prototypical woman is a White woman. Beauty and anti-aging products are marketed to make women look like the best version of a woman, and that best version is a White or, at the very least, a light-skinned woman. Thus, non-White women were significantly less visible in the marketing of Botox and other anti-aging interventions. In her analysis of magazines and cosmetic surgery, Brooks also found that Whiteness was both dominant and invisible, illuminating what she called the "powerful absent-presence of race" in that Whiteness was universally assumed and implied in constructions and prescriptions of hegemonic femininity.[103]

Aside from a handful of articles in *O, The Oprah Magazine*, *Vogue*, and *Marie Claire*, the majority of articles that mentioned racial or ethnic variations in Botox use came from *Essence*, a magazine with a predominantly Black female readership. *Essence* published a total of nineteen articles mentioning Botox between 2000 and 2013.[104] Much of what I read in these articles mirrored themes that emerged in White-centered publications. For example, articles warned against going overboard, advocated a natural look, and cautioned about going to an inexperienced practitioner.

However, because of its primarily Black women audience, there were significant and explicitly racialized departures from this script. Most of the articles in *Essence* touched on the fact that the proverbial "Black don't crack" was only true up until a certain age and that more and more African American women were turning to Botox. Reporting on the rise of Black women in their forties, fifties, and sixties getting Botox, one article, entitled "Is Plastic Surgery the New Black for Black Women?" observed that Black women began using Botox significantly later than their White counterparts because "we have thicker skin and more melanin, so we don't have a lot of wrinkles until we're older. However, because of this, there is a rise of Black women getting more Botox, typically around ages 40–60."[105] Drawing on images of celebrity Botox users, including actress and former beauty queen Vanessa Williams and talk show host Wendy Williams, some articles contended that improving economic status and workplace success among Black women was leading to a growth in plastic surgery consumption. The aforementioned article, "Is Plastic Surgery the New Black for Black Women?" reported that, as Black women rose in the professional ranks, they were "making more money and becoming more educated" about cosmetic enhancements.[106] Thus, much like articles in White-centered magazines, discourses in *Essence* around Botox assumed an upper middle-class body, highlighting the extent to which Botox is about cultivating appearances of class distinction.[107]

Although there are no official statistics on social class and cosmetic enhancements, the monetary expense of such procedures suggest that it is a relatively privileged practice. Averaging approximately $300–$400 for one procedure and needing to be continuously topped off two to three times a year, injections potentially cost upward of $1,000 in one year. Botox is not exactly cheap, yet it is significantly more affordable (in the short run) than surgical procedures like face-lifts and brow-lifts. As such, Botox is aggressively marketed as affordable and accessible. Even though marketing, media, and medical discourses have increasingly normalized nonsurgical anti-aging practices, most women are without the time or resources to provide themselves with even the minimum of what such a regimen requires. Further, since Botox is framed within discourses of personal responsibility, the many women who cannot afford Botox risk being labeled as "lazy" and "neglectful."

What Happens When the Body Is Male?

The number of male Botox consumers in the United States more than tripled from 2001 to 2013—to almost 385,000, or 6% of the total Botoxed population.[108] While some applaud this as a sign that men are seizing their right to self-improvement, most social and feminist critics view men's involvement in this terrain as part of the universal capitulation to consumer capitalism,[109] and others worry that men are falling into the same cultural traps as women.[110] With men, aesthetic clinics and physicians are beginning to realize that they are ignoring an untapped consumer base and are finding innovative ways to market to them. Walter Kennedy was a strikingly handsome Washington, DC, dermatologist and former college football player whom I interviewed in 2013. Only a few short months prior to our interview, Dr. Kennedy had opened the first men's aesthetic clinic in the country. About his experience, Dr. Kennedy explained:

I think there's a lot that we can do as providers in dermatology, you know, to actually enhance the awareness that it's okay for guys to want to look better, I mean beyond all the pressures you know. . . . Men are becoming increasingly more cosmetically conscious. Men's skin-care products are the fastest growing segment of the cosmeceutical market. . . . So my theory with medical aesthetics is that they just really haven't been marketed to. When Botox was FDA approved in 2002, the companies or the physicians targeted the most interested patient population, which was women, and I think that's changing. . . . So I have taken the initiative and tried to kind of create a space and really seek them out and start marketing to them, so I started a men's laser and cosmetic center.

Kennedy's pioneering business venture is one of many indications that the marketing of cosmetic enhancements to men is on the rise. An entire article devoted to reporting on the new trend of men going under the needle appeared in *Time* magazine in 2009.[111] Aptly titled "Boytox," the article talked about how men's use of Botox had stirring implications for gendered norms of appearance, since the vertical creases between the eyebrows and the horizontal lines on the forehead have long been seen as markers of masculinity. Practitioners told me about how careful they were when injecting men with Botox not to "feminize the masculine face." For example, as dermatologist Ivan Camacho explained, "The most important thing when you treat a man is that you want to make sure that whatever you do, you keep the masculine features of the face, you don't want a man looking like a woman." Cultural ideologies about gender, specifically that masculinity should be always constructed in opposition to femininity, were literally written onto men's faces by practitioners. Injecting Botox "correctly" on men meant not simply maintaining the "masculine features of the face" but preserving a corporeal façade of masculinity untainted by the feminization of beauty ideals.

Yet, even as providers told me how important it was to use Botox on men so the masculine features of the brow were maintained, their narratives also indicated that the popularity of Botox was gradually transforming how we think about masculine features and aging men's facial wrinkles. The brow creases that were once viewed as masculine and distinguished are increasingly becoming reconfigured as lines that make men appear worried or tired, lines that are seen as a rather troublesome liability in the midst of economic downturn and heightened job competition. As the "Boytox" article in *Time* magazine reported, "One of the many things the laid-off cannot afford is to look their age."[112] Said Washington, DC, dermatologist Walter Kennedy, "You don't want to be the one who looks the oldest, and you don't want to be the one looking tired." Affirming this trend was also South Florida dermatologist Alex Weinstein, who stated that, "although it seems odd, there's a lot of men that are doing Botox, especially with the way the economy is, people are more concerned with maintaining their youthful appearance and being able to get jobs or look like they look active enough or young enough to maintain a high-energy level at work, and that seems to be a big motivation why guys are getting it done is to have that appearance." For men, the privileging of a youthful face that exhibits health and vitality has supplanted the importance of seniority in the workplace.

The "Crisis" of Masculinity and the Rise of the Metrosexual

A dominant theme in masculinity studies has been devoted to understanding how men negotiate feelings of having lost control against a cultural and historical backdrop of shifting gender relations.[113] In a prolific cultural history of manhood in America, the sociologist Michael Kimmel documents how, since the early nineteenth century, the rapid pace of urbanization, industrialization, and other social and political change have caused men to feel a loss of power and control over a world where gender relations were no longer fixed and stable—a perpetual condition that Kimmel refers to as a "crisis" in masculinity.[114] One of the ways by which men have always negotiated this "crisis" in masculinity has been to seek comfort in controlling the only thing they could—their bodies. It is useful then to examine the rise of men's Botox use against this "crisis" of masculinity, in which men experience uncertainty and anxiety regarding shifting gendered norms and expectations.[115] Studies have found that men who seek cosmetic enhancements construct themselves as active and rational consumers seizing control over their aging bodies against a contextual backdrop pervaded by gender uncertainty.[116] For example, Michael Atkinson's conversations with men who underwent cosmetic surgery in Canada revealed that cosmetic surgery was a response to a collectively felt loss of established hegemony due to the current "crisis" in masculinity.[117] Similarly, in her analysis of cultural and medical texts, Fraser found that, "for men, a reaffirmation of masculinity as ambitious and strongly-work oriented creates space for an alliance between masculinity and cosmetic surgery."[118]

Mirroring these findings, men's magazines and Botox providers who were seeking to expand their business to male consumers have often framed Botox use as a masculine and rational body management strategy that could help them cope with increasing competition in the workplace from women and younger applicants.[119] Masculine discourses about Botox have framed it as a shrewd business tactic and have situated it within the "rhetoric of career enhancement,"[120] thus allowing men entrée into this otherwise feminized terrain. Constantly referenced in magazines was men's uncertainty about how to navigate a workplace where gender relations were in flux. For example, Marian Salzman, a co-author of *The Future of Men*, a pseudointellectual commentary about an emerging breed of man, told *Esquire* what the future holds for American men: "You will work for a woman. . . . In the future, your boss will likely be a woman. And she'll be better educated than you."[121] She also predicted to her readers, "You will look more like Joan Rivers. Men will unapologetically embrace a whole array of products and procedures that will keep them looking and feeling younger. In their 30s and 40s, men will turn to moisturizers, hair thickeners, a little nip and tuck here and there, collagen, Botox."[122] Women's real or imagined boundary crossings into masculine social territories were used to fuel men's "anxiety" about their masculine identities, selves, and bodies.[123]

Another theme in masculinity studies has interrogated how dominant practices of masculinity adapt to changing social and historical conditions by appropriating from femininities and other less powerful, or marginalized, masculinities.[124] The metrosexual man is one such example of this appropriation.[125] A masculine archetype that emerged in the 1990s, the metrosexual is a cosmopolitan man who is polished, sophisticated, fashionable, and concerned with proper skin and hair care.[126] Alleging that the metrosexual is "just as much a meditation about class as he is a new embodiment of manhood," Michael Kimmel critiques the metrosexual archetype as "depoliticized consumerism masquerading as freedom."[127]

Men's lifestyle magazines such as *GQ*, *Esquire*, *Men's Fitness*, and *Men's Health* have instructed the new metrosexual man on proper aesthetics and style.[128] In recent years, Botox has garnered small but significant attention in these publications. Narrative frames about Botox in these magazines has revealed how men were told to use aesthetics to augment and sustain their power within the current "crisis of masculinity." In addition to constructing men's aesthetics as a way to appropriate class status, men's magazines emptied Botox of its association with femininity. For example, an article in *Esquire* read, "Botox is not just manly now, it's going to change the world. . . . Though it used to be known as strictly a chick thing, a kind of poor woman's face-lift, it has turned out to be much more."[129] Given cultural stereotypes that link masculinity and violence, it is perhaps not surprising that so many magazine articles about Botox drew upon violent tropes and warrior narratives to redefine Botox from a pampering cosmetic practice to a masculine testament about one's ability to withstand a painful body ordeal. An article in *Men's Fitness* proclaimed, "It's more masculine to get jabbed a couple of times a year than to load up on a thousand different creams and potions."[130] Similarly, in a personal narrative presented in *Esquire* magazine that explored the author's experience of using Botox for the first time, he wrote: "Dr. Pearlman's assistant is wiping my face and smiling like I'm a little boy whose face is dirty. It's bloody, actually. . . . I can feel the nerves dying, curling into themselves like when you spray weed killer on a dandelion in your driveway."[131] Infusing Botox with warrior narratives about blood, death, and pain allowed men's lifestyle magazines to resist feminization and position their readers as unequivocally masculine.

Medicine and the media are machineries of knowledge production that powerfully influence our ideas about appropriate aging, beauty, gender, bodies, and self-care. They also profoundly mold how we think about and what we know about Botox. Nourishing Allergan's already aggressive and successful advertising campaign, the dominant discourses circulating within these institutions project Botox as a regulating presence in our cultural landscape and using Botox as a normalized way of performing femininity and of embodying neoliberal citizenship. Serving as ghost marketers for Allergan, journalists, physicians, and other Botox providers have extolled Botox's positive effects and promoted it as a rational, practical, and necessary practice of responsible self-care. They endorse the belief that it is a moral violation not to uncritically embrace Botox or anti-aging medicine more broadly as they simultaneously validate the precarious assumption that aging, or at least the appearance of it, is a disorder or a pathology. As a medicalized impairment, aging is a condition that we are told we can prevent, an ability that is not only desirable, but also obligatory. However, the expectation that we can or should "fight" or "battle" aging in any way belies a lack of consideration for how this alleged obligation takes place in a socially stratified society in which many of its citizens do not even have access to basic health care. With more extensive marketing devoted to women across class lines, Black women, and men, it is likely that increasing numbers of Americans will be fed the message that Botox is a moral imperative. As such, the economically and socially marginalized will likely experience further shame and disadvantage for not using Botox, or for bargaining for Botox, or for failing to achieve the natural, effortless look that comes with the high price of a skilled injector.

2

The Turf War over Botox

Dr. Richard Kramer was a dentist whom I interviewed in May 2014. Almost completely bald with enormous beady brown eyes, Dr. Kramer made up for his small stature with his generous and exuberant personality. I came across Dr. Kramer after conducting a Google search of "dentists who do Botox" in one of the cities I used for recruitment. He replied to my introductory e-mail promptly, and within a week I was in his office conducting an interview about his recent foray into Botox. Dr. Kramer offered Botox injections as "an added service to his patients" and only charged ten dollars per unit, which was considerably less than the rate of plastic surgeons, dermatologists, and even some medical spas. Like Dr. Edelstein, another dentist whom I interviewed a few months earlier, Dr. Kramer told me how dentists were "natural injectors" since they understood the anatomy of the face and worked with needles on a regular basis. However, unlike Dr. Edelstein, who did not use Internet marketing or have Botox brochures in his waiting room, Dr. Kramer aggressively advertised Botox injections both on the Internet and in his office. In addition to using Botox for the therapeutic treatment of temporomandibular joint disorders (TMJ), Dr. Kramer started integrating Botox Cosmetic into his practice at the request of his wife, who wanted free injections for herself and reduced prices for her friends.

Dr. Kramer had recently completed a two-day course on Botox with the American Academy of Facial Esthetics and at the time of the interview had only injected a handful of his patients. When I asked him about foreseen complications, he responded,

> There are not many complications that can occur, unless you don't know
> what you're doing. Unless you get the wrong muscle which anyone can

do, or unless you burst a capillary in the forehead or inject into the capillary, but that could happen to anyone. Those are one of those risks and complications that can happen to anyone. It's not a dentist versus cosmetic surgeon. One would not know how to handle that better than the other. The risks of injecting into the wrong muscle or bursting a capillary are legitimate risks of Botox. However, they are risks one learns to avoid with practice and experience.

The recent two-day course that Dr. Kramer took did little to prepare him for dealing with complications that other providers with extensive training and experience were well equipped to handle.

Later in our conversation, when I asked Dr. Kramer if he injected himself, he responded that he did not because he tried once, his hand shook, and he missed. When I wanted to talk to him about different injection techniques for men and women, he replied that he had so little experience injecting that he wasn't able to speak to that just yet. Finally, when I inquired about his youngest Botox patient, he told me that she was twenty-nine and then continued, "And she . . . to me really didn't look like she needed it, but she has already had it, so I didn't have a baseline to compare it to. And it's really not up to me to decide whether or not she needs it or not."

Consider how antithetical Dr. Kramer's account is from the dermatologists and plastic surgeons I spoke about in the previous chapter, who saw it as their job to inscribe their view of normalcy and beauty onto the bodies of their patients. Similarly, contrast this with the more experienced practitioners who spoke in detail about how important it was to use Botox on men in such a way as to maintain the masculine features of the brow or else risk feminizing the face. Finally, note that Dr. Kramer was not comfortable enough to inject his own brow—whereas almost every plastic surgeon and dermatologist I interviewed injected himself or herself regularly—and you have a cautionary tale about Dr. Kramer's insufficient training. I am not saying that Dr. Kramer will not one day be a skilled injector with years of practice, experience, and further training.

Rather, I draw upon our conversation to illustrate the extent to which a supplier-induced demand permeates our current era of cosmetic medicine, as growing numbers of medical, health, and wellness providers seduce consumers with bargains on Botox and other cosmetic procedures.

Dermatologists, plastic surgeons, magazine articles, and Allergan's pharmaceutical marketing literature consistently warn consumers that bargaining for Botox by going to an inexperienced provider is a dangerous risk. Some of these concerns are legitimate, as my conversation with Richard Kramer elucidates. In this chapter, however, I show that much of this concern for patient safety is more about dermatologists and plastic surgeons wanting to protect their lucrative turf.

Because Botox is so often the stepping-stone into the broader realm of cosmetic bodily enhancement, it sits at the center of the competitive, commercial sector of clinical medicine in America.[1] Changes within medicine, the economy, and the health-care industry have powerfully shaped the supply of practitioners willing and eager to provide Botox injections. Allergan's aggressive marketing campaign has not only stimulated increased demand for Botox, it has led to more competitive pricing and an intraprofessional turf war around the drug. On one side, there are the dermatologists and plastic surgeons. On another side are the growing numbers of other licensed physicians—for example, gynecologists and family doctors—who are interested in a piece of the pie. Finally, there are the dentists, aestheticians, nurses, and medical assistants who in many states can inject Botox legally, often without supervision from a licensed physician.[2]

Although the overwhelming majority of Botox providers learn the contours of cosmetic injection applications by taking courses with Allergan's educational team, practitioners interested in integrating Botox into their existing practices do not necessarily have to take a course through Allergan. There are an abundance of non-Allergan-sponsored training courses that offer injection certifications, and several of these certifications authorize practitioners to purchase Botox through Allergan. There are also various Internet training services that offer online live interactive aesthetic training, some even twenty-four hours a day. Marketed to medical professionals looking to supplement their existing income, these Internet sites, such as Future Aesthetic Service Training, provide a two-hour online Botox Basics class for $695. Online instructors described as "business medical professionals" and "entrepreneurs and self-starters" are available to offer guidance in injection techniques and entrepreneurial advice with opening and managing aesthetic businesses and medical spas.[3] In addition to these for-profit aesthetic training courses, there are also countless free YouTube tutorials demonstrating how to inject Botox. A Google search on "How to learn to inject Botox Cosmetic" yielded thousands of video results, and a Google image search on "How to inject Botox" revealed pages and pages of facial maps and diagrams resembling paint-by-number portraits of women's faces. A quick scan of these images and videos would lead one to believe that Botox is a relatively safe, simple, and straightforward cosmetic procedure, one that any medical or aesthetic professional is qualified to perform. And some might agree; many of the dermatologists and plastic surgeons with whom I spoke supported this claim. However, the collective caveat, epitomized by Abraham Martin, a New Orleans plastic surgeon, was that "Botox is easy to do but hard to do well." Elaborating on this stipulation, dermatologist Sonya James explained, "It's not rocket science, but at the same time, it's not like you can just look on the Internet and find the Google map of someone's face and figure out where to put Botox. . . . But that is what the medi-spas and these aestheticians who don't even have a college degree are doing; they are often just following a diagram that they found on the Internet." With an abundance of online, YouTube, and two-day crash courses available to interested Botox providers, and absolutely no standardization of content or any recognized measure of competence,[4] came considerable disagreements about who was best trained to inject Botox, who could provide the best results and safety, and who best understood beauty, facial anatomy, and symmetry. Later in this chapter, I discuss these disputes more in depth, but first I want to consider how we got here in the first place. How did we get to this point in history where physicians, a once-noble profession dedicated to caring for the sick, are presently battling over which specialty is best qualified to administer aesthetic medicine? A look at the structural shifts around the reconfiguration of the American health-care system, as well as changes in physicians' compensation structures and the increasing commercialization and deregulation of American medicine, provides insight into the social and economic forces that fuel the turf wars around Botox.

The Rise of Commercial Medicine

Our current model of commercial medicine—where physicians and pharmaceutical companies can advertise directly to consumers and compete for profit—is of recent origin.[5] Until 1975, physicians, lawyers, and other learned professions were protected from federal antitrust laws and were protected from the free-market ideology and corporate forms of organization that characterized most other sectors of the economy. In fact, the American Medical Association's (AMA) first code of ethics in 1847 banned patient solicitation. The AMA thought that commercial medicine would pose a challenge to their struggle for professional status, and leaders in the association believed that advertising and patient solicitation would threaten their long-standing efforts to convince the American public that medicine was not a commodity. As late as 1976, the AMA had an explicit ban on advertising. Then in 1975 the Supreme Court ruled in *Goldfarb v. Virginia State Bar* that lawyers and other learned professions were not exempt from the Sherman Antitrust Act, which made it illegal to prohibit business activities that reduced competition in the marketplace and restrained trade. Soon after, the Federal Trade Commission (FTC) used the *Goldfarb v. Virginia State Bar* ruling to file an antitrust complaint against the American Medical Association's ban on direct advertising, charging them with restraint of trade.[6] In 1978, the FTC declared that the AMA ban against advertising and marketing was a violation of the Sherman Antitrust Act, and

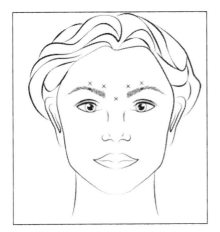 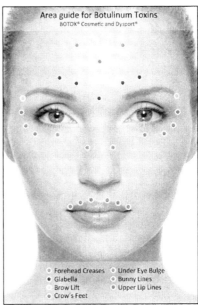

Some diagrams found easily online intended to show where to inject Botox.

medicine—specifically cosmetic medicine—became the commodity it is today.

Initially, physicians, especially cosmetic surgeons, did not welcome the FTC's overturning of the ban on advertising. They asserted that opening the health-care industry to free-market competition would threaten the existing regulatory system in which professional associations had control over access to training, hospital privileges, and peer referral in order to protect vulnerable patients from exploitation by unscrupulous physicians.[7] However, it wasn't too long before the new model of market competition took force, restructuring health care into a competitive marketplace where patients are reconfigured into consumers who are expected to rely on dubious comparisons of cost and quality of care in order to form judgments about their health-care providers.[8]

Nowhere is this reconfiguration more apparent than in the field of aesthetic medicine. Unlike the vast majority of medical specialties that operate in a seller's market based on patient need, medical aesthetics are based on a buyer's market where practitioners actively seek out otherwise healthy patients who pay them big money for cosmetic procedures.[9] In today's cosmetic medicine industry, physicians no longer hold all the power over consumers. The once-dominant doctor/patient model where doctors exert authority, has been transformed into a provider/consumer model, where the consumer's choices hold the most power. Patients are now consumers, and the stigmatized or diseased body has been replaced with the consumer body, or "a body with spending power."[10] In cosmetic surgical culture, the doctor is now a servant, a metaphorical suitor who "must woo his client, win her, and then hang on to her."[11] In our current ethos of commercial medicine, patients are expected to be informed and knowledgeable clients, educated consumers who are no longer entirely dependent on a single physician for information. Consumers of health care and wellness have unprecedented choices and information and find themselves awash in a media landscape of copious medical advertising.[12]

In a poignant sociohistorical analysis of the commercialization of cosmetic surgery, Deborah Sullivan documented how cosmetic medicine, because of its lucrative payout and amorphous boundaries, has had to rely more heavily on marketing for its survival than any other medical specialty.[13] The first paid advertisements appeared for cosmetic surgery in print media in the 1970s. By the late 1980s, the selling of cosmetic surgery was routine. Not all welcomed this change; one prominent leader in the American Society of Plastic and Reconstructive Surgeons lambasted the field of elective aesthetic surgery for resembling "the midway of a cheap carnival, complete with flashing colored lights, gaudy trappings, and loud barkers."[14] Seemingly overnight, advertising became the norm for the cosmetic surgical industry, and by 1997 the marketing department of the American Society of Plastic and Reconstructive Surgeons had a one million dollar budget.[15] Around the same time, a surge of private health-care marketing firms began to appear, offering public relations and advertising services to physicians and clinics looking to promote their work and broaden their consumer base. These firms alleged that selling cosmetic enhancements was akin to selling an automobile or a house and required long-term and blatant advertising. Since advertising generates the perception and illusion of need, in only a few short decades the cosmetic surgical industry began to do what all commercial ventures do: They began to create a demand for cosmetic surgery instead of merely responding to it. We now find ourselves in a cosmetic medical industry of supplier-induced demand, in which physicians and other aesthetic experts use their "culturally recognized superior knowledge" to stimulate demand.[16] This entrepreneurial aspect of the cosmetic surgical and enhancement industry sets it apart from conventional medical practice.[17]

Taken together, this provider/consumer model and era of supplier-induced demand has resulted in Botox providers using mass-marketing efforts to draw in business and distinguish their services from the competition. Dermatologists, plastic surgeons, other physicians, and even dentists extensively advertise their Botox services in their offices and on billboards, magazines, newspapers, television, and the Internet. Many dermatologists send monthly e-mails to their patients, offering specials on Botox, dermal fillers, and other cosmetic procedures. Some cosmetic surgeons run promotional seminars in country clubs or go to beauty salons and spas to promote their practice. Others turn to social media, offering daily promotional deals, and some have Facebook, Instagram, and Twitter pages that advertise promotions and specials to their followers.

In addition to increasing advertising and patient solicitation, there are other forces that have fueled the supply-induced demand for aesthetic medicine. As a result of changes in the health-care system during the last three decades, there has been a vast increase in the number of physicians with increased specializations and subspecializations, while the number of physicians who practice general or family medicine has significantly dwindled. With more and more physicians facing intense competition in their narrow specialties, elective procedures that are paid for out of pocket are areas of practice that are increasingly attractive to all types of doctors, not just those employed in cosmetic surgery or der-

A Botox promotion ad.

A "Botox Fridays" ad.

Ad for a Botox "Lunch and Learn" for new Botox users.

matology.[18] Free trade within medicine allows all licensed physicians to legally perform office-based cosmetic medicine, regardless of whether they are board certified in cosmetic surgery or dermatology. The increase in physicians reeling from declining insurance reimbursements along with reduced demand for noncosmetic services has intensified doctors' interest in the lucrative realm of cosmetics. This move allows physicians to "escape the corporate transformation of the health care system . . . devoid of third-party regulatory oversight and paperwork."[19]

Practitioners can make big money providing Botox. As with any elective procedure that is not medically necessary for functioning and survival, cosmetic Botox is not covered by health insurance, and thus physicians do not have to wait months to be reimbursed by insurance agencies. Because of this, not only are increasing numbers of dermatologists and plastic surgeons offering Botox, but growing numbers of obstetricians and internists are also beginning to integrate Botox into their practices. Disenchanted by managed care and diminishing reimbursements, these doctors are looking for a way to supplement shrinking incomes.[20]

Although physicians are still financially well off relative to the majority of Americans, cuts in their compensation have been such that the lifestyles that they have become accustomed to are under siege. Consequently a growing number of ob-gyns, family doctors, and emergency room physicians are offering Botox, with some even opening and directing their own medical spas in order to supplement their declining incomes. Even though the majority of nonspecializing Botox providers are likely ethical, responsible, and conscientious, their reputation is being eclipsed by the growing contingent of profit-driven and business-minded practitioners who have arisen out of America's commercialized medical system.

The Battle over Botox

Turf wars have a long history in American medicine, and the battle for lucrative medical territory is nothing new. Obstetricians have replaced midwifery and later general practitioners in the claim to childbirth, orthopedists and neurosurgeons battle over the spinal column, psychologists and psychiatrists clash over prescribing privileges, anesthesiologists and nurse anesthetists are in conflict over profitable medical turf, and radiologists are in tireless defense of their new specialty.[21] These territorial clashes tend to flare up with transformations in the health-care system and when new technologies enter the scene.[22] Nowhere has this been more evident than the case of cosmetic medicine.[23] Sullivan's sociological investigation of the expansion and commercialization of cosmetic surgery revealed how the occupational territory of cosmetic medicine has always been susceptible to invasion by other specialties. The battle over who is competent to provide cosmetic surgery and enhancements continues today as "practitioners from different medical disciplines sit uncomfortably together" in a rapidly growing industry with nebulous boundaries.[24] Consumers, tantalized by the promise of eternal youth, find themselves in an unregulated world, flooded with a multiplicity of Botox providers with very dissimilar qualifications.

When I spoke with Miami-based dermatologist Jonathon Black during the American Academy of Dermatology's annual meeting in 2013, he expressed his frustrations with the flooded marketplace of Botox providers:

> This is something that we as a specialty, dermatology, are struggling with. Initially it was kind of in our hands, then the economy took a dive, and plastic surgeons started doing it because they needed to survive because people weren't doing ten- or fifteen-thousand-dollar surgeries, breast surgeries, or face-lifts as often, so it was a way to keep revenue coming in. But now the challenge has expanded. Ob-gyns are doing it, and dentists are doing it, people who are not trained at all are doing it. And what this means is that now people are price shopping, you know. . . . and there's the Groupons and the medi-spas. So this is one of the struggles for dermatologists, we have to fight to show people that we are the best, that we are the safest, and we're trained specifically in this that we are kind

of experts in this field, us and facial plastic surgeons. We have to get the word out there that you should be coming to us rather than the Groupon people.

Almost all of the dermatologists with whom I spoke were critical of the growing numbers of nonspecializing doctors and other practitioners providing discount aesthetic procedures. Still, some dermatologists were sympathetic to their colleagues in other specialties who they knew were growing increasingly frustrated with declining reimbursements, medical insurance bureaucracies, and managed care. Miami dermatologist Rebecca Steinberg said:

I think that the reimbursement of health care is absolutely playing a role. It's the reality of health care today. If you are seeing your patients but you are not getting paid, how can you sustain your practice? You can't keep your practice with no money. So, can I really blame the internal medicine doctor who is seeing fifty patients a day and not getting paid anything, and he realizes he can make lot of money if he starts doing laser hair removal and Botox? I can't really blame them. But if you do decide to do this, then you better be trained and know exactly what you are doing.

Then, a few minutes later, she joked, "The two months of OB-GYN that I did in medical school, to me, don't qualify me to deliver a baby." Even as Dr. Steinberg recognized that shifting institutional forces more so than unscrupulous doctors were to blame for the flooding of cost-cutting Botox providers, her narrative was filled with precautionary undertones that denigrated her competition's lack of qualifications, training, and skills.

Dermatologists and plastic surgeons talked about the importance of using educational marketing to inform the public about the importance of responsible doctor shopping over price shopping. Yet they were also adamant that individual consumers should be held accountable for their own cosmetic wellness. The late celebrity cosmetic dermatologist Frederic Brandt told me, "I always say, initially people were too afraid about the safety of Botox, and now people are too nonchalant about it." Dermatologist Jonathon Black stated, "I try to tell patients, Be reasonable with your clothing, be reasonable, you know buy things on sale, or consignment, but it's your face, you only have one face, you only have one skin, you know, be careful." As with any other exercise in responsible consumption, Botox consumers were expected to carefully research the qualifications, background, and safety of the Botox provider—not unlike shopping for a car or a house.[25] Thus the onus is always on the consumer to participate wisely and responsibly in the doctor-shopping process. Those who foolishly opt for the bargain price over the qualifications of the provider are dismissed as deserving of their misfortune. Abraham Martin, the New Orleans plastic surgeon, derided bargain shoppers: "Anybody who would go to a dentist for their Botox is just asking for trouble. I mean, would you go to a plastic surgeon to get a filling?"

Although Botox injections were significantly more expensive when purchased from a dermatologist or plastic surgeon, these doctors maintained that their extensive medical training was worth the premium. Jacob Schwartzman, a former plastic surgeon and practicing dermatologist, who charged three hundred dollars for every thirty minutes of his time, defended the cost: "I've done face-lifts, I've taken the skin off of faces, I know where the muscles are. I know when I see somebody where to put the relaxant and the filler. And you take somebody who has gone to a weekend class or two weekend classes, it's different than doing a three-year residency and having the experience." Dermatologist Rebecca Steinberg compared going to a nonspecializing physician for Botox to "getting a haircut for thirty bucks at Supercuts" instead of "getting a haircut by a top stylist who obviously has the experience and training." Many of the physicians I interviewed expressed frustration at the trend toward price shopping for Botox injections and other cosmetic procedures and saw this as a crucial threat to the integrity of their profession. They hailed their expertise with injectables as superior to other specialists who lacked their extensive training and warned that many of these nonspecializing physicians were diluting their Botox or cutting costs by purchasing counterfeit Botox from foreign suppliers.

Miami dermatologist Jonathon Black told me how, in late 2012, the FDA wrote to over 350 medical practices that bought unapproved versions of Botox from suppliers owned by the distributor firm Canada Drugs and told them to stop administering it to their patients.[26] What is more, the FDA released this list to the public as a means of warning consumers about the circulating illegal Botox supply. When he told me about these recent events, Dr. Black rejoiced in what he saw as a small victory for legitimate Botox providers. He told me that this is like the FDA putting "a big scarlet B on their foreheads that they're selling fake Botox."[27]

Even as plastic surgeons and dermatologists alike expressed frustration at the growing numbers of nonspecializing physicians offering bargains on Botox, most realized that things weren't changing any time soon and conceded to this territorial tug-of-war. Despite the fact that Botox and other aesthetic services brought in a great deal of revenue for dermatologists, the seduction of this supplementary income wasn't enough to persuade them to allow their cosmetic practice to supplant their medical practice. Except for Dr. Rumi Acevedo and the late Dr. Frederic Brandt, all of the other dermatologists with whom I spoke opted to keep their practices primarily medical, allowing for only a small percentage of their services to be cosmetic. Dermatologist Jacob Schwartzman told me that he allowed cosmetics to be only 10 percent of his practice because he did not want to compete with the plenitude of nonspecializing physicians opening medical spas in his city. He elaborated:

I'm not competing with an ob-gyn who's got physician assistants doing their injections like the clinic down the street. They advertise beautifully, they do a great job, but that's not who I'm going to compete with. And I've tried competing with them; I ran an ad once that said, A dermatologist doing open-heart surgery, how ridiculous is that? You know, how ridiculous would that be, because, if you needed open-heart surgery you would

go to a specialist, and if you want skin care, you would come to a dermatologist. But the next month, that ob-gyn group ran an ad that said, If all
you want is Botox, why do you want to sit next to—and they had a picture
of a kid crying with a wart on his finger—why would you want to be in a
waiting room with a bunch of kids with warts? So I realized I wasn't going
to win that battle. So I just stopped fighting it.

Although Dr. Schwartzman's efforts inevitably failed, his story brings to
light the new marketing tactics used by medical spas to promote their
growing business. Such aggressive advertising has pushed dermatologists and cosmetic surgeons, some of whom had never advertised until
this point, to retaliate by promoting their own medical practices in print
and Internet advertisements. Such ads, which Sullivan has referred to as
"edvertising," are fashioned under the protective pretense of educating
consumers about the risks of going to an unscrupulous or unqualified
practitioner.[28] In consequence, consumers find themselves drowning
even further in a barrage of more advertisements that further energize
the cultural imperative of aesthetic medicine.

What Defines a Qualified Injector?

Most of us would agree that watching a YouTube video, taking a two-
hour online course, or following a diagram from Google does not qualify
one to be a skilled Botox injector. But does this mean that one has to be
a dermatologist or plastic surgeon to be able to provide good injections?
Since the training among the medical and aesthetic professionals who
were legally permitted to inject Botox was anything but uniform, there
were considerable disagreements about who was best trained to inject
Botox, who provided the best results under the safest conditions, and
who best understood beauty, facial anatomy, and symmetry.

My conversation with dermatological resident Dr. Deborah Jaye highlights the complexity and the tensions involved in trying to define who
was best qualified to perform and provide Botox injections. We began

the conversation on this topic with her telling me about the extensive training in injectables that she was currently receiving in her residency program. For the first six months, residents observed attending physicians and then moved to practicing on one another until they were finally allowed to provide discounted injections in the resident clinic once a week. By their third year, many of the residents were excellent injectors. Admitting that many of the third-year residents who performed regular weekly injections at the clinic might be better trained than some of the more seasoned dermatologists in town, Dr. Jaye acknowledged the advantages of coming of age in the current dermatological era of neurotoxins and fillers. She conceded that even though a dermatologist could be practicing medicine for decades, this did not necessarily mean that he or she had as much experience as a resident who was learning and practicing cutting-edge injectable techniques on a regular basis. The following explanation from Dr. Jaye revealed how the process of defining a qualified injector was fraught with tensions and contradictions:

> What defines a qualified injector? Well, it's hard to say, I mean someone who is a family medicine doctor could take an extensive training on Botox, has done it for twenty years, and maybe they are just as good as a dermatologist or a plastic surgeon. But then the scary part is that they could have just gone and taken a one-day course. . . . And I guess I would rather a dentist do that than the aesthetician, because at least they have the background knowledge of the anatomy of the face and things like, that but it's still somewhat bothersome that people can do that, but I guess eventually they'll practice enough and probably be good at it, they'll see their own consultations. I think with dentists it's the same thing, you know, they are medically trained, they know the facial anatomy, so I'm sure there are some dentists who are excellent at it, but I just think you need to look at people's backgrounds. But I guess I am pretty okay with any M.D. as long as the training is appropriate, but I think the problem comes into, How can the patient compare these people and know really what their training was? And I just feel like, I just worry about the patient

safety and if the patients think any doctor is totally qualified because they are a doctor.

Like Dr. Jaye, the majority of providers with whom I spoke did not always have consistent and agreed upon messages about what qualified a skilled Botox injector, and often there were inconsistencies that emerged in individual narratives. Where some argued that a specialty in dermatology or plastics was obligatory, others affirmed that practice, training, and experience were more important. Where some insisted that advanced medical training was required, others argued that having an aesthetic eye was paramount.

The theme of possessing an aesthetic or artistic eye was one that reverberated through many of my conversations with practitioners, regardless of their specialization or their experience level. These practitioners likened their entrée into cosmetic medicine as akin to an artistic calling. For example, Rumi Acevedo, a doctor of osteopathy, first completed a residency in family medicine before he went into cosmetic dermatology and told me that his decision to switch fields and complete an additional residency in dermatology was a result of his "passion for beauty, aesthetics, and symmetry." Scholars who have documented the long-standing association between art, aesthetic beauty, and cosmetic medicine have shown how the repertoire of the artist places the surgeon—or in this case, the injector—above the status of the ordinary technician, elevating his or her prestige to that of "creator and sculptor."[29]

Not surprisingly, it was nonspecializing physicians, nurse practitioners, and dentists who were more likely to tell me that an artistic eye was a necessary, if not a required, virtue for a skilled Botox injector to possess—and one that could potentially supersede formal medical training. For this group of practitioners, sterile images of needles and neurotoxins were strategically replaced with passionate metaphors of artistry. Saran Naslam, a nurse practitioner with years of training and experience with Botox, told me, "It's not just putting a needle in a face, it's an art, it's a knowledge, and it's a conscience." Likewise, Paul Edelstein, a Miami

Beach cosmetic dentist who recently began integrating Botox injections into his practice, shared that "the truth of the matter is you have to have an artistic eye, and what I have found is that there are plenty of cosmetic dentists and plenty of plastic surgeons that don't have that artistic eye, and plenty of plumbers who do, if you get what I am trying to say." The guiding sentiment among this group of nonspecializing practitioners is that it is neither the diploma nor the concentrated training that distinguish the great injectors from the mediocre ones; rather it is the eye for aesthetics and beauty that matters most. This handful of practitioners communicated their proficiency in facial injections as if it were an indefinable talent, like that possessed by a master sculptor.

Mirroring findings from a scholarly analysis of medical and popular publications that documented how cosmetic surgeons were often depicted as creative artists *and* expert technicians,[30] the vast majority of dermatologists and plastic surgeons emphasized that injecting Botox was a matter of *both* medical-scientific knowledge and of talent. A skilled Botox injector was required to have intimate knowledge of art and science and be proficient in each. Dermatologist Alex Weinstein told me how "you use the science to paint the palette, so to speak. There is definitely an art to it, there's no question, but there is also the science." Insisting that the possession of an artistic eye alone did not suffice, these doctors maintained that injectors required medical expertise to be able to gauge their patients' facial anatomy and facial asymmetries. Dermatological resident Dr. Deborah Jaye further elucidated this point:

It's definitely both, a science and an art. But the science so important in that you need to know the anatomy of the face, and you have to know how to dilute the Botox, and what strength you want to put in different areas. And you have to make sure to go over people's past medical history. Like we just had a woman who came in who had a history of myasthenia gravis, which is an autoimmune condition where their muscles become paralyzed and they have ptosis of the eye and things like that. Certainly that would be a person you would never want to do Botox on. You need

the scientific knowledge that you can really only get from years of school-
ing and training.

Thus, the ingenuity and subtlety of the injector as artist is dependent
on the technical and scientific skill of the medical expert. Used as a rhe-
torical device in the turf wars around Botox, the dictum that an injector
should be a medical expert with an artistic eye functioned to restrict the
number of qualified Botox practitioners. The lack of a medical degree
or absence of a specialization in dermatology or plastic surgery minimized the authority of dentists, nurses, and nonspecializing physicians
over Botox. The primary reason for this, according to dermatologists
and plastic surgeons, is that, while artistry is important, medical knowledge and training in what to do in the event of a complication is more
important than solely having an aesthetic eye. For instance, dermatologist Rebecca Steinberg stated, "Anybody can inject Botox. It's not that
hard. The issue is, What if anything goes wrong? Do you know how to
correct it? Do you know what not to do? And what not to inject? How to
prevent complications?" Struggling to command their authority in the
tug-of-war over Botox, these physicians affirmed that years of specialized medical training and experience were mandatory in order to ensure
the safety of their patients.

Explaining why he thought that plastic surgeons and dermatologists
were the only ones qualified to inject Botox, Michael Rosenblum, a plastic surgeon, told me that

> there are good reasons why you shouldn't go to a doctor who is not a
> dermatologist or plastic surgeon because they usually don't do formal
> training for Botox, maybe they read an article, maybe they did a weekend
> course on Botox, but they are doing it solely to make more money, they're
> not really going out and learning how to do it, during their residence,
> they're not putting it as part of their formal training. It's literally like they
> are learning how to stick people in the face with needles just to make
> more money. Whereas a plastic surgeon or a dermatologist, they've gone

through the process of learning all about cosmetic surgery and cosmetic medicine. I know that I will not sound objective because I'm a plastic surgeon, it sounds like I'm trying to keep my market share, but the bottom line is that you shouldn't go to somebody that's learning how to do something just so they can make more money.

The plastic surgeons and dermatologists I interviewed saw their entrée into Botox as a natural extension of their specialized practice and did not see their provision of Botox as something they were doing for financial gain. Yet, when others outside of their specialty offered Botox, they were painted as unscrupulous providers looking to make a quick buck.

However, it was not only dermatologists and plastic surgeons who articulated this concern. Carol Farelly, a nurse practitioner who worked at a medical spa in Orlando, told me that, "as a patient, I would never go to someone who is looking to accentuate their financial situation. I would only want to go to someone who is passionate about it and that has the eye. Anybody can inject, but there is a difference in someone who has the eye and the passion and someone who is doing it for a buck." Mindful of their encroachment on other physicians' lucrative turf, those Botox providers who were not dermatologists or cosmetic surgeons constructed elaborate justifications to neutralize their participation in medical aesthetics. Such accounts allowed these nonspecializing practitioners to align their behavior with culturally acceptable ideals in order to defuse what some might perceive as ethically treacherous conduct.[31] Centered on the maintenance of a moral self, their accounts were persuasive efforts designed to convince themselves and others of their credibility as ethical actors who were not in the Botox business for financial gain. Roberto Torres, an emergency medicine doctor who owned and operated a medi-spa told me multiple times that he and his partner "were not in this for the money":

I like to think of the ER as what I do for regular, you know, sort of a day-to-day thing, and the medi-spa side of it is a passion that we do, so we don't just try to crank clients out, so we don't bring you in and okay it's time to go, it's not our primary financial stream. Yes, we make the money, but it's more like a labor of love, we take our time with our clients. I like to talk to them, get to know them. I get to ask them about their kids, what they do. In the ER that doesn't happen. . . . When you see someone in the ER it's their worst day, it's never a good day for them. When they are here they are happy, it's a good day for them.

Dr. Torres's emphasis on the moral rewards over the financial benefits of the medical spa was a discursive strategy designed to convince himself and others of his occupational credibility. All providers, regardless of whether they were dermatologists, plastic surgeons, ER doctors, nurse practitioners, dentists or ob-gyns, made money with Botox, whether they admitted it or not. Likely aware of this dissonance, Dr. Torres and many other practitioners repeatedly said that they were not in the business of Botox purely for financial gain but, rather, because they enjoyed making people happy, had a passion and an eye for aesthetics, or because they were providing for the common good.

Articulating their participation in the lucrative realm of aesthetics through such morally acceptable language provided physicians and other medical professionals the sense of self-legitimation necessary to maintain their integrity as persons who are supposed to serve the sick. Consider Dr. Richard Kramer, the dentist whom I introduced in the beginning of this chapter who represents a new, entrepreneurial breed of health-care providers. Dr. Kramer told me that he began providing Botox Cosmetic because he felt that, "the more providers that are providing it, the better access people have to it, and if it's something that we do as health-care providers, that is beneficial to our patients, why would we want to limit how many people can get it?" With economic forces pushing health-care providers to unexpected territories that violate many of the social norms of the medical profession, doctors, dentists, and nurses, who are at least somewhat interested in preserving their image as servants of the public good, find themselves constructing narrative accounts that justify their new business ventures in ways that negate detrimental consequences to their selves and their profession.

The Rise of the Medi-spa

New York City dermatologist Bruce Katz coined the term "medi-spa" when he opened Juva Skin and Laser Center in 1999.[32] Rapidly growing businesses, medi-spas—or medical spas—are a hybrids between medical clinics and day spas.[33] According to the American Medical Spa Association, "Medical spas operate under the full-time supervision of a licensed medical professional in a spa-like setting. When visiting a medical spa, patients can be pampered with traditional spa services but also have the option of getting medical services like Botox, laser hair removal, and medical-grade skin therapies. The medical professionals of the med spa are licensed, educated and trained in the medical procedures and treatments provided to ensure the highest level of care for every patient."[34] The International Spa Association estimates that there are approximately 1,750 medi-spas operating across the country and that this number is growing exponentially every year.[35] The rapid growth in the medical spa market is primarily due to physicians from specialties other than dermatology and plastic surgery, and even business-minded nonphysicians, opening up and directing medical spas. Medical spa staff can also come from varied fields and backgrounds, ranging from nurses, physician assistants, medical assistants, and aestheticians. In many medical spas, nonphysician personnel can inject Botox, sometimes without the direct supervision of a physician.

There has been very little time for laws and regulations to catch up to this rapidly expanding infant industry. Currently, the regulatory language regarding medical spas is limited and vague, and since they are regulated on a state-by-state basis, they lack national standards and oversight. States have very different requirements for the type of medical professionals who can be owners or medical directors of medical spas and for type of medical or aesthetic professionals who are permitted to provide Botox injections and other procedures.[36] In many states, any licensed physician can open and direct a medi-spa, regardless of his or her residency training or board certification. Critics have pointed out that these vague regulations have led to a surge of physicians untrained in dermatology or cosmetic surgery opening their own medi-spas or, worse, serving as ghost doctors for businesspeople who require a physician on paper to supervise the facility. According to media reports, these ghost doctors receive monthly retainers and can sometimes earn rather hefty supplementary incomes without having to be on site.[37] A 2008 survey by the American Academy of Facial and Plastic Reconstructive Surgery revealed that more than 75 percent of its doctors said that they were aware of a medi-spa with a medical director who was not on site performing, or even overseeing, medical procedures.[38] In a *Marie Claire* article colorfully titled, "Doctors without Borders," one dermatologist stated that many medical spas "have businessmen running them, hiring people to administer treatments who would normally be checking out your groceries."[39] At the RealSelf website (www.realself.com), devoted to cataloging personal stories and reviews of elective cosmetic treatments, Florida physician Michael Sinclair was quoted as saying that "a blind psychiatrist sleeping in the back of the medi-spa technically allows the medi-spa to do every procedure you can think of."[40] "It's the difference between four years of medical school and four to five years of residency versus beauty school," said Timothy Flynn, former president of the American Society for Dermatologic Surgery Association.[41]

As dramatic exaggerations, these claims about concerns for public safety obfuscate the political and economic interests fueling the turf war. That said, however, there were some data to suggest that the lack of regulation and limited oversight of medi-spas have compromised patient safety and resulted in errors and complications. A 2007 survey conducted by the American Society for Dermatologic Surgery Association reported that 56 percent of dermatologists said they had seen an increase in patients with complications from cosmetic procedures like burns, nerve damage, and scarring.[42] Many of the dermatologists and cosmetic surgeons with whom I spoke echoed these sentiments, sharing stories about patients coming to them with unpleasant experiences in medical spas, asking them to fix a botched Botox or dermal-filler procedure that they had gotten elsewhere. In response to this, the American Academy of Dermatology has issued a statement about increasing standards for medi-spa regulation, lobbying for increased transparency and full disclosure in communicating the level of licensure and training of providers of medical aesthetic care.[43]

Since this is a relatively new area of legislation, the regulatory language around medi-spas is changing each year.[44] And although states varied considerably in their regulations, several have also begun to focus more intently on the issue of medical-spa safety. The call for increases in state regulation were initially sparked by Massachusetts state senator Joan Menard, who, during a trip to her dermatologist, listened as her doctor told her about patients he was treating for burns and scars inflicted by inexperienced people using laser equipment. In response to what she saw as serious lack of oversight, Menard formed the Medical Spa Task Force that included physicians, nurses, electrologists, estheticians, cosmetologists, and attorneys.[45] After agreeing about who was qualified to perform which procedures and what level of oversight was appropriate to ensure patient safety, they crafted a bill demanding refined definitions, tighter physician supervision restrictions, and increased accountability. But in 2009 the bill failed to pass.[46]

Similarly, in California, a medical-spa bill sponsored by state assembly member Wilmer Amina Carter (D-Rialto) would have demanded stronger supervision for corporate entities that own the larger medical spa chains.[47] It would have increased mandatory fines for safety violations and lapses in physician oversight. However, the bill was vetoed twice, once in 2009 and again in 2010. In September 2010, after the bill passed successfully through the California House and Senate, then-governor Arnold Schwarzenegger vetoed the measure, calling it redundant and unnecessary. In a letter following the veto, Schwarzenegger explained, "I believe the members of the board want to protect patients.

I just don't agree that the board's time is better spent on medi-spa en-forcement when other physicians should be more quickly investigated and prohibited from practicing medicine when they have caused serious patient harm."[48] Thus far, efforts at regulating medical spas have been thwarted by the pharmaceutical lobby and by critics of increased gov-ernment scrutiny and control over commercial medicine. Moreover, as former governor Schwarzenegger's statement reveals, medical spas have not been seen as causing serious enough harm to necessitate regulatory control, and governors and legislators, who were predominantly men, dismissed claims about patient safety as frivolous complaints by vain, ir-rational women who were complicit in their own botched procedures.[49]

Moreover, skeptics of the governmental regulation of medi-spas argue that behind the claims about safety needs for patients "lurks the spec-ter of self-interest" by dermatologists and plastic surgeons who want to maintain control of aesthetic medicine and the financial rewards that come with it.[50] Since dermatologists and plastic surgeons don't want to be undercut in the market by less costly providers, the push for stricter regulations is not so much about patient safety as it is about physicians looking to protect their turf. The American Medical Spa Association re-futes the notion that a medical director needs to be a dermatologist or trained in dermatology to effectively oversee a facility and administer Botox. Eric Light, executive director of the International Medical Spa As-sociation, stated that "there is no data to support the idea that one kind of physician is a better medical director than another. The facts are that medical spa procedures, when compared to the rest of the medical world, are extremely safe."[51] Challenging the dermatological lobby, which has tried to make accredited continuing medical education mandatory, Light maintained that the training courses provided by drug manufacturers, such as Allergan, were enough to provide sufficient education.

Although Allergan distributes Botox only to licensed physicians, in-cluding osteopaths and dentists, any registered nurse, nurse practitioner, or physician assistant can sign up for a training seminar through the pharmaceutical company. When I interviewed Saran Naslam, a nurse practitioner at a medi-spa in Miami, she explained that, because Allergan always wants to keep its injectors up to date, it regularly sent out trainers and clinicians to teach her and her staff about new cutting-edge techniques. Similarly, Carol Farelly, a nurse practitioner at a medi-spa in Orlando, told me, "There are always different techniques to learn, there is always a new patient that throws something different on the table. So, in order to keep up, throughout the year I read hundreds of articles, do hours of hands-on training, and I listen to CD modules, watch DVDs, and go to dermatology and various aesthetic conferences." Aesthetic education does not necessarily have to involve the formal training of specialized residencies or even medical school; rather, there are various ways to educate practitioners about injection techniques and patient safety. However, reports about dermatologists and plastic surgeons using their professional authority to thwart nonphysicians from pursuing their continuing education were frequent. For example, Carol Farelly told me about an experience when she was refused entry into a workshop facilitated by a well-known dermatologist who wouldn't allow any nurse practitioners or physician's assistants to enroll. Similarly, when I attended the American Academy of Dermatology's annual meeting in Miami Beach in 2013, even as a registered guest, I was not permitted to attend certain symposiums, presentations, and workshops because they were sanctioned only for dermatologists and licensed physicians.

When I spoke with Roberto Torres, the emergency medicine physician who ran a medical spa in New Orleans, he confided that a rival dermatologist threatened to send the state medical board to his business to do a thorough inspection. I visited this particular medi-spa somewhat frequently during the course of my research, and I got to know Dr. Torres fairly well. Each and every time I visited the medi-spa, either he or his partner, another emergency medicine physician, were physically present and actively engaged in the day-to-day dealings. These were not the unscrupulous, absent businessmen portrayed in media accounts. Even though Dr. Torres repeatedly told me how he believed in increased oversight and regulation of medi-spas and was confident that his business met all state regulations, the possibility of being shut down by begrudging competitors was a looming threat. In using controlled gatekeeping, these examples illustrate how dermatologists and plastic surgeons reduce the competition for jurisdiction over aesthetic medicine. Furthermore, these stories suggest a paradoxical finding in which, despite the fact that the dermatologists wanted the medi-spas to be as transparent as possible, the dermatologists themselves were cloaked in secrecy and refused to let other practitioners into their world.

The Larger Implications of the Botox Turf War

Botox is at the fore of a competitive commercial sector of clinical medicine in America. Botox Cosmetic might be on the cutting edge of commercial medicine in America, but it is certainly not alone. Elective treatments for hair loss, impotency, weight control, and insomnia are just a few of the other areas of medicine aggressively marketed by physicians and advertised by pharmaceutical companies. Understanding how the pharmaceutical industry and physicians use their culturally recognized superior knowledge to influence the demand for Botox advances knowledge about how the "medical-industrial complex" continues to enhance its corporate profits through selling the promise of youth, beauty, and the illusion of control.[52]

Dermatology and plastic surgery professionals, who have had longstanding control of aesthetic medicine and authority over Botox, protect their turf from the threat of open-market competition through varied institutional control mechanisms. Physicians from different specialties are more invested in debating what qualifies as a good injector than in reflecting on their role in the aesthetic industry. As these different groups wage war with one another in the battle over Botox, they further fuel the cultural and moral imperative that is aesthetic medicine. Failing to recognize their own power as gatekeepers in a system that contributes to women's and, increasingly, men's sense of bodily failure that comes with age, each of these players participate willingly and eagerly in a very profitable industry that is created and sustained by the anxieties and fears that Americans have about their aging bodies.[53]

The turf wars over Botox have some compelling consequences with respect to the reproduction of gender inequality. The first has to do with the regulation of medical spas. It has thus far been women politicians who have advocated for medical-spa regulation and male-dominated political bodies that have shot these efforts down. Male politicians do not see medical spas as causing serious enough harm to necessitate regulatory control, dismissing claims about patient safety as frivolous complaints by vain, irrational women. The second and, perhaps, the most obvious way that the Botox turf wars are fundamentally involved with and reflective of gender power dynamics is that, as with all other cosmetic medical practices, consumers are predominantly women and practitioners are predominantly men. Feminist scholars have long argued that cosmetic medicine is a "technology of gender" that reproduces traditional elements of female passivity and male dominance.[54] However, unlike cosmetic surgery, which is performed primarily by male surgeons, Botox is a procedure that is frequently performed by dermatologists, a medical specialty that is 46 percent female.[55] Furthermore, ob-gyns, nurses, and physician's assistants—specialties and occupations that are largely female—now also provide Botox injections. The fact that so many of those who perform and provide Botox injections are women complicates much of the existing feminist scholarship on cosmetic surgical culture. Feminist scholars need to ask how gender constructs are replayed in Botox clinics when providers are women. Some scholars, like the Australian sociologist Rhian Parker, suggest that the increase in women practitioners will do very little to challenge the dominant system because women practitioners still work very much within the male paradigm that governs medical involvement with women's bodies.[56] Even though the gendered ramifications that result from the growing collective of women Botox providers have yet to be determined, these emergent shifts beg us to reimagine and rethink long-standing connections among gender, power, and cosmetic surgical culture.

3

Becoming the Botox User

When I interviewed Myka Williamson in New Orleans in 2012 she was thirty-one and had just had her first child. Prior to the last five months of her pregnancy, Myka was a yoga instructor in New Orleans and in San Francisco. A strikingly tall blonde, Myka was the kind of woman who turned heads without trying, the epitome of effortless perfection. Myka and I had met a few years earlier through a mutual friend, and when I told her that I was working on a book about young women who use Botox, she agreed to talk to me about her experiences. On an uncharacteristically cold afternoon for New Orleans, Myka and I met for lunch at a casual sushi restaurant in her neighborhood. Donning a beige chunky cable knit sweater, long draped leather earrings, skinny jeans, and distressed motorcycle boots, Myka greeted me with a generous hug. We caught up on life, she showed me pictures of her son, and then after the small talk had subsided, we started to talk about Botox. When I asked her to tell me about her first time, she recalled how her turning point into becoming a Botox user happened on a summer day in San Francisco two years earlier when a friend of hers invited her to a party at her house. She elaborated:

> It was a Botox party, so that kind of was a little risky, not doing it at a doctor's office but at someone's house. But I was kind of feeling like I had nothing to lose, and you know, it was experimental, and I wanted to try it. The girl, my friend, she had it done before and just raved about it. So I guess there were probably about eight of us, she had us over for wine and food and stuff, and the doctor came with these two really attractive nurses. You could tell that they all did it, and it looked good. They gave us a really good deal, I guess. It was about $250 for each of us.

When I asked her if she had ever thought about using Botox before her friend approached her about the party, Myka confessed that, even though she was curious, it was unlikely that she would have sought it out herself, as she always imagined that Botox was something that she would be doing when she was older. Then, when I inquired if she had used Botox again, Myka responded that she had, one other time, and that she was eagerly anticipating the day when her son would stop breastfeeding so that she could use it again.[1]

The First Time

Neither unique nor remarkable, this story shares much in common with many other first-time tales I heard during the course of my research. Decisions about whether to become a Botox user were prompted by a range of motivating factors, emotions, and situations. For some, this transition was triggered by a specific moment, such as finding out about a bargain on Botox or spontaneously attending a Botox party, and for others, it was motivated by the more gradual process of seeing one's self progressively age. Where Myka's entrée into Botox consumption was sudden, spontaneous, and impulsive, other users' transitions were gradual and calculated. Even though Myka had elicited a silent curiosity about Botox prior to her first time, she required the extra push that her friend provided. Her story highlights the importance of social networks in the process of becoming a Botox user to provide valuable socialization through the transmission of shared knowledge. It also illustrates how a transitional moment, like finding out about a good deal on Botox or hearing about it from a friend or doctor, activated users' consciousness to try Botox. Each of these moments prompted a qualitative change that reorganized people's sense of self and their external behavior. Even though I discuss each of these motivations separately in order to distinguish among them, I emphasize that the transitional moments and processes that trigger an individual into becoming a Botox user are at once distinct, interrelated, and overlapping.

The Seduction of a Bargain

Getting a good deal on Botox was the most important factor emphasized in users' first-time narratives. Botox is not cheap, and many people were not ready to spend upward of $300 on a procedure they had not yet tried. Some users' decisions to begin using Botox were prompted by receiving daily deal e-mails for Botox from online marketplaces such as a *Groupon* or LivingSocial. Nicole Garcia, a strawberry blonde cosmetologist who split her time between Atlanta and Miami and who was twenty-eight at the time of our interview in 2013, told me she began using Botox after receiving a Groupon offer for a local medical spa. Similarly, Ellen Regis, a feminist anthropology professor from New England with a preppy sophisticated style whom I interviewed in 2013, told me that she was already planning on getting Botox before she turned thirty-six when her concerns about her appearance and aging face became too substantial to ignore. When she received a LivingSocial deal a few months before her thirty-sixth birthday, she immediately purchased the deal and booked her first Botox appointment.

Others with whom I spoke said they began using Botox because they got a good deal from friends who were plastic surgeons or dermatologists. For example, when I interviewed Katherine Turner in 2010, she was thirty-four and was managing a high-end clothing store in Miami. Katherine was from North Central Florida, spent a few years in Colorado, and had finally settled in Miami Beach three years prior to our interview. Katherine began using Botox regularly two years earlier when one of her close friends, a plastic surgeon, kept telling her that she had to try it and that she would love it. He gave it to her for free the first time.

Similarly, Francesca Girod, one of the oldest women in my sample, was sixty at the time of our interview in 2011. When I asked Francesca how she became introduced to Botox, she told me that she started to use it after a visit to her dermatologist and longtime friend, the late Dr. Frederic Brandt. She recalled how one day in 1995 she confessed to Dr. Brandt that she was upset about the way her face looked but was adamant that she didn't want any surgery and did not want to commit to anything major or excessive. Thrilled to demonstrate his recent foray into injectables, Dr. Brandt gave her Botox in her brow and Restylane, an injectable dermal filler, in her lower face. He refused to take her money, telling her it was an early birthday present. Alejandro Suarez-Levin, who was twenty-eight when I interviewed him in 2010, had a story similar to Francesca's and Katherine's. Alejandro, a gay cosmetologist who was usually dressed head to toe in designer clothing, reported spending over an hour a day on his beauty routine. His first experience with Botox happened two years earlier when he was at a plastic surgeon's home, coloring the hair of his wife. The three of them were talking about Botox, and he admitted he never tried it but was curious. The doctor responded that he had some stashed in his freezer and gave him some injections in his brow for free.

These accounts mirror sociological research findings on illicit drug subcultures; often users were given their first taste for free or for a bargain.[2] However, as the following story from thirty-two-year-old Jules Meyer elucidates, this discounted taste was usually a onetime transaction—one that left the user thirsty for more. A stylish, outgoing woman from Miami, Jules was thirty-two when I interviewed her in 2010 and was working as a concierge in a hotel. Our interview occurred during a difficult and tumultuous time during Jules's life. Her once lucrative career in finance had ended after the 2007 recession, and she was back at home living with her mother, trying to make ends meet. In between her finance career and her concierge job, Jules worked for a year in medical sales. It was through her networks in medical sales that Jules was introduced to Botox because a medical spa that she was working with offered her 50 percent off of Botox injections.

I have spoken with Jules regularly about Botox since our first interview four years earlier. At the time of this writing, Jules is still an avid Botox user. Even though she has since gotten back on her feet and is now a successful marketing director for a hotel chain, over the years she has had to economize, finding creative, even irresponsible and dangerous, ways to sustain her Botox habit. For example, in 2011, she told me she was fervently awaiting her tax return so she could get Botox again even though she was drowning in credit card debt. In 2012, she told me how she and her mother went to a Botox party where a doctor from Colombia injected a small group of mothers and daughters at a discounted rate.

A Bonding Ritual

Another transitional moment that prompted users to initiate Botox injections was being invited to a Botox party or having a friend or family member ask them to accompany them for injections. In my interviews, I heard several stories about girlfriends getting together to try Botox and mother-daughter Botox-bonding experiences. Often, the first time was instigated by finding out about bargain Botox and combining it with the social bonding ritual that came with friends or family members trying it together. My first time, I was invited by a dermatologist to her house, where she kept a stash of Botox in her freezer for her friends and family members. I brought a girlfriend with me, and we held each other's hands as the needle approached our respective foreheads. There was something oddly girly and exciting about doing it together, reminiscent of the social bonds that came with slumber parties and sleep-away camp. I was scared and anxious at the thought of someone sticking a needle into my forehead. But because the experience occurred outside of a clinical setting, in the home of somebody I knew, and because it was shared with a close girlfriend, this otherwise precarious medical procedure was reconfigured into a lighthearted girlish beauty ritual.

Other users' first-time narratives mirrored this experience. Ryan Callahan, a thirty-year-old gay psychology professor in 2014, told me about his first time trying Botox a few months earlier with his female best friend.[3] Recalling the experience with fond memories, he reminisced about their trip to the medical spa, comparing it with shopping trips they used to take with each other when they were in graduate school together.

Eighteen of out of the thirty-five users I interviewed tried Botox for the first time with a friend, and four women tried Botox for the first time with their mothers. I interviewed mother and daughter Lola and Sophia Guzzetta on separate occasions a few weeks apart from one another. During both interviews, each told me about how Lola, a vivacious Italian American woman who had an interior decorating practice in Miami, took her daughter Sophia, a fashion executive, to get Botox for the first time during one of her daughter's holiday visits home from Manhattan when Sophia was only twenty-four. Likewise, Nicole Garcia, the cosmetologist who split her time between Miami and Atlanta, tried Botox with her mother when she was twenty-six after they both purchased a Groupon deal from a local medical spa. That the first time trying Botox for so many was a collaborative and ritualistic experience reveals how the process of becoming a Botox user was intimately interwoven with other relationships.

Happenstance

Other participants talked about their first time trying Botox as a rather happenstance occurrence. Some told me that they had heard about it from friends. Maria Beth, a thirty-four-year-old ex-swimmer who worked in finance, told me that she was complaining to some girlfriends one night over dinner about the vertical wrinkle on her brow, which she blamed on years of competitive swimming, when a few of them told her she could get Botox to fix it. Maria Beth was stunned at the suggestion because she never figured herself as the "type of woman who would get Botox."

Others shared that they began using Botox rather spontaneously during a medical visit to their dermatologist. For example, Valentina Diaz, a spiritual, adventurous thirty-five-year-old woman who had immigrated from Argentina to Miami over two decades prior to our interview in 2012, told me that her first time was completely unplanned. During a trip to her dermatologist office to treat a skin problem, Valentina saw

You share just about everything with your BFF. Now you can share your BOTOX® COSMETIC experience!

Ads encouraging Botox users to bring friends to try the procedure.

the pamphlets on Botox in the waiting area and impulsively decided to take the plunge. Similarly, when I spoke with an old college friend, Izzy Dershowitz, a graphic designer from Fort Lauderdale, in 2010, she shared that she recently decided to try Botox when she was at her dermatologist's office for a routine skin cancer screening.[4] Reflecting on her first time, Izzy recalled, "I looked around the room, I saw the pamphlets, I thought about my growing number of friends who were doing it, and I thought to myself, Why the hell not?"

When I spoke with forty-one-year-old Penelope Lombardi, an Italian American nurse and aesthetician from New Orleans, in 2013, she told me how she started using Botox after she hosted a microdermabrasion party at her house where every single woman at the party was raving about Botox. Already swearing by regular microdermabrasion treatments and chemical peels, which her Louisiana nursing license permitted her to administer to herself and to others, Penelope was apprehensive about trying Botox because she was fearful of possible side effects from using the neurotoxin. However, a few days after the party, after she remembered how "the voices and faces of the women kept reverberating in my head," Penelope decided to book her first appointment for Botox. She has been using the product regularly ever since.

Many of the women and some of the men with whom I spoke characterized their first time as being rather happenstance—they were invited to a party, they heard about it from a friend, their dermatologist recommended it, they saw a deal on Groupon, or they were fortunate enough to try Botox for free. However, a closer look at these stories revealed that the moment these individuals found themselves with a needle in their forehead was anything but a random occurrence.

I now turn to some of the reasons behind why these women (and men) tried Botox and eventually became regular users. I found that users were drawn to Botox because of several intersecting social forces: They were profoundly bothered at the sight of their aging bodies, they were highly invested in their body projects, they were positioned within communities of practice in which investment in one's body was encouraged rather than stigmatized, and they were target audiences of Allergan's multimillion-dollar marketing campaign.

Perceptions of the Aging Body

When I asked my participants what they thought about the physical aspects of aging, the responses I heard were pretty bleak. Angela Salgado, a thirty-five-year-old petite and stylish Colombian woman whom I interviewed in 2014, replied, "I hate it. I don't want to age at all." Myka Williamson, a former yoga instructor and the type of woman who turns heads without trying, said, "I think of saggy skin. It's gross. It sounds horrible to say but it freaks me out. I don't want to look like that, wrinkly and saggy." Virginia Rudner, a 5'10" leggy blonde from Miami with an Ivy League education who was a successful New York real estate agent, half-jokingly responded, "When I think about aging, I think about my plastic surgeon on speed dial!" The women with whom I spoke viewed their aging faces as embodied failure, and wrinkles represented the most noticeable part of this decline. Moreover, these women were especially critical of the wrinkles on their foreheads, illustrating how the availability of Botox can produce an acute body-mapping consciousness, drawing attention to the forehead and making women focus on their brow creases when perhaps they would not have otherwise.

Dakota Wagner was a thirty-two-year-old, financially struggling social worker with an edgy yet feminine style who also sang in an indie-rock band on the side. When I interviewed her in 2012, she told me that she had wanted Botox for a long time because she noticed "I have this wrinkle in between my eyebrows that made me feel like I looked really old. I would notice it in the mirror, or when I would see my reflection in like a car window or something." Other women's narratives were also laced with assertions that these particular wrinkles were associated with negative emotions and oldness. Hillary Larkin, a spirited and athletic blonde woman who had recently moved from New York to Los Angeles, told me, "I'm noticing I'm looking older, like when I look at photos on Facebook. I'm like, Oh my God, I look old! And I look angry! And I always notice the stupid crease between my eyes, and I'm like, Ugh, that's the Botox wrinkle." These narratives echo findings from sociologist Laura Hurd Clarke's interviews with older women on their experiences of aging before and after the development of nonsurgical cosmetic procedures. The older women she interviewed in 1999, prior to the development of Botox and dermal fillers, spoke about their forehead wrinkles as "a general and undifferentiated category of facial creases."[5] Her interviews with women in 2005, after the rise of these technofixes, were textured with claims that brow creases and wrinkles around the mouth were particularly repulsive. Definitions of unacceptable wrinkles corresponded with developments in aesthetic medicine.

While some women talked about noticing their aging faces in mirrors or photographs, others told me they looked to their mothers for fleshy reminders of what awaited them with impending age. Sophia Guzzetta told me, "I think my mom is beautiful. But she does have a really prominent line between her brows, and I was telling her the other day that I make that face all the time, so obviously I need to be careful I don't get the same crease." Courtney Richards, a thirty-two-year-old new mother living in coastal Mississippi, echoed Sophia's observation. She confessed that she saw her mother as a mirror into her future, and she did not like what she saw. "My mom's forehead is so wrinkly. . . . It's fine for her, but I do not want to look like that when I get older. I mean I don't necessarily want it to be completely flat, but definitely not as wrinkly as my mom's, for sure. That's why I use Botox, to prevent me from looking like my mom, or from looking like a wrinkly shar pei [dog]."

Attention to these women's responses about aging clarifies the complex nature of the meanings they attached to their present, past, and future embodied selves. The process of viewing their own aging faces through the lens of their mother's creases and wrinkles propelled the development of their self-identities as Botox users. Mothers' aging faces were used as warnings, as cautionary mirrors showing how their beauty would eventually fade.[6]

Acutely aware that a major component of their social capital was largely derived from their ability to achieve and maintain a youthful body, women, more so than men, talked about their anxieties about impending creases, wrinkles, and sagging skin. Allison Harris, a forty-two-year-old self-described good Southern woman from rural Louisiana who was a broadcast journalist in New Orleans, told me, "Men age and they look distinguished and women age and they, they don't age gracefully, we just die. We don't look distinguished we just look old." The few heterosexual men with whom I spoke were also aware of the social benefits they gained from the gendered double standard of aging. For example, in 2010, when I interviewed Seth Burke, a thirty-five-year-old Jewish businessman from Miami who had used Botox twice at the request of his younger girlfriend, he admitted that "men become more stable and more financially stable, more attractive to women as they get older. Because of this, I don't feel or fear getting older in the same way a woman would."

Whereas heterosexual men articulated fewer anxieties than their female counterparts about the visible effects of aging, gay men's narratives and fears about aging were more similar to the women in my sample. The sociologists Kathleen Slevin and Thomas J. Linneman have documented how the double standard of aging is a privilege reserved for heterosexual men. Embodied ageism is ubiquitous in gay communities because gay male culture puts a very specific body on a pedestal, and this body is young.[7] The three gay male Botox users with whom I spoke were profoundly troubled by the sight and thought of their aging bodies. For example, Barrington Marx, a thirty-five-year old publicist from New York, lamented, "Once you hit thirty, you are invisible as a gay man. It's much worse for us than for women." Alejandro Suarez-Levin, the cosmetologist, admitted, "I am definitely trying to hold on to youth. Look, I'm twenty-eight now, I mean, I'm getting older and I don't want to show that I am aging. . . . because if you don't start taking care of it now, when are you going to start? By the time you are older, it is already too late." Even though at the time of our interview Alejandro was in a long-term relationship with a man eight years his senior, at only twenty-eight he had an arsenal of expensive face products and had already dabbled in multiple cosmetic nonsurgical procedures.

Ryan Callahan, the psychology professor from Maryland, departed from the narrative that gay subcultural norms carried all the explanatory power for his dissatisfaction with his aging body. Observing that his adult life was primarily spent in graduate school and in academic circles, Ryan explained that he did not have many gay male friends, and even among those he did have, he "did not socialize in a circuit where there was a great deal of body shaming." More salient to him than his gay identity and his compliance with gay subcultural norms was his occupational identity and his recent identity transition from graduate student to professor. He explained:

> My experience is not driven by gay male body conscious norms. . . . It
> doesn't feel that simple for me. That's not consonant with my experience,
> it's just that I have always thought of myself as young, and as a young gay
> man, and all of a sudden you wake up and you aren't a young gay man
> anymore. I've got gray hairs in my beard and I'm in my thirties and no-
> body's looking at me thinking, "Look at that really young guy" anymore.
> They're thinking, like, "Look at that man." And people call me sir all the

time, and my former professors don't think of me as young anymore, my students don't think of me as young, they think of me as their professor.

As Ryan complicates the reductionist assumption that gay men engage in body modification practices because they face acute social pressures from subcultural norms, he also illuminates the interpretive process of how body and self are constructed through imagined reflected appraisals. Ryan's identity transition from student to "sir," fueled in part by imagined valuations from his colleagues and students, unsettled images of body and self. His attraction to Botox played on his desire to hold onto his embodied identity as a young gay graduate student. For Ryan, Botox was rooted in recovering, rescuing, and conveying the real (younger) self. Opening up the possibility to manipulate relationships of body and self, Botox was an intervention in identity, a practice that was used to align his inner and outer self. Feeling dissatisfied at the sight of his aging body, and in a desire to restore his appearance as an indicator of character, Ryan actively responded to ideologies of youth and beauty privilege, using Botox to transform his body—or, more precisely, his face—into the person he felt like inside.

Investing in Body Projects

The quest to embody the feminine beauty ideal can be dangerous, all consuming, expensive, and painful. Feminist scholars have long been interested in trying to make sense of women's complicated relationships with their bodies and their participation in beauty culture and have documented the many ways in which women's bodies become implicated in an all-consuming project that often entails spending money, sacrificing time, and enduring pain.[8] Fashion, makeup, hair and nail maintenance, diet, exercise, and elective cosmetic surgeries are just some of the forms of bodywork that go into sustaining the aesthetic exterior of the body.

Contemporary consumer beauty culture puts acute pressure on women, and increasingly men, to improve every aspect of their bodies, augmenting the body's role in identity production. For example, almost all the women with whom I spoke went for weekly manicures and monthly pedicures. Some also incorporated regular spray-tanning sessions and facial or bikini waxes into their beauty routine. Hair removal was a critical issue for many women, and approximately a third of the women in my sample had undergone some type of laser hair removal either on their bikini lines, legs, underarms, or facial hair. Some participants also went for biannual keratin treatments, a popular procedure that temporarily defrizzed and straightened hair, using toxic formaldehyde to achieve the result. Others had professional eyelash extensions. A small minority also treated themselves to regular facials, intense pulsed light (IPL) photorejuvenation facials, microdermabrasion, chemical peels, and cellulite removal treatments.[9] Finally, some participants also had cosmetic dentistry—two participants had a full set of veneers, four had gone to their dentists for professional teeth whitening, and ten others used some over-the-counter whitening treatment.

Participants' bodies were projects to be worked on as part of their identity, plastic entities honed by vigilance and hard work. The production of their selves was sustained by the continual transformation of their bodies and investing in their body projects provided them a means of self-expression and a way of increasing the control they had over their bodies and their selves. However, this investment in embodied cultural capital did not come cheap: A month of regular manicures and pedicures can cost about $100, and a spray-tanning session is about $30–$50 with results lasting for approximately a week. Bikini waxes can cost approximately $50 a month. Facial waxing is significantly less expensive and usually costs $10 for removal of upper lip or eyebrow hair. Keratin treatments can run anywhere from $100 to $300 and last about three to four months. Eyelash extensions are $200 for the first application and need to be reapplied every two months at $75 a pop. Laser hair removal, which is permanent, can cost anywhere from $200 to $800, depending on the body part and the provider. Facials, microdermabrasion, and chemical peels cost approximately $60–$100 each. Professional teeth whitening runs about $300, over-the-counter whitening strips or gels run around $20–$50 at the local drugstore, and veneers can cost thousands of dollars.

Participants also colored and styled their hair; frequented gyms, fitness clubs, and yoga or Pilates studios; and spent a great deal of money on facial creams and serums. When I asked many of these women and even some of the men to calculate their monthly or yearly beauty expenses, some of them nearly dropped to the floor after realizing how much they were spending on their aesthetic upkeep. When I asked twenty-eight-year-old Alejandro Suarez-Levin to calculate the amount of money he spent on beauty and health expenses he looked at me and replied in a very serious tone: "You know how Lady Gaga says 'born this way'? Well, that's bullshit! It takes a lot of money to look this good!"

As the feminist cultural theorist Meredith Jones notes, we now live in a makeover culture where care of the self is always about self-improvement, enhancement, and becoming something better. In makeover culture nothing satiates our desire to be better versions of ourselves, and because our bodies are perpetually downgrading on us, the pursuit of upkeep is endless.[10] For the women and men with whom I spoke, the work that went into maintaining bodily perfection was never-ending—manicures, laser hair removal, hair color, and artificial tanning were accompanied by Botox and, for some, dermal filler and even cosmetic surgery. A handful of my participants had moved onto dermal fillers and two had collagen injections in their lips. What is more, many of the young women in my sample had also undergone elective cosmetic surgery. Ten women had breast implants, five had elective rhinoplasty, two had their ears pinned back, and five had liposuction. With regard to the men in my sample, one had a full set of veneers, one had recently undergone SmartLipo laser liposuction,[11] two had their noses reconstructed, and one had cheek implants and lip injections.[12]

The women and men in my sample conformed to beauty ideals in that they were for the most part White and thin, but equally important was that, for many, their attractiveness was also the result of a lifetime of beauty maintenance projects. Appearances were central to these women's and men's identities and their self-worth; they thus constructed selves and bodies that were dependent on preserving their attractiveness. For these women and men, attractiveness was a for-purchase commodity, and the technologically engineered body was a sought-after possession. Requiring significant investment and self-care, their bodies were actively worked upon entities suspended in a relentless pursuit to cultivate a youthful attractive appearance.[13]

Social Networks and Social Support

Many Botox users had close relationships with others who used also Botox or had used other types of cosmetic enhancements. One reason for this was that having family members and friends who engaged in similar body modification and enhancement practices undermined the stigma against these types of bodywork.[14] In addition, support for body modification and enhancement by family and friends usually contributed to interest in trying Botox.

Family Influences

A large group of users had family members who were recipients of at least one cosmetic surgical intervention.[15] Hillary Larkin, the spirited blonde woman living in Los Angeles, told me that her mother gets regular Botox and Juvederm injections and had her breasts lifted a few years ago.[16] Hillary's twenty-seven-year-old sister had recently gotten Botox for the first time in preparation for her wedding. Virginia Rudner, the Ivy League–educated New York real estate agent, divulged that her father had had a nose job, a chin job, an eye-lift, and a face-lift. Virginia told me that her mother was fearful of the knife but not the needle, and the two of them have gone for Botox injections together. Barrington Marx, the gay publicist from New York, declared that his family is "very liberal with regards to cosmetic surgery" and that his mother "has taken more shots to the face than Mike Tyson." Deeply immersed in makeover culture, many users' parents and other family members' bodies were in a perpetual state of becoming something better.

Some users' parents even encouraged them to try Botox. When she was contemplating trying Botox, Izzy Dershowitz called her mother from the dermatologist's office, assuming that her mother would be a voice of reason and tell her she was crazy for wanting Botox at age thirty-two. Instead, Izzy told me, her mom encouraged her to try it. Other women told me that their mothers not only encouraged their Botox use but also were the ones responsible for motivating them to do it in the first place. When I interviewed Madison Cooper, the daughter of a plastic surgeon, in 2012, she was thirty-eight and had tried Botox for the first time three months earlier. She explained that her mother would always tell her to relax her forehead when she was growing up. "Relax your face, relax your brow, she would always say. Until, one day, she said to me, 'Just look at the crease on your forehead, you need to do something about that.' So she is the one who told me I had to do it." Similarly, Nicole Garcia, who tried Botox for the first time at twenty-six, told me, "I started using it because my mom actually told me I needed it. I always make this confused face when I am watching TV, and she is the one who noticed it and always pointed it out."

That so many of the Botox users I interviewed came from families where cosmetic surgery and enhancements were normalized and even encouraged highlights the extent to which bodies are crucial to the intergenerational transmission of class distinctions and hierarchies. Families from the dominant social classes are more likely to have the disposable time and money to invest in their bodies and their children's bodies, whereas working-class people, with little leisure time and disposable income, lack such an advantage.[17] The intergenerational transmission of physical capital contributes to social inequality in that those from more economically privileged families have the monetary and cultural resources to invest in their bodies and their appearance—an investment that, as I discuss later in this chapter, is so often converted into economic capital.[18]

Peer Influences

Many of the users with whom I spoke found themselves embedded in peer groups in which Botox injections were gradually becoming a normalized cosmetic intervention. When I asked Hillary Larkin why she began using Botox, she responded, "Everyone else is doing it. I guess it's becoming almost like part of our culture where everyone just does it, so I wanted to try it for myself." Similarly, Seth Burke, the thirty-five-year-old Jewish businessman from Miami, told me, "I think Botox and stuff like that has woven its way into our culture as the norm, as sick as that might be."

The pressure to use Botox was particularly acute in certain cities where its normalization and mainstreaming were especially evident. Eighteen of the Botox users I interviewed lived in Miami, New York, or Los Angeles. Sophia Guzzetta, the thirty-one-year-old fashion executive who was raised in Miami and at the time of our interview was living in New York, reflected on the aesthetic norms of these two cities: "Miami is like one of the most aesthetically altered places in the United States, where you have like all these beautiful women who are like walking around the beaches with like no clothes, no cellulite, and no nothing, and certainly no movement in their head. And then I go to New York and you also have to be really conscious of how you look. Everybody has Botox there, and now it's a lot more accepted to use Botox for women our age." Similarly, when I asked Dawn Goldstein, a thirty-four-year-old broadcast journalist and former beauty queen, about life in New York, she explained, "I think living in New York is a very bizarre bubble, with different standards than the rest of the country." She then told me about a charity event she attended a few weeks earlier: "It was like literally the whole room had Botox. So, instead of asking who in my social circle uses Botox, it's a matter of finding the person in the room who doesn't use Botox."

As with families and friendships, place matters for the production of meanings around appearances and acceptable bodywork. Women in

Miami, New York, and Los Angeles told me that their decision to begin using Botox would likely be very different had they lived in a different city. For example, Miami resident Jules Meyer, who began using Botox at thirty, exclaimed, "Let's say I lived in Kansas or somewhere, I would probably never have to do this shit. . . . But that's not my life. I live in Miami Beach." Mara Siffman, also a Miami Beach native, told me, "My sister-in-law, she doesn't wear any makeup, but even she gets Botox, I feel like everybody just does." My conversations with this group of users illustrate the importance of social networks for constituting intersubjective understandings of the body. Finding themselves trapped in social networks that made them feel like they had to keep up with their peers, many of these users' stories were interspersed with narratives of hopelessness. Furthermore, these stories also illuminate how meanings of acceptable body modification and enhancement are constantly evolving and shifting. In these users' (albeit limited) social worlds, Botox was no longer seen as a stigmatized body practice for the overly vain and frivolous; rather, it was reconfigured as a rational solution to the problem of aging.[19]

The New Face of Botox Consumers

Not all the users whom I interviewed came from families and peer groups where cosmetic surgical culture was encouraged, normalized, or accepted. Nor did all users spend significant time, energy, and money on their own body projects. Maria Beth, the ex-swimmer, told me that she has "never even had a facial" and that she "goes to work with very little makeup and wet hair." Nor did all the participants in my sample have the disposable income to afford Botox. For example, social worker Dakota Wagner painted her own nails and toes, rarely went for haircuts, styling, and coloring, and did not belong to a gym. At the time of the interview, Dakota did not have health insurance. Jules Meyer also didn't have health insurance and was in considerable debt when I interviewed her in 2010. Yet recall how she told me that the first thing she was going to spend her tax refund on when she got her hands on that money was a refresher of Botox. Similarly, Courtney Richards, the thirty-two-year-old new mother living in coastal Mississippi, told me that she survived on drug-store creams and lotions, rarely went for professional manicures, and got her hair cut and styled two to three times a year at most. She explained to me that, prior to getting pregnant and having a child, she frequented hair and nail salons and was a regular at her local fitness center. Now, as a new mother, she saw these luxuries as wasteful expenditures that could be better spent on her child. But, she confessed, "I'm keeping the twice a year Botox injections, I can't really live without them!"

For some women, Botox was something they skimped and saved for, and they viewed it as an important expense worth sacrificing other indulgences. Elizabeth Sana, a recently divorced thirty-eight-year-old Latina from New Orleans, told me, "If it was between a new dress and Botox, I would totally go with the Botox. To me it's like I'd rather have no lines and an old dress." Similarly, Vivienne Mann, a thirty-seven-year-old single mother from New Orleans, explained that "Botox is not something I would go without food for, but if I had to pick between eating ramen noodles for a week or Botox, I would pick Botox." Even though some women users with whom I spoke did not have the disposable income to afford regular Botox injections, they viewed Botox as a critical enough expenditure for which they were willing to cut corners in other parts of their life.

Similarly, even though many of the women I interviewed lived in cosmopolitan urban centers like Miami, New York, and Los Angeles, others resided in smaller cities and suburbs. Moreover, a significant minority of women told me that very few people they knew had ever tried Botox or had cosmetic surgery. For example, Allison Harris, the Louisiana broadcast journalist, told me that only a handful of her friends had tried Botox and that nobody in her family had ever had any cosmetic enhancements.

Thus, although the users in my sample shared some similarities, they were not all alike. While many lived in cosmopolitan cities, some did not. While many had disposable incomes and were part of the leisure class, some were not. While many came from families and peer groups in which a cosmetic surgical culture was normalized, accepted, and even encouraged, some did not. But each and every one of these users lived in locales where medical spas were popping up in strip malls next to Starbucks and Whole Foods. These users were part of the growing number of consumers who got promotional e-mails that sold them bargain Botox. These were the people who were exposed to offers for Botox at their dermatologist's or even their dentist's office. While the majority of these users were not rich, they were also not poor. They might not always buy their groceries from Whole Foods, but they were not shopping at the Piggly Wiggly. These women users might not be able to afford the clothing on the pages of *Vogue, Marie Claire,* or *Harper's Bazaar,* but they were likely to read these magazines or, at the very least, flip through them while in line at the market, in their physician's waiting room, or at the nail salon. These users are the demographic target for Allergan's vast advertising campaign, and they represent the new faces of the rapidly growing population of Botox consumers.

4

Negotiating the Botoxed Self

The perfect combination of prom queen pretty with sophisticated con-servatism, Dawn Goldstein is 5'9", has big blue eyes, and has a perfectly coiffed blonde mane. As a former beauty queen, she was socialized early on to learn that her social currency largely derived from her ability to achieve and maintain a youthful, beautiful face and body. From a very young age, Dawn was taught how to cultivate her appearances through exercise, dieting, makeup, and other kinds of bodywork in order to look young, healthy, and pretty. When Dawn was twelve years old, she was sent to a plastic surgeon by her father to have her ears pinned back. When she was fifteen, she learned to count calories. When she was twenty-eight, she had laser hair removal on her bikini area, legs, and underarms. And when she was thirty-three, she began using Botox.

On the surface, Dawn Goldstein fulfilled every societal stereotype of a Botox user: She was a former beauty queen, she was always impeccably groomed, and she was thin, tall, and attractive. However, my three-hour conversation with the thirty-four-year-old Dawn proved that such one-dimensional assessments and stereotypes miss some critical insights about women who use Botox, obscuring the complexities of women's social psychological decision-making about their aesthetic labor. Dawn, a self-identified feminist, spoke at length about the tensions permeating her decision to use Botox and about her frustrations with the ubiqui-tous cultural pressure to accommodate to societal norms of feminine attractiveness. As a former beauty queen, Dawn always had to be very conscious of her face and her body. Now, as an adult and a successful broadcast journalist, she was even more aware of the cultural pressure she faced to preserve her youth and beauty. Frustrated at the amount of money, time, and effort she spent on her appearances, she joked that her bathroom vanity was littered with enough expensive creams, lotions, and serums to fill the cosmetic section of a department store. Dawn also bemoaned the fact that almost every woman she knew had used Botox, including her co-workers and close friends. Furthermore, she spoke extensively about her adoration for her grandmother, a woman who lived well into her nineties without any cosmetic interventions. She shared that, despite a lifelong preoccupation with her appearances, she believed in "aging normally, naturally, just like my grandmother. She had so many beautiful wrinkles, lines and creases, and that is what always made her so stunning." Disappointed that she did not see the option to grow old in the way her grandmother did, Dawn was insistent that these days it was difficult, if not impossible, for women to be able to age naturally without the help of technological fixes. Ultimately, when she turned thirty-three and found that her monthly facials and expensive creams would no longer suffice, she resigned herself to trying Botox. Dawn was adamant that, if she were not on television each day, she would have likely made a different decision about using Botox in her thirties. She spoke at length about how she traversed this "inner struggle" and how eventually her desire to stay on television superseded both her feminist ethics and her desire to age "naturally."

To Botox or Not to Botox: Traversing Tensions

Consistent with Dawn's experience, research has found that adherence to feminist ideologies does not buffer women from participating in beauty culture. Deborah Rhode, a Stanford law professor, explored the feminist movement's complicated relationship to anti-aging beauty work.[1] Her findings revealed that, even among women with strong feminist orientations, the difficulties they experienced with gendered ageism in the workplace often superseded their feminist politics. Rhode cited one feminist icon after another who dyed her hair, used Botox, or went under the knife as soon as she began graying and wrinkling.[2]

Even though almost half of the women mentioned that they were frustrated with their complicity with oppressive, unreasonable feminine beauty norms, only a small handful self-identified as feminists. Perhaps because some feminist-identified women felt guilty for engaging in hegemonic beauty practices, their justifications about Botox and their broader participation in beauty culture became significantly more nuanced with their feminist sociopolitical orientation. Not surprisingly, the woman most critical of her participation in gendered beauty practices was Ellen Regis, the feminist anthropology professor. During a two-hour Skype interview, Ellen spoke with me candidly about managing the complicity of the cultural norms of femininity with her feminist ethics. She confided:

> This is something that is so fascinating to me, and I am sure obviously to you, given what you are doing. Like just how profound the impact of cultural norms of attractiveness particularly in terms of femininity are and how complicit I am in the process. People talk so freely and are so blasé about how these are just ideals or norms, and like you have the choice about that whole kind of individualistic frame that is so dominant in our culture, and it is like no, it's big, and it's so powerful. I am just awed by how powerful these norms are in terms of keeping the decisions that I have made around this stuff. . . . Like I am very invested, it's a very big part of my gendered identity, in terms of my performance of normative femininity and accommodating to norms of attractiveness and stuff like that. But I don't think that that means that I am stupid or I am somehow, you know, more a dupe than other people, I very much resist that critique.

Discursively shifting the frame from the individual to social structural pressures, Ellen's justification was produced in part by desires to rationalize and compartmentalize the competing meanings of Botox. There were multiple ways of understanding Botox, and often it was difficult, if not impossible, to rationalize their coexistence. Such competing meanings made the decision to go under the needle a tension-fraught compromise.

Additionally, residual attitudes about the fact that Botox was a derivative of the most toxic toxin on the planet continued to lurk, and some people expressed fears about having a poisonous substance injected into their heads. These users struggled with how to reconcile their fondness for Botox with its potential health risks. Penelope Lombardi was a nurse and facial aesthetician who exercised five days a week and ate a strict vegetarian diet. She was a self-described "health nut" who was conscious about everything she put in her body. I met Penelope in 2012 when I began to go to her for microdermabrasion treatments and facial chemical peels. In 2012, when I told her that I was conducting interviews with women who used Botox, she was adamant that she would never inject a toxin into her brow. In 2013, only one year later, Penelope sat down for an interview with me and discussed her regret at not beginning Botox injections earlier. Reconsidering her previous position on the toxic properties of Botox, Penelope rationalized that "all drugs are toxins if used in incorrect doses."

Similarly, Shannon Giles, a thirty-two-year-old marketing director from Massachusetts whom I interviewed over the phone in 2011, stated, "I also am very hesitant of the fact that this was only FDA approved in the past decade, and I worry about what the long-term effects are." In 2012, when I asked Rachel McAvoy, a thirty-year-old meteorologist from Minnesota, if she ever thought about the fact that Botox was a toxin, she replied, "I know, it's funny. I eat organic food, I make sure its hormone free, antibiotic—um—free, you know, um, pasture fed, you know, everything, but then I inject poison into my face." She continued to tell me, "I am hardened about it; like in twenty-three years when all of us start going crazy and we all get some disease, I'll be like, 'Oh man, who thought that was a good idea?' But I don't really think about it, it doesn't keep me up at night or anything like that."

As these accounts suggest, the cosmetic wellness of the external aesthetic body frequently took precedence over caring for one's actual health. In the same way some of these women engaged in strict caloric restriction and excessive exercise to preserve their thin physiques, many of them also overlooked the potential long-term dangers of Botox in favor of the immediacy of an attractive unlined face. In fact, only one person with whom I spoke, Robert Moskowitz, the heterosexual man from Seattle, stopped using Botox because of health concerns. Robert had a law degree but spent most of his time traveling the globe, receiving Botox injections in his native Seattle but also in Buenos Aires, Bangkok, and in Melbourne. Then, a year prior to our interview, when Robert was thirty-five, he visited a naturopath who advised him against using Botox, since it was a derivative of the most toxic substance on the planet. With a great deal of remorse, Robert promised that he would never again inject the toxin into his face. The privileges of heterosexual male embodiment were such that Robert's subjectivity was not produced within the same unattainable beauty standards as his women counterparts, nor was he going to face the same public shame and invisibility when his aging face no longer displayed qualities of youthfulness.

Thus, even though some women were concerned with the potential health dangers of the toxin, they starting using Botox and continued to use it because of the exceedingly high value they placed on their appearances. Indeed, the most prevalent concerns among users were fears of ugliness and aesthetic inauthenticity. The Louisiana anchorwoman Allison Harris lamented, "I was really worried, I was like, What if it shows on television? What if I'm one of those one-in-a-million people who get [a] bad reaction and then I can't go on air?" Myka Williamson, the former yoga teacher, explained that "there's a fear with Botox that you're gonna look different, but in a bad way, you know, that it's gonna look fake, that people are gonna tell, you know, that you're not gonna be able to move, you know, just that kind of thing." Anxious that their inauthenticity might be discovered, many women were terrified that others would find out that their beauty was not genuine, real, or natural. Worse, women feared that they would appear perverse, ugly, and temporarily disfigured.

Even as feminist ethics, health concerns, or aesthetic fears pulled some women away from Botox, their investment in normative femininity pushed them toward it. The tensions, fears, and anxieties around becoming a Botox user were ultimately overshadowed by the risk of looking irresponsible, unattractive, or old. Ultimately, despite variegated tensions, the cultural privilege attached to youth and beauty created much too compelling of a reason for each of these individuals to use Botox.

To Tell or Not to Tell: Disclosing the Botoxed Self

As conscious and self-reflective actors, Botox users interpreted the social meanings of their Botox use and the consequences these meanings had for their identities and for their interactions in multiple institutional contexts. Relatedly, the ways that people disclosed their Botox use was shaped by their gendered, sexual, and classed social locations and by their identities in multiple institutional contexts. First, because talk about body cultivation is typical to middle-class femininity and is seen as a pleasurable bonding ritual among girlfriends, many of the women in my sample were open and truthful to their girlfriends about their Botox use. A smaller number were open to family members, and those who were often had mothers who were also recipients of cosmetic interventions. For women, the most common person from whom they kept their Botox use a secret was their husband or boyfriend. The two most common reasons for this were, first, the desire to keep their aesthetic labor invisible so their beauty could appear effortless,[3] and, second, the fear that their male partners would disparage them for spending hundreds of dollars on what they would see as a vain and frivolous procedure.

When I asked Dakota Wagner how open she was about her Botox use, she said, "I guess I'll tell anybody, except I wouldn't tell a man I was trying to date or anything!" Angela Salgado, a petite Colombian woman in her mid-thirties, kept her Botox use a secret from her fiancé for years, and when I asked her why, she laughed and replied, "He would die if he knew I was spending over $300 on this shit!"

Others confessed that they hid their Botox from work colleagues. For example, Ryan Callahan, the gay psychology professor, confided how he would never disclose his Botox use to the vast majority of his colleagues or want graduate students to know he used Botox. Similarly, Ellen Regis, the feminist anthropologist, talked at length about her dissonance negotiating her private identity as a Botox user with her public professional identity as a critical feminist scholar. For Ryan, Ellen, and myself, our professional identities were structured around shared meanings that coalesced around a critique of youth-oriented beauty culture. Acutely aware that our professional colleagues perceived Botox users with the stigma of gratuitous vanity, each of us decided to manage this stigma through nondisclosure.

The interactional strategies for attempting to balance the expectations of our professional identities with the societal demands of youth and attractiveness reveal the nuances involved in negotiating the fluid and shifting images of vanity, especially since our experiences stand in such sharp contrast to the experiences of those in service professions such as cosmetology, real estate, and fashion and in media, where the normalization of Botox was most palpable. This group of Botox users chose to bare all, in terms of exposing their Botoxed bodies. For example, when I asked Rachel McAvoy about disclosing her Botox use, she proclaimed, "I am not embarrassed at all! I'll tell anyone who asks. And even the ones who don't ask!" Amanda Castillan, a thirty-two-year-old Colombian woman who was raised in Miami, told me, "Oh yeah, I told all the younger girls I work with, I told them I do it and they should start now before it's too late."

These contradictory strategies of disclosure expose the situational contingencies of the stigma of vanity. Many women and gay men with whom I spoke detected that societal attitudes about Botox were changing and that, at least in their limited social circles, it was a practice that was increasingly normalized. Barrington Marx told me that in 2003, when he first got Botox, "people thought I was out of my mind, but now it's a whole different world out there." When I asked him if he told his friends or family about his Botox use, he answered, "Look, I'm not one of those people that . . . you know . . . when everyone says, 'How do you look so young, it seems impossible?' I'm not one of those people that says, 'Oh, you know it's just lots of water and portion control.' I think it's important to be open and honest and spread the good word. And also take pride in self-preservation, you know, there's something to be said for taking pride in growing old gracefully, but if you want the boy next door, go next door. That's not me." Reveling in the pride of vanity, Barrington's response illuminates how disclosing the Botoxed self to others can be a form of classed identity work that presents the appearance of a hardworking, successful, and deserving self.

Given cultural mandates about hegemonic masculinity, it shouldn't be any surprise that the few heterosexual men with whom I spoke were less likely to divulge their Botox use than were the gay men and heterosexual women in my sample. Although they were open about it to their family, they were highly secretive about this to their male friends and to most of their girlfriends. The following narrative from Robert Moskowitz, the lawyer turned global explorer from Seattle, whom I interviewed in 2014, reveals the performative strategies of managing the stigma of Botox use for heterosexual men:

> I mean, I try not to tell anyone for two reasons, because (a), you're embarrassed, and (b), you want it to seem like you are so youthful looking and that you're just special and that you're just so young looking. You want them to believe that that's who you are. You don't want them to think that you're doing Botox. Like, I've told some of my good friends, but that's just because we were talking about it, and it kind of got to that, but yeah, definitely something I would avoid telling my boys, for sure. I don't want to be seen as girly or feminine, especially among my more homophobic friends. There is this idea that guys shouldn't be worried so much about their appearance, and to do so is like, you know, effeminate or gay or weak. So I just don't talk about it.

Robert's chagrin about his Botox use underscores how the stigma of vanity pervades constructions of hegemonic masculinity, since for men, vanity is viewed as a "swerve into the feminine" and is equated with homosexuality.[4] Robert's Botox consumption is potentially threatening to his hegemonic masculinity, since, as a heterosexual man, his sense of self worth is not supposed to be tied to how he looks. Keeping his Botox use a secret allows him to maintain the appearance of hegemony without his presumed heterosexuality falling under suspicion, and it protects him from the powerless aspects associated with a feminine culture of beauty. Although social scripts about hegemonic masculinity are shifting to the extent that it is expected for heterosexual middle-class White men to take care of their appearance, there is a limit to how much work they should put into their body projects. Botox injections are not yet seen as socially acceptable for the majority of heterosexual men.

Accounting for the Botox Self

Despite its increasing normalization, Botox still sits at the margins between acceptable and unacceptable bodywork. Occupying a threshold area, Botox straddles a liminal space between makeup and plastic surgery. Women are allowed to enhance their beauty with a certain culturally appropriate set of techniques. At the present moment, things like concealer, hair color, and nail polish fall within the realm of normalcy. For some women, Botox is situated within the standards of concealer, but for most others, it does not fit within the normative realm. And men's decision to use Botox is an even trickier conundrum to navigate. Because of this, Botox demanded some justification from its users.[5]

Body Entrepreneurs: Navigating Intimate and Commercial Marketplaces

Thinking about the women and men with whom I spoke as "body entrepreneurs" is a useful lens through which to conceptualize Botox users, as the body and the way it is presented and cultivated is a form of capital that can add value and prestige to the self. Enhancing physical bodies can augment an individual's position in the social and economic order. For example, some women told me that their decision to begin using Botox was motivated by a desire to maintain their physical attractiveness, boost their self-confidence in social situations, and improve their chances in an already limited heterosexual dating pool. Demographic shifts like the later age of marriage and increasing divorce rates mean that women are single for much longer. Moreover, reigning heterosexual scripts are such that men generally date and marry younger women. Thus women are not only spending more time as single unmarried adults, they are navigating a heterosexual dating pool alongside other, younger contenders.

Amanda Castellan, the 32-year-old Colombian woman who was raised in Miami, affirmed that "we're not getting married at the age of twenty-three anymore; we're waiting until we are older. So we still need to date for much longer, and we want to look young while we're doing it. And not to mention, people are getting divorced more. I have friends, women who are becoming single after their divorce, and they just have to get that refreshment of Botox to maintain their competitive edge in the dating pool." One of the ways that Virginia Rudner, the thirty-year-old Ivy League–educated New York real estate agent, accounted for her Botox use was through this competitive frame. She elaborated, stating that "other women, they are your competition, that's who like you're next to. If you are having dinner with another couple, and his wife looks fantastic, and you are, like, looking at her, and you think, Wait, I can look like that, but you don't, then there's a problem."

Many women who were single and in their thirties or forties lamented that they saw themselves as aging out of the heterosexual dating market; they spoke about contending with younger, fresher looking women and feared the prospect of getting older without a male partner. The foreboding possibility of a permanently unmarried future governed women's aesthetic choices. Even within a changing gender and sexual landscape where middle-class women are expected to defer marriage and family formation until their early-thirties to focus on education and career investment, there is still no cultural discourse that imagines middle-age single life as an enriching or positive lifestyle.

The aging process can have dire social and economic consequences for all women, but this pressure is exacerbated for those who already have beauty privilege. For women who are accustomed to turning heads when they walk into a room, the fear of becoming invisible and irrelevant with age and accepting what the sociologist Erving Goffman called "nonperson treatment" can be devastating.[6] Although these women were aesthetically privileged before Botox, penetrating their everyday realities were relentless and intrusive thoughts of aesthetic failure, embodied ugliness, and the comparative evaluation of their own beauty with others. The meanings they constructed about their bodies and their beauty were derived from their social interactions with other women whom they saw as equally, if not more, attractive. Although the slight change that Botox made in their appearances might seem like a tiny distinction, for these women it was a sensible and rational solution to the problem of their fading attractiveness.

I found that it was significantly more likely for women to speak about Botox as a means for achieving workplace success than success in the romantic realm, as the desire for career advancement was configured as a more socially acceptable reason to participate in feminine beauty culture. Women spoke about Botox as a means for improving the enterprising self and as a practical and necessary upgrade to maintain their competitive edge in the workplace. Shifting the location of competition from the feminine realm of relationships to the masculine territory of career investment suggested that feminist values of financial independence from men were important sources of women's identities. However, financial success was often accompanied by a retro femininity. Although many of these women had gained access to occupational fields from which their mothers were once excluded, their bodies continued to be routinely disciplined and policed in the workplace. One reason for this is that employment-based ageism significantly disadvantages women more so than men, and women are significantly more likely to cite appearance-based age discrimination in the workplace than are their male colleagues.[7] Because employers frequently perceive women as being older than their same-aged male counterparts, women can attempt to circumvent these disadvantages by focusing on their appearances and trying to look as young as possible.[8] And doing so is financially consequential. Economists have documented a "beauty premium" for which women who comply with current cultural standards of beauty receive higher incomes than those who do not.[9]

Furthermore, many jobs either implicitly or explicitly require women to meet specific standards of attractiveness, and women are expected to engage in aesthetic labor in order to meet workplace appearance standards. A sociological term that elucidates the connections between organizational contexts and individual bodywork, "aesthetic labor" is predicated on the expectation that workers cultivate their appearances in exchange for direct or indirect economic rewards, and it accentuates the expectations for specific forms of bodily presentation within certain workplaces.[10]

Women in the service economy were especially likely to mention the importance of engaging in aesthetic labor for their careers. Katherine Turner, a manager at a Miami high-end boutique, told me, "Appearances are central to this job. My face is like my business card. There is no way I can afford to look tired or old." Likewise, when I asked Jessica Johnson, a Miami Beach hairdresser in her early forties, about her Botox use, she replied, "How am I supposed to have people take me seriously in this job if I don't look the best I can look? I charge over $120 for a freaking haircut! I have to look the part. I am selling myself here." The sociologists Christine Williams and Catherine Connell have argued that the workers employed at upscale retail stores and high-end beauty salons are a large component of what is purchased; they literally embody the intended cultural meanings associated with the products and services sold in the shop. Rewarding those workers who embody the style and image of the workplace adds to the "mystification of commodities, attributing value and meaning to things, while obscuring the unequal and unjust social relations that produce them."[11] In this way, the commodification of workers' corporeality naturalizes those embodied distinctions that are shaped by social inequality.

As Dawn Goldstein's story foreshadowed, the theme of Botox injections being a career investment was also particularly evident among the broadcast journalists in my sample. Allison Harris of Louisiana shared, "With my situation, a lot of it does have to do with the job. I mean, I want to be able to stay in this business for a while; I'm not independently wealthy. I need a job. And the longer I can preserve my appearance and as much youth as I can, the longer I'm going to be able to stay in the business for years and years and years." Shunning age-defying procedures like Botox was risky, especially as it was one of the few tools women had at their disposal to continue to hold power in an unequal occupational system.

In order to succeed in their workplace, women felt they needed to look better, fresher, and more confident. Reflective of American values of industriousness and hard labor, these women spoke about investing in their bodies to sustain their competitive edge in commercial economies. As body entrepreneurs, they took pride in their initiative, risk-taking, and hard work by couching their explanations of aesthetic labor within masculine tropes of competition. They fashioned themselves as ambitious and motivated careerists. On the one hand, aligning femininity with such brazen determination contrasts with the stereotypical constructions of traditional middle-class femininity as docile and passive. On the other hand, the source of these women's power still came from their beauty and bodies, revealing how women's entrée into male-dominated occupations has not corresponded with the freedom to abandon the pursuit of an externally derived feminine beauty ideal.

It's a Personal Choice: Communicating Agency

Through self-surveillance and conscious assessments, these women and men decided to use Botox as a means to preserve their attractiveness and youth and enhance their own social and cultural power. It is vital to emphasize, however, that where each of these individuals was competent, deliberate, and autonomous, their autonomy was constituted within circumstances not of their making. Couching their accounts about Botox within the logic of individualism and autonomy was one discursive strategy that Botox users employed to see themselves as active and self-governing subjects.[12] For example, when I asked Barrington Marx, the gay publicist from New York, if he ever felt the pressure to hold onto his youthful appearance in order to attract younger men, he retorted, "Absolutely not! I am doing this for myself and myself only." Others with whom I spoke also distanced themselves from those whom they saw as using cosmetic enhancements to please others in an attempt to enhance their own legitimacy. Allison Harris, the Louisiana broadcast journalist, shared how she thought it was problematic when a woman got Botox—or any other cosmetic procedure, for that matter—to gain male attention. For her, body enhancements were okay only if a woman was "doing it for herself." It was unacceptable, even denigrating, for a woman to use Botox as a means to please or keep her intimate partner.[13]

Echoing this conviction, Izzy Dershowitz, the Fort Lauderdale graphic designer who at the time of our interview was planning her wedding, told me that "Botox for me was a personal choice. I may have a husband soon, but at the end of the day I only have myself. I have to be happy with myself, that's the most important thing. If it takes a little needle in my head, a little pain, then fine." Later in our conversation, Izzy continued to make the connection between her recent Botox injections and the breast augmentation surgery she had fifteen years earlier. "The boob job, well, that was like the best thing I ever did for myself. You know, people are against this and against that, but when they realize what it can do for your self-confidence, it's worth it. Like the money, the surgery, the pain, that was all worth it. It's just like Botox, if it can make you feel better about yourself and make you happier about yourself, then do it." These accounts are consistent with modern norms about middle-class femininity that condemn women's aesthetic labor if it is driven solely by the pursuit of pleasing a man or securing a husband. The modern autonomous heterosexual woman performs aesthetic labor to please herself; becoming more desirable to men is an added bonus or an extraneous by-product of this work.

Others emphasized that they used Botox, not because they were dissatisfied with their body, but rather as a means to preserve their comfort with their appearance. Interwoven throughout their accounts were constructions of the self as an autonomous, self-governing agent. Alejandro Suarez-Levin, the twenty-eight-year-old gay cosmetologist, maintained, "Look, it's a personal choice. You know, I don't look at it as me being not happy with myself. . . . It's me seeing some things I don't like, but it's not necessarily me being unhappy. So, I say, if it makes you a little bit happier, go ahead and do it." Ryan Callahan, the gay psychology professor, said, "For me, using Botox is not about fixing what I hate about myself, it is about preserving what I like about myself." Similarly, Madison Cooper spoke extensively about growing up with a father who was a prominent plastic surgeon and a mother and older sister who had taught her to take full advantage of the opportunities this presented. She told me how she learned—perhaps significantly earlier in her life than those without a plastic surgeon for a father would—that, if you have the technology and the financial means to be able to alleviate any sort of self-esteem issues, then the prevailing attitude should be "go ahead and just do it!"

Accentuated throughout these accounts was the idea that there was little reason not to embrace any technology or procedure that could make people look, and consequently feel, better, particularly if they could afford it. Feminist scholars studying women's conformity to beauty practices have argued that discourses of autonomy and choice obscure the economic, social, historical, and medical context that makes such a "choice" possible. Women's (and I would argue, men's) agency and their personal choice to begin and continue using Botox occurs within a web of structural inequalities and within contemporary makeover culture, where ideologies of personal transformation and opportunities for enhancement are ubiquitous features of everyday life but are only accessible to a privileged handful.[14]

In a similar vein, a substantial number of women and men with whom I spoke articulated their Botox user identities by using the language of responsibility, learned expertise, and resourcefulness. In his book, *Drugs for Life: How Pharmaceutical Companies Define Our Health*, the medical anthropologist Joseph Dumit surmised that medical consumers are now supposed to be smart, resourceful, educated, and utterly committed to taking charge of their health.[15] Model medical citizens should piece together careful consideration of expert research and advice and execute control over their bodies. Consistent with this conclusion, many Botox users in their twenties and thirties prided themselves on having the foresight to begin using Botox regularly and prophylactically as a way to prevent future deep wrinkles from forming.

In 2013 I interviewed thirty-one-year-old Reed Hammell, a quiet brunette who worked in the non-profit industry in the United States and abroad. As we sat in a café, she told me the story about her first time using Botox. Six years earlier, she had started to notice a faint line between her eyes. She approached her dermatologist and told him she wanted to start using Botox to prevent the line from growing deeper. Her dermatologist told her that, although—theoretically speaking—continuous Botox use might have the potential to prevent a deeper line from forming, he was hesitant to inject her because, at twenty-five, she would be his youngest patient to date. But Reed insisted, telling her dermatologist that she was not taking no for an answer. Against his better judgment, her dermatologist agreed. Six years later, with a creaseless brow, she proudly announced that her dermatologist has since apologized for his reluctance to inject her and commends her proficiency and foresight.

A substantial number of other Botox users colored their narratives with discourses of responsible and preventative self-care. For example, Rachel McAvoy, the meteorologist from Minnesota, justified her decision to begin using Botox with claims that it is preventative: "I always say it's a preemptive strike." Likewise, twenty-eight-year-old cosmetologist Alejandro Suarez-Levin expertly explained, "If you start early it totally prevents these lines from getting deeper, I mean I would have started earlier if I knew. I mean, look at my twenty-two-year old assistant, she just started going for Botox. I think she is really smart, starting before the lines even form."

Such discourses of responsibility were used to legitimate engagement in consumer beauty culture. Moreover, they promoted neoliberal ideologies that depended on individual subjects to take responsibility for realizing and securing their own well-being. Consequently, the problem of ugliness, and thus the solution, became situated at the level of the individual. By relying on tropes of rugged individualism to justify their Botox use, these women reproduced social inequalities that further stigmatized and devalued women who either refused to do the same or who lacked the financial means to participate in beauty culture.

Finally, a handful of participants framed their Botox user identity through the language of empowerment. For example, gay psychology professor Ryan Callahan spoke at length about how rewarding it was for him to finally be able to afford an indulgence like Botox after spending his entire twenties in graduate school and buried in student debt. He elaborated, "It was a fun reward. And something I have been waiting to do. I mean, it's not like I didn't get Botox last year because I wanted to wait until I was thirty. I didn't get Botox last year because I couldn't afford it. That's it. And now I can, and it's fun, and I can't wait to do it again."

Similarly, Katherine Turner, the high-end boutique manager in Miami, told me that "it feels really good to know I can spend my hard-earned money at the spa, I can go get that massage I want and get that touch-up of Botox. I mean, I earned this, nobody is buying these things for me." It is vital to note that the postfeminist promise of empowerment is largely commodified and tied to the possession of an attractive youthful body.[16] Consider this narrative from Penelope Lombardi, the nurse and facial aesthetician:

I think Botox is empowering to women. Botox builds confidence and makes you feel good about yourself. Now women can feel like they're doing something for themselves. And it empowers women. I do believe Botox is empowering to women because appearance means a lot, and we are a vain society, so I think it's empowering to women. If you can do that, you feel powerful.

Here women's empowerment is stripped of any political liberation and reduced to their ability to consume the necessary practices designed to possess an attractive youthful body. Articulating empowerment through this postfeminist ideology, Penelope excludes women who are unable to live up to narrow standards of feminine beauty, like poor, overweight, or unattractive women and those women who are unwilling to embrace and pursue these narrow standards.

Botox users are agents of their own beauty, as well as beauty objects, in that their agency subsists in the process of navigating and managing societal norms that are perceived to be fixed and enduring—they are seen as beyond the individual's control. Any possibility of individual or collective resistance is rejected in favor of surrendering to beauty culture and participating in the game, even though they didn't make the rules. Thus, no matter how individuals framed their decisions to use Botox—as a choice pervaded with tension, or as a strategy for developing the enterprising self, or as an autonomous choice, or as responsible self-care, or as an empowering practice—the consequence is the same: Each and every one of the women and men with whom I spoke ended up reproducing some of the cruelest aspects of beauty culture. By ultimately deciding to participate in an oppressive youth-oriented beauty culture, these women reified the structural expectations for which they denied responsibility. Through their efforts to make themselves better versions of themselves, they validated appearance as an indication of character and sustained an oppressive system that rewards a narrow visual display of bodies and punishes all others.

5

Being in the Botoxed Body

At barely five feet tall, Madison Cooper was the portrait of a postmodern punk pin-up girl. The daughter of a plastic surgeon, she had already had breast implants, a nose job, and her ears pinned back by the age of twenty-five. At around thirty, Madison discovered her affinity for tattoos and had begun to spend what would eventually be thousands of dollars marking the entire right side of her body with elaborate Orientalist art and symbology. No stranger to body modification, Madison was both the canvas for her father's flourishing South Florida surgery business and her tattoo artist's blossoming career.

When Madison was thirty-eight, and at the advice of her parents, she decided to try Botox. From the time Madison was a small child, she told me how she would notoriously furrow her brow and wrinkle her face. Whether she was watching television, reading a book, or immersed in a deep conversation, Madison could always be found scrunching her diminutive face, an expression that once bore a sense of childlike inquisitiveness. Madison told me how her mother, the dutiful wife of a plastic surgeon, had always reprimanded her for scrunching her brow, warning her that this expression would leave an undesirable line in between her eyebrows. Just as her mother warned, the line began to faintly appear in her early thirties. Madison told me how she began to see that she "was constantly looking confused or like I was thinking really hard, and I noticed that after I had a thought, the line was still very prominent on my forehead after I wasn't thinking. It was so intensely still very visible on my face." When Madison hit her late thirties, her signature inquisitive expression and the resulting wrinkle no longer seemed cute. As she grew older, Madison explained that the expression she once perceived to be an adorable look of curiosity suddenly looked more like an unpleasant angry scowl.

The wrinkles associated with aging, especially the lines between our brows, are particularly disconcerting to women because these are the lines that can cause us to look angry, bitchy, and irritated. And these are precisely the very lines that Botox is designed to "fix." A few days after trying Botox to "fix" her troubling lines, Madison looked in the mirror and was flabbergasted at the results. Observing that the brow wrinkle that had troubled her for so many years had all but disappeared, Madison was in awe of the way Botox "calmed" her forehead and "lifted" her brow. Relishing the glow of her newly placid face, Madison spent the next few days tirelessly trying to furrow her brow, but no matter how hard she tried, her paralyzed muscles would not allow her to scowl. She remembered how "I couldn't do it, and because I couldn't scowl, it could not create that line that had been there for so long. It was such a nice thing to notice in the mirror—that line now completely diminished."

Other participants with whom I spoke reiterated this sentiment, and many users reveled in their smoother, calmer looking faces. Virginia Rudner, the Manhattan Ivy League–educated real estate agent, told me, "I didn't imagine it would give me the result that it did, which is that, not only does it make me not be able to move my forehead, but it made the fine wrinkles that I did have completely disappear." Amazed at the subtle but detectable visual difference in their faces, users had countless superlatives to describe their newly Botoxed brows. Time and time again, I heard responses like "I looked refreshed," "calmer," "glowing," "younger," "more awake," and "just better looking."

However, when I asked users to describe how their Botoxed face felt, they often struggled to find the words to capture the sensation. When they finally were able to summon the words, their descriptions oscillated between feelings of pleasure and peculiarity. First-time users told me how it felt like "a post-it on your forehead," "a piece of masking tape," and "localized paralysis." Many expressed a sense of corporeal unfamiliarity with their new facial architecture. For example, Angela Salgado, the petite Colombian woman in her mid-thirties, explained, "It was the weirdest feeling I have ever felt because all of the sudden you feel like your muscles are tightening. I mean you know. I'm like, it's like you literally feel like somebody injected some stiffening stuff, which they did, into my brain." Over the next few days after injection, as Botox seeps into the face, it starts to smooth the brow by paralyzing the muscles that control facial movement. The result is that the ability to fully express oneself becomes impeded. Robert Moskowitz, the heterosexual lawyer turned world traveler from Seattle, described the sensation as "feeling like granite basically, like it feels like very immobile, like your forehead just feels heavier." He then told me how a few days after using Botox he sensed that he had significantly less range in his ability to make facial expressions and observed that it was "like running with heavy weights on. . . . You're just like slower."

My own experience with Botox mirrored these narratives. As I became acquainted with my newly Botoxed face during the early weeks of my adjustment period, I, too, could not believe how awake and refreshed I looked. The creases on my brow had all but disappeared and I had this added space between my eyes and my eyebrows that never made me look tired, even after a night of insomnia or too much red wine. I loved the ways my eyebrows had a permanent but slight lift, even more so when I smiled, and how my eyes, which I always thought were too small for my face, were open just a little bit wider than normal. But it also felt strange and foreign in the way I imagined a permanent piece of Scotch tape must feel between one's eyebrows. My range of facial motion and expression felt stunted. I kept trying to scrunch the upper part of my face and furrow my brow. I would stare in the mirror, desperately trying to scowl using only my eyes and my brow. But, alas, this proved to be impossible. The entire top half of my face felt occupied and invaded by a foreign substance.

Although I was still very much able to move my face and express emotion, I soon realized that I was only able to express *certain* emotions. The curious thing was how easy it was for me to look bright eyed and happy but how rarely I looked upset, anxious, or perplexed. It wasn't long after the high of my overarched brow and wide eyes subsided that I soon began to worry about how I was now going to give someone a disapproving look, crinkle my brow to express frustration at my students or colleagues, or signal to my friends that I was annoyed or confused. A few of the other participants with whom I spoke voiced similar concerns. Jessica Johnson, the Miami hairdresser, told me that, at first, she wondered how she was going to express her sense of irritation to her colleagues. Shannon Giles, the sales director from suburban Massachusetts, confessed that she wasn't sure people would find her funny anymore, since her sense of humor and ability to make people laugh came more from her facial expressions than her mediocre jokes.

In a 2002 interview, Jean Carruthers, one of the "discoverers" of Botox Cosmetic, told *Vancouver* magazine, "I haven't frowned since 1987. I have a picture of it."[1] Before I tried Botox myself, I wondered if this was in fact true, or if it was a Botox urban myth. In order to gauge this, I decided to ask participants to frown during our interview, an activity that proved to be quite amusing for all parties involved. The first time I did this it was with Nicole Garcia, the Miami-based cosmetologist in her late twenties. After countless attempts to scrunch her tiny face, she eventually gave up, laughed uncontrollably, and screamed, "Oh my God! I can't!" In reality, Nicole could frown using the facial muscles on the lower part of her face, but her facial expression on the upper half still looked sprightly and unwearied. Other participants were also able to curve their lips down and produce a frown with the lower part of their face, but they were unable to wrinkle their brow and emote with the top half of their face. What resulted was a mismatch between the top part of their face and the emotional expression of the bottom half.

Though not completely, Botox does, to a perceptible extent, inhibit the face's ability to visibly express negative emotions such as annoyance and anger. The physiological reason for this effect is that, when we express negative emotions like anger or aggravation, we pull our eyebrows together and push them down. The muscles that are responsible for this action, the corrugator supercilii muscles (colloquially referred to as "frown muscles"), are the muscles that we use Botox to impair. By paralyzing these muscles, Botox prevents this brow-lowering action, but it does not actually limit our ability to frown; more precisely, Botox inhibits our ability to scowl or grimace.

No More Bitchy Resting Facework

Sociologists have long speculated about the meaning of human faces for social interaction. In the 1950s, the sociologist Erving Goffman developed the concept of facework to refer to the ways that human faces act as a template to invoke, process, and manage emotions.[2] A core feature of our physical identity, our faces provide expressive information about our selves and how we want our identities to be perceived by others.[3]

Botox's effect on facial expression may be particularly enticing to women, who from early childhood are taught to project cheerfulness and to disguise unhappiness. Historically dislocated from the public sphere, from political power, and from leadership positions, women are penalized for looking speculative, judgmental, angry, or cross. Male politicians and CEOs are expected to look pissed off, stern, and annoyed. However, when Hillary Clinton displays these same expressions, she is chastised for being unladylike, as undeserving of the male gaze, and criticized for disrupting the normative gender order.

Nothing demonstrates this more than the recent viral pop-cultural idioms "resting bitch face" and "bitchy resting face." For those unfamiliar with these not so subtly sexist phrases, "resting bitch face," according to the popular site *Urban Dictionary*, is "a person, usually a girl, who naturally looks mean when her face is expressionless, without meaning to."[4] This same site defines its etymological predecessor, "bitchy resting face," as "a bitchy alternative to the usual blank look most people have. This is a condition affecting the facial muscles, suffered by millions of women worldwide. People suffering from bitchy resting face (BRF) have the tendency look hostile and/or judgmental at rest. Their expression does not necessarily reflect how they are feeling inside. BRF can ruin friendships and first impressions, start fights and kill an atmosphere."[5] Resting bitch face and its linguistic cousin, bitchy resting face, are nowhere near gender neutral.[6] There is no name for men's serious, pensive, and reserved expressions because we allow men these feelings. When a man looks severe, serious, or grumpy, we assume it is for good reason. But women are always expected to be smiling, aesthetically pleasing, and compliant. To do otherwise would be to fail to subordinate our own emotions to those of others, and this would upset the gendered status quo.

This is what the sociologist Arlie Russell Hochschild calls "emotion labor," a type of impression management, which involves manipulating one's feelings to transmit a certain impression.[7] In her now-classic study on flight attendants, Hochschild documented how part of the occupational script was for flight attendants to create and maintain the façade of positive appearance, revealing the highly gendered ways we police social performance. The facework involved in projecting cheerfulness and always smiling requires energy and, as any woman is well aware, can become quite exhausting. Hochschild recognized this and saw emotion work as a form of exploitation that could lead to psychological distress. She also predicted that showing dissimilar emotions from those genuinely felt would lead to the alienation from one's feelings.[8] But, enter Botox—the neurotoxin that can seemingly liberate the face from its resting bitch state, producing a flattening of affect where the act of appearing introspective, inquisitive, perplexed, contemplative, or pissed off can be effaced and prevented from leaving a lasting impression. One reason Botox may be especially appealing to women is that it can potentially relieve them from having to work so hard to police their expressions.

Even more insidiously, Botox may actually change how women feel. Following the early work of Charles Darwin and William James, scientists have long suggested that facial expressions, like frowning or smiling, can influence emotion by contributing to a range of bodily changes that in turn produce subjective feelings.[9] This theory, known in psychology as the "facial feedback hypothesis," proposes that the control of facial expression produces parallel effects on subjective feelings. Specifically, expression intensifies emotion, whereas suppression softens it. If, as the facial feedback hypothesis states, facial expressions not only convey emotion but also produce it, then it follows that blocking negative expressions with Botox injections should offer some protection against negative affect.

In 2009, Andreas Hennenlotter, a German scientist, and his colleagues conducted an experiment to test this very hypothesis.[10] Hennenlotter had his female subjects, half of whom had Botox and half who served as a control group, imitate angry expressions in an MRI scanner and found that those with Botoxed-impaired brows were unable to do so. Compared with the non-Botoxed women, these women had significantly lower levels of activity in their left amygdalas, suggesting that making an angry face affects the amygdala, a key neural region for anxiety and anger, through feedback from the facial muscles and skin. These findings provide evidence for the importance of facial feedback on emotion and lend support to the theory that Botox can be used to lessen feelings of anger and anxiety.[11] Taken together, Hennenlotter's experimental study and Hochschild's qualitative work on flight attendants point to some of the principal attractions of Botox. Functioning as an emotional lobotomy of sorts, Botox can emancipate women from having to vigilantly police their facial expressions and actually reduce the negative feelings that produce them, all while simultaneously offsetting the psychological distress of alienation described by Hochschild.

All of this has implications, too, for our interactions with others. Research suggests that emotional displays have effects on the autonomic nervous system of the people with whom we are communicating because people have a tendency to mimic the facial expressions of the others with whom they are interacting.[12] Thus our facial expressions may influence, not only our own emotions, but also the emotions of those who are reading and responding to our facial expressions.[13] Substantiating a physiological basis for the transmission of emotions during social interactions, these findings from psychological research help to shed light on why

Botox appeals not just to women but also to their intimate partners, children, and co-workers. Botox rescues these others from having to negotiate interactive facework with their irritated wives, mothers, and bosses. As the mimetic faculty of facework can be tiring, part of the attractiveness of Botox lies in the fact that these others can sit back and enjoy a woman's company without the performance demands of affective labor.

And this can have some peculiar consequences. Ellen Regis, the anthropology professor, told me how her teaching evaluations soared after she got Botox. She half-jokingly proclaimed that, because she was no longer able to emit that "what the hell are you talking about look" in class, her students now found her friendlier and more deferent, qualities that somehow made her a better professor than the one she was one semester earlier, when she could furrow her brow and express intellectual skepticism. Ellen's once-expressive face—one that represented the dangerous and angry woman or—more appropriately, the feminist killjoy—disrupted student's expectations about how a young White middle-class gender-conforming woman should look and perform. Her placid Botoxed face was likely seen as more attractive to students because it allowed her to comply with moral imperatives of feminine happiness and to restore the harmonious social order of the classroom. Moreover, Ellen's professorial dossier will inevitably reflect this imaginary pedagogical improvement, as teaching evaluations are important factors for promotions and tenure. Her experience thus turns the spotlight on the material consequences that ensue from gendered appearance surveillance.

When Pain and Pleasure Collide

As I have already stated, the primary seduction of Botox is that does not merely reduce the face's ability to emote in the present; it prevents the appearance of emotion from occurring in the future and leaving a lasting facial impression. One way that is does this is by training faces not to furrow or frown. Izzy Dershowitz, the graphic designer, told me that after getting used to the feeling of Botox, "My face knows not to make these expressions now. It's pretty amazing actually." Similarly, when I interviewed Miami Beach mother of two Mara Siffman after five years of regular Botox use, she explained that her face no longer is capable of certain expressions. She says, "You just learn, you know, your face knows not to make those expressions or movements that are going to cause those wrinkles."

In preventing faces from recording affect, emotion, and expression, Botox also constituted subjectivities, such that selves now found fault in scowling and in expressing doubt, annoyance, and anxiety. After my second time getting Botox I noticed a splitting ache above my right eye every time I attempted to furrow my brow, so much that it conditioned me to associate this painful stimuli with my attempt to glare. Training and disciplining the face, Botox conditioned its users to find fault in expressing those emotions that indicate annoyance or skepticism. The very act of scowling or glaring for users became vilified, for this act was seen as enabling further wrinkles and creases to etch deeper into subject's brows. Epitomizing how modern technologies become constitutive of self-policing subjects, Botox is an example of the ways that disciplinary institutions are literally embodied by consumers.[14] In much the same way that the constraining corsets of the Victorian era reshaped female torsos by compressing their waists, Botox inscribes gender power relations on the flesh by intervening in the physiological functioning of the body.[15] Thus, in addition to imbuing feminine bodies with cultural norms and values, Botox provided subjects with technologies of the self through which to intervene in their own bodies' natural processes and to mold them to achieve a culturally valued aesthetic.[16] Subjecting their bodies to constant monitoring, objectification, and discipline, users engaged in a perpetual self-monitoring and mastery of their own bodies. Thus, in a Foucaultian sense, Botox users became their own jailers.[17]

Botox can cause discomfort and headaches for the first few weeks, especially when users are becoming newly acquainted with their lack of facial mobility. Another common side effect that users reported enduring was facial bruising. Mara Siffman remembered having to "cake concealer" over her black-and-blue brow for a week. When I asked if the bruises hurt, she exclaimed, "What? After two C-sections, and breast implants, a little bruising from a needle is nothing!" In 2012 when I asked thirty-four-year-old New Yorker Lauren Schwartz how she felt about the black-and-blues that resulted from Botox, she responded, "Pain is beauty, right?"

Redemptive accounts and warrior narratives that confronted notions of docile femininity colored my conversations with Botox users, revealing how pain and masochism are necessary features of the optimization of the feminine body. Where masochism has always been a necessary component of femininity,[18] this is even further exacerbated in our current makeover society, where the good neoliberal female citizen is a suffering self who minimizes and normalizes the pain and discomfort of aesthetic labor. Thus the minor pain and bruising that potentially accompanied Botox was seen as worth the risk. For some, however, bruising was so commonplace that they didn't even see this as a potential hazard; they saw it more as something that simply came with the territory. When I asked thirty-seven-year-old single mother Vivienne Mann about the potential risk of bruising, she laughingly retorted, "Bruising? I mean, that's par for the course. What do you expect when you are dealing with a needle in your face?"

Bruising, however temporarily embarrassing, is but a minor side effect compared with some of the other side effects people endured. For instance, in addition to dealing with perpetual bruising, self-proclaimed health nut Penelope Lombardi had debilitating headaches every time she went for a fresh Botox injection. "The one thing I don't like about it and I dread is I get these headaches, and I feel very heavy, and I do feel not everyone experiences this, but I do because I can't move my eyebrows as much as I did before. It feels heavy, it feels like they're dropped a little bit, and it's a heavy feeling. The headaches lasts about three to four days, and whenever I get [injections into] the glabella lines, I still feel very tender when I touch it, and there's bruising and swelling." Admitting that her debilitating headaches and weeklong bruises were not enough to convince her to terminate her regular Botox use, Penelope told me that she soon forgot about the pain once the visible effects of Botox began to appear.

Like Penelope, some of the other women with whom I spoke minimized their negative responses to Botox, and a few even forgot about these altogether. For example, when I told Lola Guzzetta that I wanted to interview her about Botox, she replied, "I love it. I love it. I love it!" After about forty-five minutes of her telling me how much she loved Botox, I asked her if she had any bad experiences with the procedure. She froze and said, "Have I got a story for you!" She then told me about the very first time she got Botox in 2002. After about two weeks of feeling an intense tightening of her eyelid, it began to droop rather drastically, so much that she had thought she had had a stroke. She went to her general practitioner, who conducted a brain scan and an entire series of medical tests. When the tests and scans came back negative, the doctor asked her if she had Botox, when she told him that she had, he explained that these stroke-like symptoms were actually a side effect of Botox. Lola was suffering from ptosis, a temporary side effect from Botox that is caused by damage to the muscle that raises the eyelid. As Lola recalled these events, it was evident that this was a highly stressful and traumatic experience, yet ten years later, under the intoxicating fog of Botox, she almost all but forgot this experience.[19]

One of the most feared side effects that users mentioned was the raised eyebrow effect. Often called the "Spock eyebrow," a reference to the fictional character from Star Trek who had a dramatically quizzical eyebrow, this creates a look that results in the appearance of an unnatural face that is "too Botoxed." The Spock eyebrow effect happens when the injector does not treat enough of the horizontal forehead. If the injector is well trained to deal with such a mistake, it can usually be corrected by injecting a few extra units slightly over the outer eyebrow to lower the resting tone of the muscle.[20] However, in some cases (which often might speak to the qualifications of the injector), the Spock effect can last until the neurotoxin loosens its grip, which could take weeks, even a month. Only one woman in my sample, Rachel Lipsner, an attorney in her early sixties, had to weather the full effects of the Spock eyebrow, and as soon as she noticed it taking effect, she went back to her dermatologist and had the error remedied immediately. Yet she still had to deal with a few embarrassing days of going to work with an "obviously Botoxed face" before she could make time to see her dermatologist.

Where none of my other participants shared stories of having to weather the full effects of the Spock eyebrow, many told me about girl-friends who had endured this side effect. Such women were consistently used as examples of what not to look like, as exemplars of what happens when one goes too far with Botox or when one opts for bargain Botox. In their stories, these women represented the "risky other" whose Botox consumption was "unregulated and out of control."[21] Accentuating the body of the "risky other" allowed women to construct a corporeal measuring stick against which they, the normal and responsible Botox users, were "measured, accepted, and condoned."[22] The "risky other" and the "voluntary risk taker" are narrative archetypes that have emerged out of our normalized cosmetic surgical culture in which the good and normal consumer is constructed in opposition to the surgery junkie, the addict, and the obsessed patient.[23] Responsible Botox consumers are "voluntary risk takers" who consciously navigate known risks in order to align their bodies with current notions of feminine morality.[24] As these women brave the known risks and side effects of Botox, they demonstrate their commitment to creating a female body that reflects the value of self-work in our neoliberal ethos. It is vital to point out that it is precisely these women who see Botox and other cosmetic practices as empowering, for it is these women who have the financial resources to fix, change, or edit any procedure with which they are not immediately happy.

Botox Dependence and Addiction

Since Botox's ability to keep the aging face at bay is so short-lived, some critics argue that it creates a compulsion for repetitive use. My findings reveal that this concern is not unfounded. When I attended the American Academy of Dermatology annual meeting in Miami in 2013, I visited the Allergan booth. With my guest badge draped over my neck, I approached one of the four sharply dressed female reps, made some small talk, and told her I was interested in trying Botox. Pointing to her wrinkle-free brow, she boasted that she had been a dedicated user for seven years. Then she told me, "You are going to love it, but once you start, that's it. You won't ever want to stop."

The inability to stop using Botox was a sentiment that reverberated throughout my interviews with users. For example, the first time I interviewed Hillary Larkin she told me that she absolutely hated the way her face looked and felt with Botox injections, and she was adamant that she was not going to use Botox again. However, when I saw her a year later on a visit to Los Angeles, the first thing she said when she saw me was, "I know I said I wasn't going to do it, but I got Botox again! I just had to after my last breakup!" Milestones like a traumatic breakup, weddings, and birthdays often triggered subsequent Botox use and prompted users to forget, or at the very least minimize, the negative effects they attached to their first experience. Maria Beth, the ex-swimmer, told me that, after she tried Botox the first time, she was fairly certain she would not get it again because she couldn't rationalize such a large expense. Then, less than a year later, and a month before her wedding, she decided to get injected for a second time because she did not want her forehead wrinkles to show in photographs. Other users also admitted that, even though they disliked the initial effects of Botox and never planned on using it again after that first time, they eventually became hooked. Vivienne Mann explained, "It was amazing how quickly it becomes addictive. When you start to see it wear off, it's just like you immediately need to get it done. I guess you're just used to not having any wrinkles at all in your forehead. Not being able to move my eyebrows no longer bothers me because I'm used to it five years later, and so every time I see a line now I'm like, 'Argh, what is that thing?'"

The homology to being addicted to an illicit drug is a useful heuristic device for thinking about how users become dependent on the effects of Botox. The way participants described their addiction to and dependence on Botox reflected a phenomenological use of the term, rather than the scientific definition used in substance-abuse treatment. Viewing Botox addiction through a phenomenological lens illuminates how Botox becomes an "embodied custom" that dramatically changes one's lived experience, personal identity, and sense of autonomy.[25] For example, even though users may connect negative symptoms—such as not being able to lift their eyebrows or having severe headaches—with their early use of the toxin, these are eventually considered a small price to pay for its effects. These accounts mirror those found in the sociological research on drug use, which has documented how, even though many initial experiences with drugs are often unpleasant, the user learns to redefine these effects as something to be appreciated and enjoyed.[26]

Like those of many illicit drugs, the effects of Botox were short-lived, especially when compared with more permanent surgical cosmetic procedures. Botox only "cured" the anxieties of the aging body for a few short months, so once users began to notice the wrinkles reappear, panic resurfaced. Elizabeth Sana confessed, "When I look in the mirror and I see those lines, I am on my phone with the dermatologist immediately booking my next appointment." When I asked Elizabeth how often she goes back for injections, she laughingly responded, "I am kind of crack-like about it."

Only one person in my sample, Robert Moskowitz, ceased Botox use altogether after stern advice from his naturopath. Robert, a self-described recovering Botox addict, described his dependence:

> When I was doing it, whenever I'd see wrinkles, I'd be like, Oh fuck, I gotta get back. You know like, it's such an amazing dream world that whenever you see Father Time creeping up again, you just don't want to be reminded of reality, so you just wanna go back for more. You quickly book the appointment. I would ignore the recommended time limits, I

would just go back and lie and not say at all when I last got it, just 'cause it puts you in a fantasyland where the realities of age don't really apply to you any longer, just for that temporary period, and so when that starts showing signs of eroding, you definitely have a quick urge and make a quick call to get right back in that chair and get your fix.

By communicating his addiction to Botox as akin to what happens to heroin addicts when their euphoric high comes to an end, Robert's confession illustrates the compulsion that ensues from the incessant need to satisfy the body's dependence. With Botox, users can visit an intoxicating fantasyland where the high of agelessness is an ephemeral state of being. And, just like any other drug, the initial high of Botox only satisfies users for so long.

Similar to what researchers have documented in the habituation of illicit drug users, where the addict requires increased dosages to overcome tolerance and physical dependence, so, too, can the Botoxed body develop a psychosomatic tolerance to the neurotoxin.[27] For some individuals with whom I spoke, their fixation on maintaining the illusion of a wrinkle-free face meant that the 15 units of Botox that once did the trick their first few times no longer sufficed after a year or so of regular use. Many users told me how they had to up the ante to 20 or even 30 units. For example, thirty-three-year-old Shannon Giles told me that, even though she started out using 15 units only two years ago, at the time of our interview in 2013, she needed 25 units to maintain a placid brow. Dakota Wagner also started off using 15 units, but four months later, for her second round of injections, she was up to 25 units and, two years after that, had increased to 30 units.

One reason for this increase in dosage is that, as they told me, some users were cautious about the amount with which they got injected the first time because they wanted to preserve their ability to express themselves and maintain a slightly dynamic forehead. However, only a few years later, many of these same users sought a different effect from the toxin—they sought the appearance of a fully paralyzed brow. For example, when I spoke with Mara Siffman three years after our first interview, she told me, "Now I want no movement. None. Zero." Similarly, Penelope Lombardi said that, by her third time getting Botox, she had upped the units to double the amount she used the first time, and after three years using Botox, Penelope told me that she now wanted "a bit of a Spock eyebrow" because she couldn't stand to look at her forehead with any wrinkles and loved the way her eyebrow arch looked with the lift that Botox provided.[28]

As many Botox users became increasingly comfortable going under the needle, and as their idea of what a "normal" face looked like shifted to one further away from the non-Botoxed face, they transposed the meaning of the practice from a medical procedure to a routine component of body maintenance. Katherine Turner, the manager at a Miami Beach high-end retail chain, explained that "Botox is a ritualistic part of my beauty regime. You know, it's something I factor in, like, Oh, I'm going to get Botox on this day because I have this coming up. It's just a part of my life now. Like getting your teeth cleaned, going to gynecologist once a year. For me, now I add Botox once a year." When I asked Katherine Turner if she perceived herself getting Botox injections every year for the rest of her life, she replied, "I don't see why I would ever stop." Hillary Larkin confessed, "It's like waxing. Once you're committed, you're committed. You are in it for life." We are thus seeing an emergent generation of consumers who see Botox as being on par with routinized body labor. By virtue of adding Botox injections to the continuum of bodily alterations ranging from manicures to eyelash extensions, these users reconfigured Botox as yet another practice of performing respectable femininity and doing respectable socially classed bodywork, and then came to depend on it.

A Gateway Drug?

During the course of research and writing this book, I received countless inquiries from friends asking me if they should try Botox. Responding that they should do whatever they please, I would playfully forewarn them to be cautious because Botox was a gateway drug into other aesthetic procedures. In keeping with the metaphor of the drug-dependent body, I would joke that Botox was like the marijuana of cosmetic procedures.[29] In November 2014, when I called Sophia Guzzetta to tell her I was getting Botox again, she announced, "Congratulations! First stop Botox, next stop, fillers!" Michael Rosenblum, the Baton Rouge plastic surgeon I interviewed, echoed this sentiment when he told me, "I do warn my patients, I am very clear to point out that once you start using Botox, it is a slippery slope; you're going to want to use Botox again, and as you get older, you're going to want to experiment with fillers."

One of the more obvious reasons for the progression from Botox to fillers is that individuals became increasingly comfortable with needles in their face. Another may have to do with what some physicians believe is a consequence of facial muscle recruitment, a pattern that occurs when the face, limited in its ability to express emotion in the way that once was familiar, compensates by pulling from other muscles. In other words, human faces will still find a way to make expressions by using auxiliary muscles, rather than those that have been Botoxed, thus leading to more creases, but in different parts of the face. The only remedy for muscle recruitment (other than stopping Botox use altogether) is to get injections of either Botox or dermal fillers in these areas, creating a "potentially endless cycle of technological fixes."[30]

However, the most common reason cited by users was that their habituations with Botoxing their foreheads eventually lead them to be increasingly sensitive and attuned to the other wrinkles on their faces. Rachel McAvoy, the meteorologist from Minnesota, explained, "I love Botox, but the only problem is now the attention is taken away from my forehead now, and now I'm starting to notice my parenthesis around my mouth. Like I want fillers here (pointing to nasolabial lines). The funny thing is, I always used to think like my face was too chubby when I was younger, but now I'm like, I want to put shit into my face. Now I'm saving up for Radius injections."[31] In a similar vein, three years after our first interview, Mara Siffman told me that she not only wanted a frozen forehead, she also was seriously contemplating turning to dermal fillers to plump her nasiolabial folds. Madison Cooper also admitted that she was thinking about using fillers on the lower part of her face within the next year.

It was typically unlikely for women in their twenties and early thirties in my sample to have progressed to fillers, but as they aged into their late thirties and early forties it became more and more likely. For example, Vivienne Mann and Elizabeth Sana, both in their late thirties, graduated to using fillers after years of consistent Botox use. Other women, such Rachel Lipsner and Francesca Girod, who began using Botox in their forties and fifties, used dermal fillers in conjunction with Botox from the very beginning of their foray into injectables.

My findings expose how the success the cosmetic surgery and enhancement markets depends on inducing sufferings of personal inadequacy that renders consumer behavior and consumer bodies essential to their continuation. These industries create a culture of lack that is only quenched through purchasing more surgery, more laser treatments, more filler, and more Botox. As the human body, specifically the feminine body, is increasingly presented with endless options and choices for self-transformation and enhancement, so do new expectations and anxieties about selves and bodies arise.

Like You, Only Better: Designing the Ageless and Natural Body

In her cultural critique of cosmetic surgery, Meredith Jones argued that the majority of anti-aging bodywork was not necessarily about the pursuit of denying aging; it was, rather, about designing aging or, perhaps more precisely, about designing agelessness.[32] Consistent with this, the overwhelming majority of people with whom I spoke maintained that they were not using Botox to stop the appearance of aging altogether or even to look younger; rather, they were using Botox to look like a better version of themselves. For example, Jules Meyer explained that

"I like Botox because it helps me look the best I can at my age. I'm not trying to look younger, I just want to look good for my age and not let myself go." Ellen Regis shared, "I think with Botox, it fits with my desire to want to look good for my age. I don't have some kind of, like, wholly unrealistic kind of desire to look like I'm in my late twenties." Echoing this, Allison Harris stated, "With Botox, you don't want to look like you had something done. I just want to look like I'm holding on to what I have."

A common theme that surfaced in my conversations with Botox users was how the aesthetic care of the body should be visually obvious, but not too obvious. Women spoke about being paradoxically stuck between cultural scripts that mandated they maintain their youthful appearance through rigorous aesthetic labor and those that sanctioned them for looking like they had any work done or for trying too hard. Herein lies a major paradox with respect to living in a Botoxed body: Whereas it was okay for people to *know*, at least those with whom one was close, it was typically not okay for people to *notice* anything other than a subtle, almost imperceptible difference in appearance. Moreover, even though aesthetic labor was often constructed as a sign of morality and responsibility, there was still a fine line that women had to walk in which they needed to look good, but not like they were trying too hard. As the feminist anthropologist Ellen Regis articulated, "You don't want to seem overly concerned with your appearance because then you morph into, like, one of the Real Housewives, and that's bad." Even as women are inundated with messages to subject their bodies to endless enhancement, they are only supposed to do so to the extent that this work remains invisible. In short, women *should* use Botox, but they should not *look* "Botoxed."

Dominant White middle-class feminine norms of attractiveness privilege a seemingly natural and effortless beauty, so the countless hours and monetary investment that went into my participants' body projects had to be kept hidden for their bodies to retain their value.[33] The "natural" trope was frequently invoked to denote the Goffmanian notion of "passing," in that looking Botoxed or too cosmetically enhanced was a discredited identity.[34] In order to avoid the stigma of going overboard, the Botoxed body needed to publicly pass as normal and as natural, and it was common for participants to tell me they were using just enough Botox so they would still "look natural." For instance, Sophia Guzzetta explained that "it's not like I shoot up a lot in my face, you know, just enough so that it still looks natural." Similarly, Katherine Turner shared that she didn't want her face to "look Botoxed. . . . I want a natural and fresh look. I don't want to look fake." Virginia Rudner told me, "I don't think I look Botoxed, right? I think my face looks natural." "Natural" no longer indicated a body untouched by technology; rather, "natural" referred to a body constructed through technological interventions that could not be detected, tampering with the signs of aging so subtly that these technological interventions remained hidden.[35] As the gay psychology professor Ryan Callahan told me, "'Natural' no longer means not having work done. 'Natural' means passing for having no work done." Temporal and situational, "natural" was woven throughout narratives as a discursive trope that functioned to construct oppressive disciplinary regulations for how women, and increasingly men, should navigate aesthetic rules.[36]

Hence, the rise of Botox exposes how appearance norms and stigmas evolve and change with the emergence of new technologies. Where the aging face is stigmatized for its insufficient self-care and irresponsibility, the completely creaseless or paralyzed face is stigmatized for its absurdity, narcissism, and profound vanity. Unlike some scholars who have noted a shift toward the artificial in which the obviously modified or augmented body is preferable to the organic or natural looking one,[37] I found that, in the case of Botox, the natural look was privileged over an obviously paralyzed face, and passing as an unmodified youthful face was required to successfully hide the stigma of showing too much technological intervention.

The notion of growing old gracefully was another common trope interwoven through participants' narratives, and it was frequently linked with the trope of "looking natural." For the most part, participants saw procedures such as Botox injections, lasers treatments, chemical peels, and even cosmetic surgery as helping them to grow old gracefully. For the majority of the women and men with whom I spoke, growing old gracefully usually entailed technologically tampering with the signs of aging. For example, when I asked Barrington Marx what "aging gracefully" meant to him, he replied, "I think that expression is absolute nonsense! Frankly, I don't find anything graceful about forcing the rest of society to see your face turned into a leather wallet. I don't find anything graceful about that. I think it's far more graceful to take care of yourself." Barrington's colorful response illuminates how, in our current cultural ethos, aging has a negative cultural value—and not because of physical deterioration and impending morbidity, but because sagging skin and wrinkles are culturally stigmatized.

As I detailed in the previous chapter, the women and men with whom I spoke had profoundly abysmal views of aging, and most did not see a future where they could permit their bodies to age without technological intervention. Where the truism of "earning their wrinkles" was notably absent in participants' narratives about aging gracefully, also absent was the desire to have zero facial creases and risk looking like they were trying too hard. Similar to the way that "natural" was invoked as a disciplinary trope to distinguish between acceptable and unacceptable bodywork, "aging gracefully" meant not going overboard with technological intervention. For example, Sophia Guzzetta told me, "I believe that people should grow old gracefully, so at the end of the day, I'll keep doing Botox, but I'm not going to be one of those plastic women who I see walking around Miami Beach because I think that's very scary." Similarly, Nicole Garcia said, "I don't want to be one of those ladies that looks like catwoman, like their face, like, has no wrinkles at all, like, I don't mind to have a little bit of wrinkles when I get older." "Aging gracefully" was a rather lose and elastic term that meant using enough technology to stall aging but not to stop it; it was about "stretching middle age" but also about growing older with grace and acceptance.[38] Hillary

Larkin summed up how "aging gracefully" was a term laced with tensions, contradictions, and inconsistencies:

> Aging gracefully to me is all upon how the person feels. So if a person feels like they are aging gracefully, and they are getting a ton of plastic surgery, then fine, but living in New York when you see those women hailing a cab on Madison Avenue, and their face literally left in the cab that just drove past, to me that's not aging gracefully, it's trying to stop aging in its tracks. Aging gracefully is being ok with your wrinkles, letting here and there a couple of wrinkles happen. I think my grandmother has aged gracefully. She's had a couple of little surgeries, she's had her eyes done, maybe a mini face-lift, and her neck done. . . . She just did little things to make herself feel a little bit better or a little bit younger. So, I think we have the technology, and we should use it, but we should use it moderately.

Many of the women Botox users with whom I spoke felt like they were caught between a metaphorical rock and a hard place, a damned if you do, damned if you don't mentality. Navigating this duality was a source of frustration for many of them, and some spoke candidly about their temptation to surrender and allow their aging bodies to take their "natural" physiological course. Madison Cooper admitted, "I'd like to say that I want to grow old gracefully, but being the daughter of a plastic surgeon as well as living in a town where cosmetic surgery is advertised in every magazine, billboard, and, well, corner of anywhere that I go, I know that it is probably not very likely."

Even as some women expressed awareness of the insidious impact of ageist norms and advertisements, the need to be beautiful, feminine, and socially valued trumped such critical assessments. The ever-increasing availability of anti-aging products available to women to assist them in their quest to hang on to their youthful appearance for as long as possible made refusing to use them both impracticable and unthinkable. When I asked women if they were ever tempted to stop engaging in anti-aging aesthetic labor altogether—and, specifically, if they were ever tempted to stop using Botox—the responses were dismal. Dakota Wagner earnestly responded, "That's not an option, I wish it were. So, if you can't beat 'em, join 'em, I guess," and Vivienne Mann retorted, "I wish that I could just say 'fuck it,' but I could only do that if everyone else said 'fuck it' with me." Rather than face social scrutiny and eradication, these women ultimately resigned their bodies to their ageist culture. Used to legitimate engagement in consumer beauty culture, such defeatist rhetoric was fueled by a paradoxical anxiety about becoming invisible as an aging woman and about standing out as the only woman not taking charge of her always declining body. That Botox users' narratives of choice were so frequently peppered with narratives of defeat exposes the extent to which empowerment and capitulation are two sides of the same coin when it comes to feminine beauty work. Moreover, even as the struggle to remain young and attractive by societal standards is condemned for failure, it seems that the moral imperative to care for and "fix" our wrinkles will only continue to intensify within our rapidly expanding landscape of aesthetic labor.

Conclusion

The Perils of an Enhanced Society

Botox is a feminized cosmetic practice and an enhancement drug. Just like Prozac, Viagra, and human growth hormone, Botox is a drug that enhances the human body beyond what is normal or natural.[1] Moreover, in the same way Viagra is used to construct optimal masculine bodies, Botox produces ideal feminine bodies. Predicated on blurring the boundaries between the fictive and the real, Botox represents one of many "contemporary culture conjectures in which the body and technology are conjoined in a literal sense."[2] Straddling the organic and the technological, the Botoxed body is the prototypical cyborg body, a technobody that exposes the postmodern destabilization of the human/nonhuman binary and the illusory distinction between nature and culture.[3]

The Botoxed body is "more real than real"; it is an enhanced body and a body superior to the normal body.[4] Seen as preferable to the "natural" body, the Botoxed body looks relaxed, awake, and refreshed even if it is exhausted, stressed, or anxious. In this way, Botox counterposes the flawed "natural" body with new sets of standards for deficiency and normalcy. Now, "looking like you" isn't good enough, since, with the advent of Botox, you need to be "like you, only better." Botox users' blasé acceptance of their enhanced bodies provides insight into the evolving meanings of natural and synthetic social paradigms. Like the rise of Prozac and Viagra before it, the increasing popularity of Botox troubles the normal body, making it such that society at large begins to desire and to expect a biomedical or technologically enhanced ideal.[5]

A friend recently commented to me, "I don't understand why people have a problem with Botox. America is an enhanced society. If we would just admit this, celebrate it, and move on, things like Botox would be a nonissue." I responded, "So does this mean we should indiscriminately swallow pills and ingest prescriptions, resigning ourselves to having the brains, stamina, face, and body we can afford?" She paused, only for a moment, and rejoiced, "Of course it does!"

Americans' burgeoning consumption of medicinal enhancements for a variety of previously nonmedical conditions raises important questions about who has access to these drugs, to whom they are being marketed, and how pharmaceutical enhancements perpetuate and reinforce existing class, gender, race, and age hierarchies. For example, despite recent indications that more women of color are using Botox and are being depicted in Allergan's marketing materials, for the most part, the bodies and faces of Botox are White. Even when the body is Black, however, discourses about Botox actively construct and assume an upper-middle-class feminine body. Botox is thus about appropriating and communicating a class status marked by deliberate self-production and self-transformation. Marketing discourses that claim to empower the predominantly White, well-dressed, ageless women pictured in Botox advertisements beg for a critique on how this reinforces a White bourgeois beauty norm. Even though the vast majority of Botox users are those who can afford the drug, Botox and other medicinal enhancements are increasingly marketed to broader socioeconomic demographics. Yet, issues of class privilege are absent from media discussions of Botox and in the company's marketing materials. Moreover, even though Botox is financially out of reach for the majority of women, Allergan's aggressive marketing, coupled with the rise in medical spas and the increasing promotions and bargains on Botox injections, makes it such that more women are given the option and, thus, the responsibility to use Botox. For this reason, I speculate that in the not so distant future Botox will become more of a cultural imperative than an aesthetic option for increasing numbers of women across class lines.

Regulatory discourses about "looking natural" and "buyer beware" become even more important here because many women who cannot afford the high-priced dermatologists or cosmetic surgeons will be compelled to turn to medical spas and Groupon and other discounted deals to do their bidding. Inasmuch as White middle-class beauty standards dictate that aesthetic labor be invisible, the bodies of the less fortunate may experience additional stigma for bargaining for Botox and for failing to achieve the natural look that comes with the price of a skilled and experienced injector. There may be some truth to the claim that going to a medical spa or a dentist for treatment—or using a discount promotional offer instead of seeking out a more experienced, reputable plastic surgeon or dermatologist—is the equivalent of going to megafranchise bargain-basement haircutter's instead of getting a cut by a top stylist. But the vast majority of women cannot afford to go to a top stylist for a haircut, just as not everyone can afford to go to a reputable dermatologist for Botox. My findings illustrate how women seeking out a bargain for Botox are painted as frivolous and careless and therefore only have themselves to blame for procedures that go wrong. They are shamed for doing exactly what their economically privileged counterparts are doing: following social scripts about appropriate feminine bodywork.

The rise of Botox illuminates how, in a socially stratified society like America, some forms of body modification, specifically those that are out of reach for much of the population, can further exacerbate existing social inequalities. When the collective purchases, practices, and lifestyles that go into cultivating body capital are unattainable for the majority of the population, the bodies of the economically privileged and beautiful become legitimated as moral and responsible and the bodies of the less fortunate, old, and ugly become even further stigmatized. As the sociologists Shari Dworkin and Faye Linda Wachs observe in their analysis of fitness marketing, "While once the sins of the individual were thought to be written on the flesh, simply not having perfect flesh is now viewed as a sin in and of itself."[6]

Gendered Bodies and Selves

The rise of Botoxed bodies reveals a great deal about the privileges of male embodiment. There is no doubt that more and more men are being marketed to by Allergan's vastly aggressive campaign and that there is a steady rise in the number of male Botox consumers. Nonetheless, the fact that over 90 percent of Botox users are women is a more pressing concern. While some of the men with whom I spoke might very well feel the weight of body objectification, their gender privilege still enables them to maneuver through beauty ideals and normative body standards in ways that women cannot. Even though men might feel dissatisfaction with their aging bodies, their subjectivities are not defined by their bodies in the same way as women's. This is precisely because in contemporary American society, women's subjectivities, their identities, and their very sense of selves are defined by and through their bodies and their appearances.

Botox is one of myriad body practices that manifest the sociocultural need for women to remain young, thin, and beautiful. Botox reflects and reproduces a very specific form of femininity guided by hegemonic beauty ideals. Inscribing subjects with dominant gendered meanings and values, Botox serves as an ideal site for examining what Anne Basalmo refers to as the "technological reproduction of the gendered body."[7] Botox's erasure of the brow creases and frown lines that can cause women to look angry or "bitchy" fits within a long-standing history of regulating women's bodies to accommodate to societal standards of feminine attractiveness. In much the same way that Victorian-era corsets reshaped female torsos by constricting their waists and that Chinese foot binding remade women's feet to fit with cultural standards of class and beauty, Botox inscribes gender power relations on the flesh.

Where objectification is an important component to theorizing Botox users' experiences of embodiment, so too are psychosocial processes, social interactions, and cultural interpretations. The Botoxed subject is produced within a polemical nexus of sociopolitical contexts, institutional arrangements, and structurally created demand. The Botoxed body is both culturally regulated *and* voluntarily cultivated. Employing the plurality of a both/and approach to understanding Botox reveals how Botox users are rational agents and herded conformists.

The body is a vessel for communicating how subjects perceive their selves, how they want to be perceived by others, and where they locate their selves in society. People engage in body modification practices to enhance their appearance and social status and to bring their bodies into conformity with cultural norms. Botox users are body enhancers; with thoughtful and deliberate discipline, they cultivate their bodies in ways that meaningfully demonstrate their definitions of their selves and their identities. Acutely aware that aging poses a serious threat to their self-as-attractive identities, Botox users consciously inscribe their social anxieties about aging onto their flesh, attempting to keep youthful identities from fading away. Feeling the need to keep pace with a society that places a high premium on youth and beauty, they turn to Botox injections as a rational and calculated strategy to augment their embodied cultural capital.

Rejecting labels of "passive victim" or "dupe," Botox users articulate their Botox use as an intentional lifestyle choice and a normal responsible strategy for appearance management and preservation. Reflective of the values of American consumer culture that celebrates plasticity and self-enhancement, Botox users display a body and a self that is open to change and to becoming something better. Users employ Botox as a tool for the construction of new and enhanced gendered identities that present the incessant renovation of the self. Thus Botox injections are not an end in itself; rather, they are used to convey a self that is open to transformation and improvement through the aesthetic care and stylization of the body.

Indeed, the stories in this book can tell us a great deal about the transmission of social inequality through individual bodies. First, the biographies of first-time Botox users reveal how social capital can lead to the accumulation of body capital, in that many users had connections to friends and family members who either were Botox providers themselves or who had an "in" with a provider who could give them Botox injections at a lower cost. However, unlike the cultural imaginary associated with illicit drug use, these were clean, even glamorous, affairs. Related, the body and the way it is presented and cultivated is a form of capital that can add value and prestige to the self. Because bodies are read as signs of success, they can be used to access other avenues of success. Specifically, through deliberate cultivation of their embodied cultural capital, individuals can also accumulate economic capital and social capital. Indeed, some of the Botox users with whom I spoke shared stories about using Botox to preserve their youth and beauty privilege and to maintain their competitive edge in economic and intimate marketplaces. As body entrepreneurs who strategically cultivate their appearances in order to enhance their social, cultural, and economic power, Botox users emphasize the legitimate desire for career advancement and workplace prosperity alongside desires to preserve their beauty privilege.

Although beauty is hardly objective, and scholars and laypeople disagree as to whether beauty is socially constructed or biologically based, there are certain proverbial criteria for what makes someone attractive.[8] The women in my sample conformed to these criteria in that they were for the most part White and thin, but equally important is that many of these women accomplished their beauty through a lifetime of beauty maintenance projects, spending a great deal of time and money on clothing, makeup, fitness, and body care like tanning, manicures, expensive haircuts, and cosmetic surgeries and enhancements. As such, the overwhelming majority of them have experienced the privileges that come with being good-looking; most of them have not walked through life ever having to deal with being plain, homely, or ugly. While aesthetic labor is a necessary part of demonstrating femininity, it seems to be even more compulsory for women who have higher beauty capital. The privilege that comes with being attractive is one component of embodied cultural capital, one that, by virtue of the double standard of aging, is often ephemeral. Women with beauty privilege are more likely than those who have not experienced these privileges to see aging as a crucial threat to their embodied cultural capital. As new images of their selves have emerged from their aging bodies, so have tensions between their embodiment and perceptions of its appearance to themselves and to others. Fueled by fears of becoming invisible and irrelevant with age, and motivated by desires to preserve their beauty privilege, these women resorted to Botox. The stories in this book provide us with an entrée into a world where young women, endowed with beauty privilege, work to maintain their privilege, illuminating how women's appearances can be simultaneously a source of their power and a source of their shame.

Contexts of Choice

Botox users' embodied subjectivity emerges from and is embedded within a particular sociocultural context. Instead of revealing genuine portraits of interiority or true selves, these narrative accounts tell us a great deal about the postfeminist neoliberal context in which they are situated.[9] Narrative accounts that project an agentic, responsible, and empowered subject are reflective of a neoliberal and postfeminist grammar of individualism that endorses freedom, autonomy, and consumerism, obscuring the ways that Botox users are herded by structurally created demand and cultural trends.

Botox users articulate their selves as rational and agentic consumers who are empowered to take control of their lives and their bodies. They communicate and experience selves who are able to make choices about their bodies free from cultural influences and unconstrained by social structures. Yet the illusion that choices are good so long as they are freely chosen obfuscates the structurally created demand in which such choices are offered. The decisions women make about Botox and other feminine beauty work are not made under conditions of their own making, and these decisions occur within a context in which a particular kind of femininity has become a normative requirement.

Furthermore, since the free-market neoliberal economy is remarkably proficient at creating anxieties and desires that people never knew they had about their bodies, to speak of Botox users' freedom of choice is a fallacy. As the human body is increasingly presented with endless options and choices for self-transformation and enhancement, so do new expectations and anxieties arise about selves and bodies. Thus situating these individual narratives of choice and agency within the conditions of choosing in which they are enmeshed allows us to acknowledge how agency and choice are more discursive strategies that people invoke to locate themselves as autonomous subjects than they are reality. Motivated by a desire to carve out a space for their selves where they can be seen as empowered, self-responsible subjects, Botox users cast off the rhetoric of coercion, oppression, or conformity. However, the pressures placed on Botox users to comply with hegemonic beauty norms are painfully obvious. Behind Botox users' adoption of the rhetoric of choice and agency are sentiments that their Botox use is more accurately an obligation, a necessary component of their bodily self-care.[10]

Repressive bodily discipline constitutes and organizes women's experiences of femininity in contemporary society because the postfeminist promise of liberation, freedom, and "having it all" is tied to the possession of a youthful and beautiful feminine body. Postfeminist agency as an empowered or liberated woman is predicated on mastering the gendered status quo through deliberate and conspicuous consumption, narrowly defining women's agency to how they look and what they can buy.[11] Active, autonomous, and empowered, postfeminist citizens choose to use beauty products because they make them look and feel good. It is precisely these postfeminist discourses of emancipation and empowerment that give Botox users the vocabulary to justify paying hundreds of dollars to get a poison injected into their brow and to frame this as if it were an indulgence, an afternoon of pampering, or a luxury. Neoliberal discourses of responsibility and normalization further provide Botox users a model for constructing personal narratives of the self, giving them the language to attribute their actions to their own desires and to talk about their beauty practices as if they occurred in a world unconstrained by gender inequality and social structural power dynamics. Confusing autonomy and liberation with conspicuous consumption and conformity, neoliberal postfeminist rhetoric allows Botox and other aesthetic practices to masquerade as unproblematic expressions of autonomous subjects.

Yet Botox users' perception of their free will, however illusory, is real for the construction of their selves and for how they interpret their bodily discipline. Even as they buy into discourses of autonomy and choice when their decisions are more culturally constrained than many admit, their individual narratives reveal how these discourses have a constitutive function. Fashioning narratives from available discourses and cultural resources, Botox users construct personal accounts through which they gain a sense of themselves as autonomous actors. Through adopting discourses of choice and autonomy, Botox users convince themselves that they are agentic and empowered subjects. Reigning heteropatriarchal appearance norms are such that women are worth more, and feel better about their selves, when they comply with hegemonic beauty ideals. Finding pleasure in self-transformation and enhancement, their agency not only persists in the Botox process but also is simultaneously cultivated, even magnified. Empowered at the same time that they are disempowered, Botox users become agents within an oppressive system through their participation in bodily discipline.

A False Choice: Failing at Femininity or Failing at Feminism?

I have tried to show that it is unfair to blame individual women who use Botox for their role in perpetuating the hegemonic gender order. It is true that women who use Botox sustain an oppressive gender system that values a narrow visual display of feminine bodies and that these women Botox users raise the standard of normalcy by naturalizing a youthful feminine face that is unattainable without the use of Botox. That said, I have also attempted to demonstrate that, when an individual woman refuses to engage in what (in some circles) is increasingly becoming mandatory aesthetic labor, she risks being labeled as "irresponsible," "unattractive," "lazy," and "unfeminine." In short, she fails at societal prescriptions of femininity. Until appearance is not the defining feature of feminine identity, it seems that women who refuse to participate in cosmetic anti-aging practices will continue to be devalued by mainstream social norms and will age with stigma and shame.

I have experienced both the appeal and advantages of Botox while also experiencing the shame of using it—not just for being vain but also for what I perceive as a personal failure in adhering to the core ethics of feminism. As much as I would like to be able to feel good about my choice to indulge in Botox, it feels like a false choice and much less a cause for celebration. Through the process of writing this book I have a better understanding of this false choice. My own personal conflict about whether to use Botox feels less like an internal conflict and more like an external one in which feminist narratives that (correctly) emphasize the perils of being complicit with beauty norms compete not only with a multibillion-dollar industry that benefits from women's quest for physical perfection but also with a postfeminist narrative that emphasizes choice as a source of empowerment.

METHODOLOGICAL APPENDIX

This appendix details how I went about studying the Botox phenomenon. In the pages that follow, I tell the story of how this research project came to be. I detail my research process and address the methodological decisions I made throughout my five years researching and writing this book. I discuss how my interpretation of my aging body and face shifted throughout the many years involved in this project, and I share my anecdotes about my attempts and struggles to grasp and adequately capture the cultural phenomenon that is Botox.

My Discovery of Botox

When Botox emerged on the scene in the early 2000s, I was a Ph.D. student working on my dissertation on gay men's experiences on thinking about and becoming fathers. I was in the process of conducting interviews with gay fathers when I came home to Miami one weekend and met up with some girlfriends at a party. We were in our mid-twenties, and the bulk of my girlfriends were living in Miami or Manhattan, working in finance, real estate, or fashion marketing. I chose the less-than-glamorous path of academia and was still living in a small quaint college town. While we were at this party, one of my friends, Mara Siffman, took some of us aside and told us that she had tried Botox. At that moment, I vowed to myself that if I ever finished my dissertation (which at that point didn't seem like a possibility), my next project would be a sociological investigation of Botox.

Eventually, I did finish that dissertation, and in 2009 I began work on this project. As a feminist sociologist invested in understanding how people participate in and challenge the existing gender order, I came to this project with questions initially focused on how Botox was a technology of gender and how Botox injections were being used to construct explicitly gendered (feminized) bodies and identities. As I witnessed more and more of my friends and family members using Botox, I wondered what the rise of Botox meant for norms of beauty, youth, femininity, and aging. These questions were fueled by my position as a feminist scholar critical of, but not necessarily against, body modification practices like cosmetic surgery. I had grown up in a predominantly Jewish suburb of Miami where girls got nose jobs for their sixteenth birthday presents and breast implants before they went off to college. Their mothers had eye-lifts, and their grandmothers had face-lifts. I was no stranger to cosmetic surgery, but what was different about Botox for me was that these were not young women trying to fix something that to them was broken—an obviously Jewish nose, a flat chest, or already sagging and creasing skin. This was about women my age who were trying to prevent something from happening in the future, trying to fix something that was not yet "broken." Needless to say, my sociological imagination had been piqued, and I was deeply curious about this emerging phenomenon. Why were these women doing this? How common actually was this? And where were they getting these messages that Botox was preventative?

Researching the rise of Botox and its social and cultural implications meant examining a broad tapestry of discourses *and* lived experiences. In order to capture the intricacies and complexities of the Botox phenomenon, I knew I would have to apply a diverse range of qualitative methods that went beyond simply talking to people. Of course, talking to people was important, and I conducted fifty-five semistructured conversational interviews with Botox consumers and Botox providers. Qualitative interviews are sensitive to the distinctive quality of different life experiences, the contextual nature of knowledge, the production of meaning, and the interactive character of human action.[1] Qualitative interviews were useful to explore how different actors interpreted and negotiated medical and cultural discourses about Botox. In addition to this, however, I also wanted to address and analyze the circulating medical and cultural discourses about Botox that these actors were encountering.

To do this, I collected and analyzed hundreds of mass media reports and Allergan promotional materials about Botox. I read and analyzed the Botox website on multiple occasions. I coded and analyzed articles about Botox in different magazines aimed at diverse audiences. I examined press releases and news reports from the American Society for Cosmetic Dermatology and Aesthetic Surgery, the American Society for Aesthetic Plastic Surgery, and the Medical Spa Society. I attended the American Academy of Dermatology annual meeting in Miami in 2013, where I conducted four days of ethnographic research, attending panels on cosmetic dermatology, speaking with prominent dermatologists, and seeing firsthand the vast exhibit hall where pharmaceutical, cosmeceutical, and beauty companies alike extended bags of free samples to conference attendees, hoping that they would then be marketed prominently in dermatological offices across the globe. In the exhibit hall, I was able to speak with Allergan representatives about Botox. The Allergan "booth" more closely resembled a living room with white plush carpet, modern white couches, and sleek coffee tables, where well-dressed, wrinkle-free female representatives supplied educational materials about Botox to physicians and other interested suppliers.

In addition, my analysis of Botox was also informed by my own experiences becoming a Botox consumer and living in a Botoxed body. Although I have used a scholarly perspective to guide my research and the writing of this book, my insights into Botox, beauty, anti-aging, and bodywork are informed and leavened by own experiences with my aging body. Finally, in the many years that have I spent researching and writing this book, I have had countless informal conversations about Botox with women and men, critics and proponents, and consumers and rejecters. People are curious about Botox, whether they have tried it or not, and it seemed that everybody wanted to talk about the subject with me.

Talking to People

Much of what I have to say about Botox is based on my in-depth semis-tructured interviews with a sample of thirty-five Botox consumers who had used Botox at least once and twenty Botox providers. Every single provider, except for one, was also a Botox user. Interviews typically lasted between forty-five minutes and over two hours. After explaining the nature of my project, I obtained informed consent form every participant. Participants were informed of their right to ask me questions and their right not to answer any question they were not comfortable with. No participant refused to answer any of the questions in the interview. The vast majority of the interviews took place in person, either at the participants' home or office or in a café. Other interviews were conducted via Skype or FaceTime phone applications, and only three were conducted over the telephone. One of the major advantages of semistructured qualitative interviewing is the opportunity to adjust the interview guide as one proceeds through each interview. Thus, where each participant was given many of the same questions, as the interviews progressed, I added new questions, took some questions out, and altered follow-up questions.

Interviewing Users

Scholars who have studied cosmetic surgery have documented challenges in recruiting participants because many individuals hesitate to admit that they have undergone such procedures and because physicians are bound by doctor-patient confidentiality.[2] However, I did not find that this was the case with Botox. The primary reason for this was that I began recruitment in 2011 by interviewing my close friends in Miami. I solicited interviews by telling everybody I knew about my study, both in person and through social media, and much of this initial recruitment took place through my social networks. Most of these early interviews were with people I knew, and some of them were people I knew well—friends, friends of friends, families of friends, and even family members.[3]

Starting with my social networks, conducting research from this position allowed me to capitalize on my subcultural capital as someone who was intimately familiar with an initial group of women my age who used Botox. The experience of doing this kind of insider research was uniquely different from traditional research methods in that many of my participants and I already had a shared investment, mutual identification, and a personal history that preceded my research, a situation that proved advantageous for fostering an organic establishment of rapport and trust, as well as easy and regular contact, and allowing for open and accessible lines of communication. That said, however, even though the "friendship as method" approach was initially an easier way to begin my research,[4] there were some dilemmas that inevitably ensued from this method, such as "an uncharted leap across the personal/professional divide [that] is bound to cause some degree of both personal and professional crises."[5] Throughout the research and writing process, I was faced with ethical questions about making use of long-lasting trusted relationships and intimate knowledge. There were other times when I found it difficult to balance my own academic credibility with my accountability and loyalty to my friendships and family. Given the levels of intimacy and trust shared by friends and family, they were likely to forget that I was recording and that I would potentially publish what they were saying. In these cases, I found it to be a useful strategy to formally seek corroboration of my interpretations from those I interviewed in order to protect our trust and give my friend-participants a greater feeling of control over their own representation. There are also many times throughout the writing of this book where I have changed some details of my friend-participants' backgrounds and biographies to minimize their socially recognizable identifications. Finally, as I already shared deep intricate perspectives with many of my participants, I continually had to take a step back from our experiences and relationships to critically examine them. Yet, despite these dilemmas and tensions, I am certain that without many of these prior shared relationships, much of these delicate personal disclosures made would not have been made.

After interviewing my initial sample of friends and acquaintances, I asked them to refer other friends, using initial contacts to secure future interview participants through snowball sampling, a widely used methodological strategy that entails asking initial participants to refer you to friends, acquaintances, or other people appropriate to interview.[6] Snowball sampling is a commonly used recruitment strategy among qualitative researchers studying hard-to-reach populations. Although a snowball sample is a nonprobability sample that is not generalizable to the populations as a whole, it is a useful to capture shared cultural and individual meanings among people who are connected by a behavior or identification.

My goal in interviewing Botox users was to understand their lived experiences and to explore the beliefs and motivations that shaped their decision to get Botox in the broader context of the beauty norms and scripts they negotiate on a day-to-day basis. I constructed a semistructured interview guide to encourage them to talk about their experiences with Botox and with other types of beauty and anti-aging bodywork and to talk about their thoughts and fears about their aging bodies. I began each interview by asking Botox users to recall their first time getting injected. I asked them to take me back to that day and to reflect on what sorts of things they were thinking about, who they were with, where they went, and if they were afraid, excited, or perhaps both. I then asked them to think about the reasons behind their decision to try Botox and their reasons for continuing to use it. I asked them about tensions, anxieties, and fears and, if they decided to tell people about their Botox use, who they decided tell and not tell. I also asked participants to provide detailed descriptions of their own beauty practices, routines, and expenses and those of their close friends and family. In addition, I wanted to understand what it was like for them being in their body. I asked them about their bodies, what they loved, what they didn't like, and what they wanted to change. I asked them about seeing themselves age and about their thoughts about their mothers' and fathers' aging faces and bodies. I also asked them about bargaining for Botox, using Groupon deals, going to medi-spas, and attending Botox parties.

In my interviews with Botox users, I drew upon feminist interviewing strategies to make the interviews flow like a conversation.[7] This was not difficult in many of my interviews since many of the women and men in my sample were friends, family, acquaintances, or friends of friends. I used a conversational style of interviewing to enhance trust and rapport and to help reduce the inequality that often characterizes researchers' relationships with their participants. Regardless of whether my participants saw me as such, I was a researcher; I was in a position of power in the interview setting. I decided what kinds of questions to ask, I carefully monitored the flow of the interview, and I steered discussion in very specific ways. That said, however, I did not expect participants to answer any question I was unwilling to answer myself. In many interviews, I shared intimate details of my life with my participants about my bodywork, my thoughts and fears about aging, and my feminist tensions around Botox and other beauty rituals.

I also concluded every interview by inviting participants to ask me questions. Many participants did ask me questions, the most common of which was if I had used Botox myself. Since I tried Botox more than halfway through my data collection, my response to these questions was different depending on when the interview took place. Before I tried Botox, participants usually asked me why I had not, and I would tell them the truth: First, it was expensive and I couldn't really afford it. Second, I already did enough things to my body and I didn't feel like adding another thing I "had to do." And finally, I would disclose my feminist tensions around Botox. Participants responded in varying ways, some agreeing with my reasoning, others telling me my logic and decision were downright wrong, and others asking me how I could understand what it feels like to have Botox if I hadn't tried it myself. After I tried Botox, I was able to share my experiences with my participants in the interview, which gave me a very different understanding of what a Botoxed face feels like and looks like. I was able to understand the visceral sensation of not being able to move my face in ways I previously could not. After a few months, when the subtle but ever-so-present wrinkles on my brow began to reappear, I was able to share with my interviewees the disappointment I felt at Botox wearing off.

Because many of my participants were people I knew, it was not uncommon for me to see them months or even years later. These impromptu run-ins provided an informal opportunity to talk more about Botox outside the context the interview setting. When applicable, and with their permission, I draw upon these conversations in my book.

Women represent the bulk of my sample of Botox users since they are the overwhelming majority of Botox consumers. I interviewed two heterosexual men and three gay men. All of the women identified as heterosexual except for one, who identified as pansexual. Although the ages of my sample of Botox users spanned from twenty-seven to sixty-two, I oversampled for women (and to a lesser extent men) in their twenties and thirties because I was most interested in the phenomenon of young consumers who use Botox "preventatively." Only three individual in my sample were over fifty years old, all of them women. Consistent with statistics on cosmetic surgery recipients, the vast majority of Botox users with whom I spoke were White. However, four women identified as Latina, and one man was Latino. Even though three women in my sample identified as Italian American, their racial category would be read as White. Every other Botox user in my sample was White non-Latino. Every single one of my participants defined themselves as middle class, except for one who identified as upper class. Five participants had advanced professional degrees, three had completed some college, and every other participant had completed college. Botox users' occupations were diverse; they included lawyers and professors, broadcast journalists, stay-at-home mothers, therapists, teachers, personal assistants, real estate agents, fashion executives, cosmetologists, and retail managers. Every single Botox user with whom I spoke made over $30,000 annually, except for one woman, and every user except for three earned under $100,000 annually.

Interviewing Providers

My goal in interviewing Botox providers was to understand how they made sense of the rise of Botox and how they interpreted their role in this phenomenon. I asked them to share their thoughts about Botox, their role as ambassadors of youth and beauty, their relationships with their clients, and their relationships with other providers. I also asked them about the demographics of their clients and if their clients came in alone or with friends or family members. I asked them questions to get at their thoughts on the increasing normalization of Botox and about whether they thought Botox was preventative. I wanted to understand how they negotiated socially and culturally constructed notions of beauty with the expectations of the women and men they injected. I asked them about what kinds of things they spoke about with their clients during the injection process. In addition, a great deal of the interview guide was designed to solicit information about how they interpreted the intraprofessional turf war among Botox providers.

I targeted particular types of providers to achieve a relatively diverse pool in terms of medical specialty, duration practicing in specialty, age, gender, and ethnicity. Fifteen providers were men, and five were women. Two providers were cosmetic dermatologists, eight were dermatologists, one was a dermatological resident, one was a practicing dermatologist and a former plastic surgeon, four were plastic surgeons, two were dentists, one was an emergency medicine physician, and two were registered nurse practitioners. Some providers had been practicing in their field for over thirty years, and others had just completed medical school or residency. Providers' ages ranged from thirty-two to sixty-eight years old. One was South Asian, one was Middle Eastern, two were Latino, and the remaining sixteen were White.

For the interviews with providers, I conducted sixteen in person and four over the telephone. The providers I spoke with on the phone were Dr. Frederic Brandt, a celebrity dermatologist who split his time between Manhattan and Miami and was dubbed "the Baron of Botox";

Dr. Ivan Camacho, a Miami dermatologist whom I met at the American Academy of Dermatology annual meeting in Miami after attending his presentation on "Men and Aesthetics"; and Dr. Walter Kennedy, a Washington, DC, dermatologist who recently opened the first men's aesthetic and skin-care clinic.

Like the recruitment for Botox users, my recruitment strategy for Botox providers began with my social networks. I interviewed friends and acquaintances from high school who were dermatologists and plastic surgeons. I also solicited interviews though word of mouth and social media postings. Next, I asked them to refer other friends, using these contacts to secure future interview participants through snowball sampling. During the process of data collection and analysis, I theoretically sampled for dentists, providers at medi-spas, providers who worked with men, and celebrity dermatologists in order to fill in gaps in research findings.

Researching Texts

In addition to interviews, I also examined marketing, media, and medical texts. Integrating analysis of cultural and medical discourses with my interview data was a way to methodologically engage Foucault's poststructuralist approaches.[8] I analyzed these texts to examine the implications of power relationships represented in pharmaceutical marketing, media, and medicine. I attended to the ways that knowledge about Botox was produced, legitimated, and maintained through discursive practices. The first step in this phase of research was to go to Allergan's advertising material. I accessed print advertisements, digital advertisements, and informational pamphlets (which are essentially advertisements). I also repeatedly perused and analyzed Botox's website over the years. I took extensive notes about the ways that Allergan presented and managed messages about Botox. I read and analyzed the product information about how Botox works, what kind of results to expect, the potential side effects and risks, and the before-and-after images.

Next, I wanted to explore how women's magazines presented Botox to their readers. I generated my sample of this first group of magazines by checking the lists of 2010 Amazon.com top bestsellers in the categories "fashion and style," and "women's interest." Magazines included in this first round of sampling included *Cosmopolitan*; *Good Housekeeping*; *O, The Oprah Magazine*; *Marie Claire*; *Redbook*; *Self*; *Allure*; *Glamour*; *Harper's Bazaar*; and *Vogue*. Because the Food and Drug Administration approved Botox for cosmetic use in 2002, I included only those articles published between 2000 and 2013. Following my selection of the sample, I electronically searched each magazine for the keywords "Botox," "Botoxed," and "Botoxing," using a search-all-text research mode.

After reading, analyzing, and coding this group of magazines, I decided to expand my sample to include magazines that don't necessarily cater to an all female readership. I expanded my search to Amazon.com top bestsellers in the categories "news," "celebrity," and "men's magazines." In this round of sampling I analyzed articles in *Newsweek*, *Time*, *People*, *Vanity Fair*, *GQ*, *Esquire*, *Men's Health*, and *Men's Fitness*. Finally, after realizing that Whiteness was assumed in all of these magazines, I added *Essence* magazine to my sample.

My final sample included nineteen magazines that I believe speak to a wide and diverse range of readers. The magazines in my sample included news sources (*Newsweek*, *Time*), cultural commentaries (*People*, *Vanity Fair*), women's interest (*Cosmopolitan*; *Essence*; *Good Housekeeping*; *O, The Oprah Magazine*; *Marie Claire*; *Redbook*; *Self*), fashion and style magazines (*Allure*, *Glamour*, *Harper's Bazaar*, *Vogue*), and men's magazines (*GQ*, *Esquire*, *Men's Health*, and *Men's Fitness*). Given that print magazine sales have dropped significantly since 2000 and that some new magazines have appeared since that time, it is likely that the top sellers in each category may have changed during the thirteen years of my sampling frame. However, I made the decision to stay with a consistent set of magazines over time so I could observe the evolution of discourses on Botox in a single publication.

My final search yielded a total of over 900 articles. *People* magazine had the highest number of articles about Botox (125), followed by *Allure* (105) and *Marie Claire* (86). Not surprisingly, men's magazines had the fewest articles on Botox, with *GQ* having a total of four, and *Men's Fitness* a total of six. I also conducted a word count of the magazines in which I calculated how many times the word "Botox" was used by the articles in each by magazine for that year. I counted the number of times "Botox," "Botoxed," or "Botoxing" was mentioned in the article title, in the subheadings, or in the body of the article. I also included each time the word "Botox" showed up in a picture caption.

Many of the articles were about Botox's noncosmetic applications, and many articles mentioned Botox in passing (especially those at the later end of the sampling time frame). That said, however, every article I read contributed to my analysis of Botox—even those that spoke about Botox for hyperhidrosis (excessive sweating) or for migraines lent empirical muscle to showing how Botox's applications extend far beyond the cosmetic. While some articles certainly offered me more quotes, data, and background information than others, all were ultimately instrumental to my analysis of media messages about Botox.

It is significant to note that media attention to Botox has increased steadily over the last twelve years; in 2000, there were only nine total articles published that mentioned Botox in all eighteen magazines, while only five years later, in 2005, there were sixty-seven articles. Magazines in my sample from 2008 had the highest number of articles mentioning Botox—eighty-four articles. In the years that followed, the conversation about Botox started to peter off, a finding that I argue lends support for its growing normalization. By 2012, there were seventy-two articles that mentioned Botox, and in 2013, there were sixty-nine articles.

Finally, for my chapter on the turf wars over Botox I collected and analyzed press releases and news reports from the American Academy of Dermatology, the American Society for Cosmetic Dermatology and Aesthetic Surgery, the American Society for Dermatologic Surgery Association, the American Society for Aesthetic Plastic Surgery, the American Academy of Facial and Plastic Reconstructive Surgery, and the American Med Spa Association to understand how these professional associations manage media messages about Botox and decide who is best qualified to inject Botox. I also conducted a Google search of the following terms: "who should be able to inject Botox," "should I go to a medi-spa for Botox," "turf wars over Botox," "learn to inject Botox," and "how to inject Botox." Much of the data in Chapter 5 comes from documents, reports, and blogs accessed from these searches.

Analysis

For my analysis of marketing, media, and medical texts, I read through each and used a grounded theory approach to discourse analysis in order to ascertain their objectives, purpose, common discourses, embedded assumptions, shared definitions, and intended audiences.[9] I approached each text asking the following questions: What is the purpose of the text? How does the text represent certain underlying assumptions? What are the meanings embedded in the text? How do these meanings reflect a particular sociohistorical context? How does the text construct images of reality? What realities does the text claim to represent? Who is the intended audience? Who benefits from the text? Using these questions as an analytical backdrop, I engaged in an initial line-by-line coding of each article to document dominant themes, patterns, assumptions, and discourses.

I analyzed interviews in a matter consistent with a constructivist grounded theory approach.[10] Immediately after conducting each interview, I wrote an extensive theoretical, methodological, and personal memo. Trained research assistants transcribed each interview within weeks after they were completed. I coded every interview. By coding each interview soon after they were conducted and by writing constant memos, my preliminary analysis of each interview informed subsequent interviews. One of the shortcomings of my coding procedure was that I was the only person who coded the interviews. However, I did have three Botox users and one Botox provider review drafts of chapters to enhance the dependability of my results and analysis. Their enthusiastic feedback and comments reassured me that I had captured their experiences with Botox in meaningful ways that were consistent with their own interpretations.

I coded each interview line by line for recurring themes and patterns. I used a constant comparative method in which I compared incident with incident, category with incident, and category with category. After the initial coding, which fractured data into separate codes and categories, I used focused coding to sift through the most significant and frequent codes in an effort to bring the data back together in a coherent whole.[11] Like all qualitative researchers, I was faced with decisions about how best to present participants and their stories. I went through many stages of writing before I was satisfied that I represented these stories and these people to the best of my ability and that my arguments and my data were consistent with one another.

My Own Experiences

Finally, my analysis of Botox was informed by my own experiences becoming a Botox user and living in a Botoxed body. When I started collecting the data for this book, I was a woman in her early thirties who engaged in what I thought to be adequate, if not very good, skin care. I washed my face with a brand-name cleanser, spent a good chunk of change on eye creams and serums, and even splurged on a few facials throughout the years. Two years into my data collection, I began to use prescription grade Retin-A (which can cost upward of $100), purchased $50 sunblock, and got monthly microdermabrasion and chemical peels, which set me back an additional $50 each. Three years into the project, I decided to try Botox. Five years in, I tried Botox a second time.

When I began this project, I told everybody who would listen how vehemently opposed to Botox I was and that I would never consider trying it. I was thirty-one. Now at thirty-six, my position on Botox has changed. During the last five years I have watched my skin lose its volume and elasticity and witnessed the arrival of new wrinkles that seem to appear daily. The countless women's magazines that I read for this book did not help me accept these wrinkles as a sign of maturity. Rather, my readings of these magazines made me feel ashamed about my aging face. In the end, it was my conversations with other Botox users that eventually convinced me to try it.

I draw upon my own experiences as data throughout this book. Rather than ignoring my desire to maintain my beauty and youth privilege, I use this as a resource. Throughout the process of data collection, analysis, and writing of this book, I would consistently ask myself questions such as, Why do I feel such shame at my aging face? How in the process of writing this book did I fall into the very cultural traps that I critique? How can I teach my undergraduate women's studies students about the dangerous consequences of beauty culture when here I am injecting a toxin into my face in the hopes of preserving youth and beauty? Where appropriate, I decided to weave my own voice and my own experiences into this book. This book then does not only represent other women's experiences with Botox, but mine as well.

Employers value the degree over ~~what~~
what went into earning it

Salary directly related to the
# of years of school they completed
rather than the final year + resulting
degree.   } Sheepskin effect
                                       (b/c diplomas
                                       are printed
                                       on velum)

HS, college
Bartender, sec guard/waiter
>35% ~ Lib arts

Students only learn the material
you specifically teach them

NOTES

INTRODUCTION

1. Hamilton and Weingarden, "Lifts, Lasers, and Liposuction," 14.

2. Except for one celebrity dermatologist whom I interviewed, all names are pseudonyms.

3. Noonan and Adler, "Botox Boom," 52.

4. Park, "Hot Shots," 90.

5. Ibid., 90.

6. Botox Cosmetic is the first drug to have the registered trademark for botulinum toxin therapy and is still the most popular. Others include Dysport, Myobloc, and Xeomin. Similar to what has occurred with Kleenex or Tampax, the brand has become synonymous with the product.

7. Allergan Pharmaceuticals, "About Botox Cosmetic."

8. American Society for Aesthetic Plastic Surgery, "Statistics, 2014."

9. Allergan Pharmaceuticals, "About Botox Cosmetic."

10. American Society for Aesthetic Plastic Surgery, "Statistics, 2013."

11. See Chapter 1 for the relationship between the cosmetic drug Botox and the disease botulism.

12. Kuczynski, *Beauty Junkies*.

13. Allergan Pharmaceuticals, "About Botox Cosmetic."

14. American Society for Aesthetic Plastic Surgery, "Statistics, 2014."

15. Ibid.

16. Kuczynski, *Beauty Junkies*, 59.

17. See Cook and Dwyer, "Small Pricks."

18. Waskul and Vannini, *Body/Embodiment*, 8.

19. For a thorough discussion of medicalization, see Bauer, "Medicalization of Science News"; Clark and Olesen, *Revisioning Women*; Conrad, "Medicalization and Social Control"; Conrad and Potter, "From Hyperactive Children to ADHD Adults"; and Conrad and Schneider, *Deviance and Medicalization*.

20. Clarke et al., "Biomedicalization," 163.

21. Ibid., 162.

22. Ibid., 171.

23. Pitts-Taylor, *Surgery Junkies*.

24. American Academy of Anti-aging Medicine, "Anti-aging Medical News."

25. Brooks, "Aesthetic Anti-aging Surgery," 233.

26. Calasanti, "Ageism, Gravity, and Gender," 11.

27. Our ambition to control aging is certainly not a new phenomenon, as gaining control over aging has been a human desire since early civilization. Throughout human history we have seen every imaginable attempt to battle wrinkles. As early as 1600 BC, wealthy Egyptians were buried with recipes to remove wrinkles to keep up appearances in the afterlife. In 1513 the Spanish conquistador Ponce de León set sail to discover the fountain of youth. In the early 1600s, the Hungarian countess Elizabeth Báthory was rumored to bathe in the blood of youthful virgins as an attempt to hold on to the beauty of her youth and reverse the signs of aging. Humans have ingested powders and potions, stretched up their faces using thread and tape, and rubbed their skin with Crisco shortening, acid, and animal blood to fight the signs of aging. See Bayer, "Cosmetic Surgery and Cosmetics."

28. Hurd Clarke, *Facing Age*, 126.

29. See Peterson, "Risk, Governance," 194; Galvin, "Disturbing Notions," 117; and Harvey, *A Brief History of Neoliberalism*.

30. Peterson, "Risk, Governance," 194.

31. Bauman, *Globalization*.

32. Ibid.

33. Giulianotti, *Sport*, 118.

34. Giddens, *Modernity and Self-Identity*, 196.

35. Shilling, *Body and Social Theory*.

36. Ibid., 5.

37. Giddens, *Modernity and Self-Identity*, 196.

38. See Balsamo, *Technologies of the Gendered Body*; Hurd Clarke and Griffin, "Body Natural"; and Gonzalez, "Envisioning Cyborg Bodies."

39. Sontag, "Double Standard of Aging," 37.

40. Ibid., 32.

41. Ibid.

42. For films, see Bazzini et al., "Aging Woman." For television commercials, see Ganahl, Prinsen, and Netzley, "Content Analysis."

43. Van Meter, "About-Face."

44. Davison, "What HAS Renee Zellweger Done?"

45. Duncan and Loretto, "Never the Right Age?"; Ginn and Arber, "Gender, Age"; and Itzin and Phillipson, *Age Barriers*.

46. Itzin and Phillipson, *Age Barriers*; and Hurd Clarke and Griffin, "Visible and Invisible Ageing."

47. Barnett, "Ageism and Sexism"; and Duncan and Loretto, "Never the Right Age?"

48. Heyes and Jones, *Cosmetic Surgery*.

49. Tarule, "Voices in Dialogue," 274.

50. Virginia Blum, *Flesh Wounds*; and Wolf, *Beauty Myth*.

51. Kathy Davis, *Reshaping the Female Body*.

52. Leve, Rubin, and Pusic, "Cosmetic Surgery," 123.

53. Bordo, *Unbearable Weight*, 24.

54. Ibid.; Brooks, "Under the Knife"; Fraser, *Cosmetic Surgery*; Heyes, "Normalisation"; Heyes and Jones, *Cosmetic Surgery*; Pitts-Taylor, *Surgery Junkies*; and Tait, "Television."

55. Gill, *Gender and the Media*, 260.

56. Meredith Jones, *Skintight*, 24.

57. Fraser, *Cosmetic Surgery*.

58. Pitts-Taylor, "Becoming/Being," 121.

59. Fraser, *Cosmetic Surgery*.

60. I use the term "postfeminist" in the same way Gill does in her analysis of postfeminist media culture. Gill argues that postfeminism should be conceptualized as a sensibility in which feminism is simultaneously taken for granted, depoliticized, and repudiated. See Gill, *Gender and the Media*, 161.

61. Leve, Rubin, and Pusic, "Cosmetic Surgery," 127; and Braun, "Women Are Doing It."

62. Heyes, "Cosmetic Surgery."

63. Leve, Rubin, and Pusic, "Cosmetic Surgery"; and Braun, "Women Are Doing It."

64. For example, some scholars have found that African American women resist the culture of thinness embodied in the White Eurocentric beauty ideal; see Hesse-Biber et al., "Racial Identity." It has also been argued that Black women resist dominant standards of beauty owing to a combination of distinct cultural ideals and perceptions of what Black men prefer; see Molloy and Herzberger, "Body Image."

65. For a review of the scholarship on women's differences in body image and bodywork among different ethnic groups, see Forbes and Frederick, "UCLA Body Project II"; and Chin Evans and McConnell, "Do Racial Minorities Respond?"

66. McLaren and Kuh, "Women's Body Dissatisfaction."

67. Dumas, Laberge, and Straka, "Older Women's Relations."

68. For findings that show that lesbians are more satisfied with their bodies than are heterosexuals, see Brand, Rothblum, and Solomon, "Comparison"; Cogan, "Lesbians Walk the Tightrope"; Slevin, *Embodied Experiences*; and Sari Dworkin, "Not in Man's Image."

69. Kaminski et al., "Body Image"; and Peplau et al., "Body Image Satisfaction."

70. Holliday and Cairnie, "Man Made Plastic."

71. Shari Dworkin and Faye Wachs, *Body Panic*, 34.

72. Ruiz, "In Pictures"; Masters, "Most Vain Cities."

73. Schuler, "U.S. Cities." 53.

74. My analysis of becoming the Botox consumer is heavily influenced by Pitts-Taylor, "Becoming/Being," 122.

75. Here I am highly influenced by Leon Anderson's five key features of analytic autoethnography. Anderson proposes that analytic autoethnography should include

complete member researcher status, analytic reflexivity, narrative visibility of the researcher's self, dialogue with informants beyond the self, and a commitment to theoretical analysis. See Anderson, "Analytic Autoethnography."

76. Ibid., 383.

CHAPTER 1. MARKETING AGELESSNESS

1. There are five types of botulism—foodborne, wound, infant, adult intestinal toxemia, and iatrogenic. Foodborne botulism is the most common and is caused by eating foods that contain the botulinum toxin. Foodborne botulism often comes from consuming home-canned foods with low acid content and is caused by failure to follow proper canning methods. See National Center for Emerging and Zoonotic Infectious Disease, "Botulism."

2. Erbguth, "Historical Notes."

3. Devriese, "On the Discovery of *Clostridium botulinum*"; and Torrens, "*Clostridium botulinum*."

4. Erbguth, "Historical Notes."

5. Ting and Freiman, "Story of *Clostridium botulinum*."

6. The Center for Disease Control estimates that, in the United States, an estimated 145 cases of botulism are reported annually. Of these, approximately 15 percent are foodborne, occurring after ingestion of tainted meat products, preserved fish, and home-canned foods. Another 65 percent of those infected with botulism are infants. Infant botulism most often occurs when a baby ingests *Clostridium botulinum* bacteria that are found in dirt and dust and sometimes in honey. The remaining 20 percent of the cases are wound botulism, which typically occurs in intravenous drug users. See National Center for Emerging and Zoonotic Infectious Diseases, "Botulism."

7. Although Justinus Kerner did propose some medicinal uses of the toxin, like lowering the sympathetic nervous system activity associated with movement disorders. See Ting and Freiman, "Story of *Clostridium botulinum*."

8. Singer, "So Botox Isn't Just Skin Deep."

9. In 1989, the U.S. Food and Drug Administration (FDA) also approved Botox for the treatment of crossed eyes and uncontrollable blinking.

10. Noonan and Adler, "Botox Boom"; and Kuczynski, *Beauty Junkies*.

11. In 1996, Jean Carruthers and Alastair Carruthers published "Treatment of Glabellar Frown Lines with C. botulinum-A Exotoxin" in the *Journal of Dermatologic Surgery and Oncology*; it was the first scholarly publication on Botox's cosmetic potential. See Ting and Freiman, "Story of *Clostridium botulinum*."

12. Singer, "So Botox Isn't Just Skin Deep."

13. Allergan Pharmaceuticals, "About Botox Cosmetic."

14. Kuczynski, *Beauty Junkies*, 42.

15. I draw heavily from Sullivan's historical analysis of cosmetic surgery. See Deborah Sullivan, *Cosmetic Surgery*.

16. There is an extensive body of literature on how the pharmaceutical lobby controls and manipulates knowledge about sickness and wellness. See Cohen, *Overdose*; Dumit, *Drugs for Life*; Carl Elliott, *White Coat, Black Hat.*

17. Brooks, "Under the Knife."

18. Noonan and Adler, "Botox Boom."

19. Ibid.

20. Ibid.

21. Corliss, "Smile—You're on Botox!" 59.

22. Gardner, "Beyond Botox," 78.

23. Park, "Hot Shots," 90.

24. Piccalo, "Taking Aim at Botox," 1.

25. Kuczynski, *Beauty Junkies.*

26. See Finzi and Rosenthal, "Treatment of Depression"; Finzi, "Antidepressant Effects," and *Face of Emotion*; and Finzi and Wasserman, "Treatment of Depression."

27. Jerry Adler and Karen Springen, "Can You Really Botox the Blues Away?"; and Janes, "Don't Worry, Be Pretty."

28. U. S. Food and Drug Administration, "Warning Letter to Mr. Peter A. Kresel of Allergan, Inc."

29. Botox is expressed in mouse units. One unit is equal to the amount that when injected will kill 50 percent of a group of test mice in an in vivo experiment. Botox injections of less than 100 units are used for cosmetic purposes in humans, and doses of less than 600 are used for other therapeutic purposes. The dosage at which Botox becomes lethal to humans is approximately 3,000 units. I am indebted to Alex Kuczynski's *Beauty Junkies* for this clarification.

30. Zeman, "Botoxed and the Boldfaced."

31. Kuczynski, *Beauty Junkies*, 50.

32. Gellene, "'Mr. Botox' Case Raises Some Brows."

33. Ibid.; Kuczynski, *Beauty Junkies.*

34. Kuczynski, *Beauty Junkies.*

35. Ibid.

36. Even though it is illegal for pharmaceutical companies to promote drugs for off-label uses, and many have been fined by the FDA for marketing drugs for unapproved conditions, these fines are minimal when compared to the dollar sums these companies are pulling in. For Allergan, a company worth billions, these kinds of punishments are a mere slap on the wrist.

37. PhRMA, "Code on Interactions with Health Care Professionals."

38. ProPublica, "Dollars for Docs: Allergan Inc."

39. Green et al., "Black-Market Botox?"; and Charles and Moore, "Botched Botox Victims Speak Out."

40. Eric Kaplan eventually published a book in 2007 about their experience, aptly titled *Dying to Be Young: From Botox to Botulism.*

41. ABC News, "Hospitalized after 'Botox,' Couple Warn Consumers."

42. Kuczynski, *Beauty Junkies.*

43. Peraino, "Beware the Back-Alley 'Botox' Scam."

44. Despite the fact that Botox is a derivative of one of the deadliest toxins on Earth, the buyer-beware repertoire was used less frequently to warn readers of other dangers of Botox. Nevertheless, there are a few notable exceptions to this pattern. For example, one article in *Harper's Bazaar* reported that warning labels indicate the possibility of "rare spontaneous reports of death" after treatment with botulinum toxin and of allergic reactions to Botox, which could cause the body to go into anaphylactic shock, resulting in death. See Schmid, "Are You Risking Your Health?"

45. Voss, "Doctors without Borders."

46. These stories are often about injectors who take the liberty to use Botox for off-label purposes not approved by the FDA, particularly tricky injections in the lower part of the face, where paralysis is a much more serious consequence.

47. Evans, "Skin Truths," 138.

48. Stein, "Nip. Tuck. Or Else," 42.

49. Ibid., 46.

50. American Society for Aesthetic Plastic Surgery, "Statistics, 2014."

51. Ibid.

52. Ibid.

53. Ibid.

54. Ibid.

55. Ibid.

56. American Society for Aesthetic Plastic Surgery, "Almost Half of Americans."

57. Ibid.

58. American Society for Aesthetic Plastic Surgery, "Statistics, 2014."

59. American Society for Aesthetic Plastic Surgery, "Almost Half of Americans."

60. Brooks, "Aesthetic Anti-aging Surgery," 233.

61. Robinson, "Youth Crusade," 246.

62. Brown, "Beyond Botox," 240.

63. Triggs and Harrington, "Botox Confessions," 64.

64. Ibid.

65. Ibid.

66. Caris Davis, "Simon Cowell Admits to Using Botox."

67. It is of interest to note that some actresses—like Kate Winslet, Rachel Weisz, and Emma Thompson—have come out as adamantly opposed to Botox and other aesthetic enhancements and have even formed the "British Anti-Cosmetic Surgery League." Other actresses confess to nips and tucks and using dermal fillers but say that they refuse to use Botox since paralyzing facial muscles interferes with their ability to reflect emotion—an essential career necessity for an actor. See Kate Sullivan, "Kate Winslet Says No."

68. Cashmore, *Celebrity Culture.*

69. Schneider, "Facing Off over Plastic Surgery," 64.

70. Kron, "Nip/Talk."

71. Beck, "Medical Spas Get a Checkup."
72. Newman, "Breakfast and Botox?" 22.
73. Figueroa, "Smile. Relax. Smile. Relax," 53.
74. For "Girls Night Ouch," see Evans, "Skin Truths," 129.
75. Patricia Adler and Peter Adler, "Tinydopers"; Goode, *Marijuana Smokers.*
76. One testimony to the normalization of Botox in the mass media is the number of times it was referenced in my sample of magazines. In 2000, the word "Botox" appeared only nine times. In 2002, it was referenced twenty-nine times. By 2008, journalistic interest in Botox peaked with eighty-four articles referencing Botox. Over the last seven years, magazine coverage of the product has remained stagnant, averaging around seventy articles per year about Botox. Other evidence for Botox's normalization is that, over the last decade, tropes about Botox as dangerous, as a medical breakthrough, and as a miracle cure gradually became replaced with tropes of normalization. The word "Botox" appeared more and more frequently in magazines but was also increasingly mentioned in passing, either as a description of a celebrity's beauty routine or as a recommendation by a beauty editor for how to fix a particular facial wrinkle.
77. Stein, "Nip. Tuck. Or Else," 42.
78. Brooks, "Aesthetic Anti-aging Surgery."
79. Brooks, "Under the Knife."
80. Haiken, *Venus Envy.*
81. Reed, "Without a Trace," 224.
82. Crapanzano, "Frozen in Time."
83. Allergan Pharmaceuticals, "About Botox Cosmetic."
84. Ibid.
85. Kazanjian, "Wrinkles We Keep," 198.
86. Reed, "Without a Trace," 225.
87. Meredith Jones, *Skintight*, 86.
88. American Society for Aesthetic Plastic Surgery, "Statistics, 2013."
89. Says Dr. Paul Frank of New York; see Erin Flaherty, "Forever Young?"
90. Ibid.
91. Scirrotto, "Botox Makes You Look Older?"
92. Fraser, *Cosmetic Surgery.*
93. Duncan and Loretto, "Never the Right Age?"; Itzin and Phillipson, *Age Barriers.*
94. American Society for Aesthetic Plastic Surgery, "Statistics, 2013."
95. Rust, "Cost and Effect," 122.
96. Newman, "Career Lift."
97. Adato et al., "Yes, I Use Botox."
98. O'Rourke, "A Shot at Youth."
99. For similar analysis, see Loe, *Rise of Viagra.*
100. Fraser, *Cosmetic Surgery*, 70–76.
101. Only within the last year has the American Society for Aesthetic Plastic Surgery begun to collect statistics on the racial and ethnic demographics of Botox users. In

2014, 76 percent of Botox users were White, 9 percent were Hispanic, 5 percent were Black, 5 percent were Asian/Pacific Islander, and 4 percent were labeled as "other." See American Society for Aesthetic Plastic Surgery, "Statistics, 2014."

102. This is corroborated by scientific research that has found that more darkly pigmented subjects show the dermatological signs of aging at a more advanced age compared with more lightly pigmented subjects. See Rawlings, "Ethnic Skin Types."

103. Brooks, "Aesthetic Anti-aging Surgery," 243.

104. Eleven of these nineteen articles either mentioned Botox in passing or in the context of medical use for migraines or excessive sweating. Therefore my analysis of *Essence* magazine comes from only eight articles.

105. Jeffries, "Is Plastic Surgery the New Black?"

106. Ibid.

107. Bourdieu, *Distinction*.

108. American Society for Aesthetic Plastic Surgery, "Statistics, 2014."

109. Featherstone, Hepworth, and Turner, *Body*.

110. Gullette, "All Together Now."

111. Stein, "Boytox."

112. Ibid., 53.

113. Kimmel, *Manhood in America*.

114. Ibid.

115. Michael Atkinson, "Exploring Male Femininity."

116. Ibid.; Kimmel, *Manhood in America*; and Featherstone, Hepworth, and Turner, *Body*.

117. Michael Atkinson, "Exploring Male Femininity."

118. Fraser, *Cosmetic Surgery*, 30.

119. Balsamo, *Technologies of the Gendered Body*.

120. Ibid., 67.

121. Salzman, quoted in Tucker, "This Is Your Destiny."

122. Ibid.

123. Michael Atkinson, "Exploring Male Femininity," 71.

124. Demetriou, "Connell's Concept," 355.

125. The term "metrosexual" was coined by the British journalist Mark Simpson in 1994 to describe a polished and sophisticated new man who was emerging in the cosmopolitan centers of the United States and Western Europe. See Aldrich, "Homosexuality and the City"; Connell and Messerschmidt, "Hegemonic Masculinity."

126. Kimmel, *Manhood in America*.

127. Ibid., 249–250.

128. Shugart, "Managing Masculinities."

129. Jim Atkinson, "Next Great Drug."

130. Gordon, "It's a Botox Blast."

131. Curcurito, "The Third Most Insane Way."

CHAPTER 2. THE TURF WAR OVER BOTOX

1. For the same argument about cosmetic surgery, see Deborah Sullivan, *Cosmetic Surgery*.

2. Handley, "Medi-Spa."

3. Future Aesthetic Service Training, "About FAST"; Voss, "Doctors without Borders."

4. Official Allergan-sponsored trainings are not described at Allergan's Botox Cosmetic website, botoxcosmetic.com; however, several other websites, unaffiliated with botoxcosmetic.com, claim to use Allergan products and list target audiences as physicians, registered nurses, nurse practitioners, physician assistants, and dentists, among others. See Molly Katz and Brian Biesman, "Becoming an Injector."

5. For histories of pharmaceutical direct-to-consumer advertising, see Hartgraves "DTC Prescription Drug Advertising"; Hilts, *Protecting America's Health*; and Ameringer, "Organized Medicine on Trial."

6. Ameringer, "Organized Medicine on Trial."

7. Deborah Sullivan, *Cosmetic Surgery*; Ameringer, "Organized Medicine on Trial."

8. Parker, *Women, Doctors, and Cosmetic Surgery*.

9. Deborah Sullivan, *Cosmetic Surgery*; Parker, *Women, Doctors, and Cosmetic Surgery*.

10. Meredith Jones, *Skintight*, 68.

11. Ibid., 66.

12. Deborah Sullivan, *Cosmetic Surgery*.

13. Or, in Sullivan's words, "edvertising"—her term for the new marketing tactics used to educate consumers about the risks of going to an unqualified practitioner. See Deborah Sullivan, *Cosmetic Surgery*.

14. Gorney, "Who Is Responsible?" as cited in Deborah Sullivan, *Cosmetic Surgery*, 139.

15. Deborah Sullivan, *Cosmetic Surgery*.

16. Ibid., 153.

17. Parker, *Women, Doctors, and Cosmetic Surgery*, 98.

18. Deborah Sullivan, *Cosmetic Surgery*, 129; Roger Levin, "Increase Profits"; Gray, *For-Profit Enterprise*.

19. Deborah Sullivan, *Cosmetic Surgery*, 83.

20. Kalb, "Our Quest to be Perfect"; Kantrowitz, "Brush with Perfection"; Voss, "Doctors without Borders," 110.

21. Deborah Sullivan, *Cosmetic Surgery*, 128. Also see Gearon and Fields, "Medicine's Turf Wars"; Leavitt, "'Science' Enters the Birthing Room"; PR Newswire, *Orthopedics This Week*; James Jones, Laurence McCullough, and Bruce Richman, "Turf Wars"; David Levin and Vijay Rao, "Turf Wars."

22. Deborah Sullivan, *Cosmetic Surgery*; Cinda Becker, "Subatomic Turf Wars."

23. Coye, "Turf Wars"; Zetka, "Occupational Divisions."

24. Parker, *Women, Doctors, and Cosmetic Surgery*, 62.

25. Meredith Jones, *Skintight*; Leve, Rubin, and Pusic, "Cosmetic Surgery"; Hilton, "Consumer-Patient."

26. Nordqvist, "Fake Botox Warning."

27. Allergan takes these claims very seriously, and prominently placed on Allergan's Botox Cosmetic website (botoxcosmetic.com) is a link with instructions on how to verify authentic Allergan-manufactured and -distributed Botox. Likely a bureaucratic effort meant to protect Allergan from legal penalties, the website advises interested consumers to see a "reputable physician" who purchases Botox directly from the company or an authorized Allergan distributor. The website also provides a link to a list of physicians who purchase their supplies from Allergan.

28. Deborah Sullivan, *Cosmetic Surgery*.

29. Quoted at Parker, *Women, Doctors, and Cosmetic Surgery*, 98. See also Gilman, *Making the Body Beautiful*; and Deborah Sullivan, *Cosmetic Surgery*.

30. Fraser, *Cosmetic Surgery*, 135.

31. Scott and Lyman, "Accounts."

32. Bailly, "The Truth about Medi-Spas."

33. I use the terms "medical spa," "medi-spa," and "med-spa" interchangeably.

34. American Med Spa Association, "What Is a Med Spa?"

35. Beck, "Medical Spas Get a Checkup."

36. American Med Spa Association, "What Is a Med Spa?"

37. Voss, "Doctors without Borders"; Beck, "Medical Spas Get a Checkup;" Handley, "Medi-Spa."

38. Voss, "Doctors without Borders."

39. Ibid.

40. See Handley, "Medi-Spa." As of May 2014, the original quote had been removed from www.realself.com.

41. Beck, "Medical Spas Get a Checkup."

42. Ibid.

43. See American Academy of Dermatology, "Position Statement."

44. At the present time, there is only one resource that offers up-to-date information on the state-specific laws and regulations affecting medical spas across the country. In 2013, in response to the need for regulatory information about "the exploding med-spa industry," the American Med Spa Association (AmSpa) partnered with local health-care attorneys in over thirty states to assemble a website that summarized state-specific laws and regulations for medi-spas "using common sense language without confusing 'legalese.'" See American Med Spa Association, "AmSpa's Laws and Regulations Resource Page"; and Skin Inc., "AmSpa Launches First Ever State-by-State Summary."

45. The task force convened for two years and examined other state laws and regulations of medi-spas and cosmetic medical procedures. It also solicited presentations from various stakeholders and interested parties, among them, cosmetic and pharmaceutical manufacturers and distributers, the Massachusetts Department of Public Health, the National Coalition of Estheticians, and the American Society of Cosmetic Dermatology and Aesthetic Surgery.

46. "Menard was met with stiff opposition from businesspeople and, in particular, cosmetologists—who feared the negative financial impact it could have on their lucrative industry." See Voss, "Doctors without Borders."

47. McKinney, "Medical Spas Face New Scrutiny."

48. Ibid.

49. For similar findings about regulatory language around cosmetic surgery, see Pitts-Taylor, *Surgery Junkies*; Fraser, *Cosmetic Surgery*.

50. Gearon and Fields, "Medicine's Turf Wars," 62, 64.

51. McKinney, "Medical Spas Face New Scrutiny."

52. Relman, "New Medical-Industrial Complex."

53. Parker, *Women, Doctors and Cosmetic Surgery*.

54. Fraser, *Cosmetic Surgery*, 30.

55. According to the American Medical Association, *Physician Characteristics and Distribution* reference guide, in 2012 there were 11,772 active dermatologists, 5,414 (46 percent) of whom were female and 6,358 (54 percent) of whom were male. According to the same data source, there were 7,726 active plastic surgeons, 1,181 (15.3 percent) of whom were female and 6,545 (84.7 percent) of whom were male.

56. Parker, *Women, Doctors and Cosmetic Surgery*.

CHAPTER 3. BECOMING THE BOTOX USER

1. No formal testing has been done on the effects of Botox on pregnant or breast-feeding women. Because of this, it is widely advised that pregnant women and women who are breastfeeding do not use Botox.

2. Akers, *Deviant Behavior*, and *Drugs, Alcohol, and Society*; and Faupel, *Shooting Dope*.

3. This stands in sharp contrast with the stories of the heterosexual men in my sample, as none went to get Botox with groups of other men. Of the two heterosexual men in my sample, one went by himself, and the other went with a girlfriend.

4. This is actually one of the ways that dermatologists bolster their cosmetic practice. Once patients are already in the exam room, physicians can promote one of their many cosmetic procedures. Often, while in the waiting room, patients will pick up brochures about Botox, laser treatments, or dermal fillers out of curiosity and ask their dermatologists how such treatments might be beneficial for them.

5. Hurd Clarke, *Facing Age*, 99.

6. In her analysis of celebrity women profiled with their mothers in gossip magazines, Jones writes that the "mother's wrinkles are presented as active and malevolent, about to invade the daughter and take her over." See Meredith Jones, *Skintight*, 99.

7. Slevin and Linneman, "Old Gay Men's Bodies."

8. Brumberg, *Body Project*.

9. Intense pulsed light (IPL) facials use laser and light treatment to improve the appearance of photo-aged skin and to remove age spots (sun-induced freckles), most benign brown pigments, and redness caused by broken capillaries through a process called "photorejuvenation."

10. Meredith Jones, *Skintight*, 57.

11. SmartLipo laser liposuction technology is a noninvasive procedure that uses a laser to liquefy fat deposits through the top layers of the patient's skin. The laser ruptures fat cells, and the resulting liquid substance is then removed through a tiny incision in the skin.

12. Alejandro Suarez-Levin had SmartLaser liposuction, Seth Burke had a full set of veneers, and Barringron Marx had elective rhinoplasty, cheek injections, and cheek implants. Robert Moskowitz did not seek out elective cosmetic surgery until he had to get his nose reconstructed following a bar fight while in college that resulted in a broken nose. In the hospital, he had the surgeon reconstruct his "Jewish" nose so that it no longer had a bump.

13. Although I cannot say for sure, I suspect that my sample is not representative of the larger population of Botox users. It is likely that, during the course of my research, I stumbled upon a sample of women and men who have significantly more cosmetic surgical and non-surgical procedures than both the general population as a whole and the population of Botox consumers.

14. These findings are consistent with research on other body-modification practices, specifically tattooing and body piercing. See Dickson et al., "Stigma of Ink."

15. While some participants' parents had undergone these cosmetic procedures decades earlier, other participants were only recently turning to cosmetic surgery and enhancements.

16. Juvederm is an injectable hyaluronic acid dermal filler used to provide nine months to one year of correction for moderate to severe facial wrinkles and folds, such as the lines from the nose to the corners of the mouth.

17. Bourdieu, "Forms of Capital."

18. Shilling, "Educating the Body," 657.

19. Unfortunately, there are no statistics on Botox consumption in specific cities, so it is difficult to know if Botox use is higher in places like Miami, New York, and Los Angeles than in other cities, though I suspect it is. However, the American Society of Plastic Surgery began collecting and reporting regional data on Botox consumption in 2014. According to these statistics, the highest percent of Botox users is in the Pacific region, which constitutes 29 percent of all Botox consumption. The South Atlantic region makes up 24 percent of Botox users; New England and the Middle Atlantic, 20 percent; Southeastern and Southwestern Central United States, 14 percent; and the Central Northeast and Northwest, with the smallest percentage, 13 percent. See American Society of Plastic Surgeons, "2014 Plastic Surgery Statistics Report."

CHAPTER 4. NEGOTIATING THE BOTOXED SELF

1. Rhode, *Beauty Bias*.

2. Ibid.

3. Erving Goffman's concept of "passing" is relevant here for conceptualizing the way these women wanted their beauty to pass for "natural." See Goffman, *Stigma*.

4. Danahay, "Mirrors of Masculine Desire," as cited in Tanner, Maher, and Fraser, *Vanity*, 7.

5. For a discussion on accounts, see Scott and Lyman, "Accounts."

6. Goffman, *Behavior in Public Places*, 83.

7. Duncan and Loretto, "Never the Right Age?; Ginn and Arber, "Gender, Age"; Itzin and Phillipson, *Age Barriers.*

8. Itzin and Phillipson, *Age Barriers*; Hurd Clarke and Griffin, "Visible and Invisible Ageing"; Barnett, "Ageism and Sexism"; and Duncan and Loretto, "Never the Right Age?"

9. Hamermesh and Biddle, "Beauty and the Labor Market." For a review, see Hosoda, Stone-Romero, and Coats, "Effects of Physical Attractiveness."

10. Williams and Connell, "Looking Good."

11. Ibid., 372.

12. This finding has been identified in other feminist work on aesthetic labor; see Bartky, *Femininity and Domination*; Kathy Davis, *Reshaping the Female Body*; Gill, "Empowerment/Sexism"; McRobbie, *Aftermath of Feminism*; Stuart and Donaghue, "Choosing to Conform"; Fraser, *Cosmetic Surgery*; and Braun, "Women Are Doing It."

13. There is a robust literature in the sociology of deviance that documents the way stigmatized or disadvantaged people denigrate and "other" those they see as doubly deviant in an effort to enhance their own legitimacy. See, e.g., my own work on drag queens in Berkowitz and Belgrave, "She Works Hard for the Money"; Berkowitz, Belgrave, and Halberstein, "Interaction of Drag Queens and Gay Men"; Patricia Adler and Peter Adler, *Tender Cut*, on the hierarchies of self-injurers; and Rochelle and Kaufman, "Fitting In and Fighting Back," on stigma management strategies among homeless youth.

14. See, e.g., Meredith Jones, *Skintight*, Rose, *Inventing Our Selves*; Gimlin, *Body Work*; and Banet-Weiser and Portwood-Stacer, "I Just Want to Be Me Again!"

15. Dumit, *Drugs for Life.*

16. See, e.g., Baumgardner and Richards, *Manifesta*; Gill, *Gender and the Media*, "Postfeminist Media Culture," and "Empowerment/Sexism"; Jeffreys, *Beauty and Misogyny*; Wolf, *Beauty Myth*; and McRobbie, *Aftermath of Feminism*.

CHAPTER 5. BEING IN THE BOTOXED BODY

1. Jean Carruthers, quoted in Smith, "Botox Diaries," as cited in Cooke, "Effacing the Face," 27.

2. Goffman, *Interaction Ritual.*

3. Synott, "Truth and Goodness"; and Talley, *Saving Face.*

4. *Urban Dictionary*, "Bitchy Resting Face."

5. Ibid.

6. Bennett, "I'm Not Mad."

7. Hochschild, *Managed Heart.*

8. Ibid.

9. Darwin, *The Expression of Emotions*; James, *Principles of Psychology.*

10. Hennenlotter et al., "Link between Facial Feedback and Neural Activity."

11. One key point to note is that there was no difference in amygdala activation pre- and post-Botox when the women imitated sad expressions because their Botox shots did not immobilize the muscles that make a sad face. Such findings contradict those by the dermatologist Edward Finzi, who has argued that Botox can lessen feelings of depression. See Finzi and Rosenthal, "Treatment of Depression"; Finzi, "Antidepressant Effects," and *Face of Emotion*; and Finzi and Wasserman, "Treatment of Depression."

12. Kleck et al., "Effects of Being Observed"; Vaughan and Lanzetta, "Effect of Modification"; and Dimberg, "Facial Reactions."

13. Hatfield, Cacioppo, and Rapson, *Emotional Contagion*.

14. Foucault, *Discipline and Punish*.

15. Balsamo, *Technologies of the Gendered Body*, 160.

16. Foucault, "Technologies of the Self."

17. Foucault, *Power/Knowledge*; and Crawley, Foley, and Shehan, *Gendering Bodies*, 87.

18. For examples, see Brumberg, *Body Project*; and Ehrenreich and English, *For Her Own Good*.

19. These findings mirror those found in the sociological research on drug use that have documented how many initial experiences with drugs, ranging from alcohol to marijuana to heroin, are unpleasant or uncomfortable. See Faupel, *Shooting Dope*, for a detailed discussion on this phenomenon with heroin users.

20. RealSelf, "How Does a Practitioner Correct?"

21. Leve, Rubin, and Pusic, "Cosmetic Surgery," 134.

22. Meredith Jones, *Skintight*, 107.

23. Pitts-Taylor, *Surgery Junkies*.

24. Lupton and Tulloch, "Life Would be Pretty Dull"; and Raisborough, "Contexts of Choice."

25. Schlimme, "Addiction and Self-Determination."

26. Saul Becker, "Becoming a Marijuana User"; and Faupel, *Shooting Dope*.

27. Weil and Rosen, *From Chocolate to Morphine*; Pierce, "Gen-X Junkie"; and Lindesmith, "Sociological Theory."

28. The fact that the majority of my participants upped their units contradicts the logic perpetuated by many dermatologists and other experts, who argue that the more you use Botox, the less you will need, since your facial muscles are learning to relax. I am not necessarily saying that these people actually need more Botox to maintain a wrinkle-free brow, but as they get accustomed to having no movement, they often want less and less movement—which means more and more Botox.

29. Whether or not Botox is actually a gateway drug is contested. Sociologists studying the relationship between drugs and society disagree about whether there are gateway drugs or if in fact there is an individual "drug-taking disposition" in which a user of any drug, legal or illegal, is more likely than a nonuser to try another drug. See Goode, *Drug Phenomenon*; and Kandel, *Stages and Pathways*.

30. Cooke, "Effacing the Face," 11.

31. Radius is a dermal filler.

32. Meredith Jones, *Skintight*.

33. Craig, "Beauty."

34. Goffman, *Stigma*.

35. Fraser, *Cosmetic Surgery*, 71.

36. Ibid.

37. Pitts-Taylor, *Surgery Junkies*; Anthony Elliott, *Making the Cut*; Gimlin, "Too Good to Be Real."

38. Meredith Jones, *Skintight*.

CONCLUSION

1. Several other products now compete for Allergan's monopoly on Botox; most popular among these are Dysport, manufactured by Valiant Pharmaceuticals, and Xeomin, manufactured by Merz Pharmaceuticals. In addition, there are increasing varieties of needle-free skin-tightening products marketed as "Botox in a jar," treatments that allow interested consumers to forgo the needle in lieu of milder and less-expensive alternatives. Some of these, like the not-yet-FDA-approved Botox Gel, are an emulsion-based form of botulinum toxin type A, and others, like Argireline and Snap-8 peptides, are creams that limit the neurotransmitters that tell people's facial muscles to move. All of these new products are marketed as cheaper and milder alternatives to Botox, but it is vital to note that they have emerged on the market as a direct consequence of Botox's rising popularity.

2. Balsamo, *Technologies of the Gendered Body*, 78.

3. Haraway, *Simians, Cyborgs, and Women*.

4. Balsamo, *Technologies of the Gendered Body*.

5. See Loe, *Rise of Viagra*; Linda Blum and Nena Stracuzzi, "Gender in the Prozac Nation."

6. Shari Dworkin and Faye Wachs, *Body Panic*, 15.

7. Balsamo, *Technologies of the Gendered Body*.

8. Etcoff, *Survival of the Prettiest*.

9. See Turner, "Real Self."

10. Leve, Rubin, and Pusic, "Cosmetic Surgery"; Joanne Baker, "Ideology of Choice"; Lippman, "Choice as a Risk"; Davies et al., "Constituting the Feminist Subject"; McRobbie, "Post-feminism and Popular Culture"; and Braun, "Women Are Doing It," 24.

11. McRobbie, "Post-feminism and Popular Culture."

METHODOLOGICAL APPENDIX

1. Denzin and Lincoln, *Qualitative Inquiry Reader*; and Esterberg, *Qualitative Methods*.

2. Gimlin, *Body Work*.

3. See Tillman-Healy, "Friendship as Method."

4. Ibid.; Owton and Allen-Collinson, "Close but Not Too Close."

5. Taylor, "Intimate Insider," 13.

6. Esterberg, *Qualitative Methods.*

7. Hesse-Biber, "Practice of Feminist In-Depth Interviewing."

8. Clarke, *Situational Analysis.*

9. Charmaz, *Constructing Ground Theory.*

10. Ibid.

11. Ibid.

BIBLIOGRAPHY

ABC News. 2007. "Hospitalized after 'Botox,' Couple Warn Consumers." May 17. http://abcnews.go.com. Accessed August 6, 2015.

Adato, Allison, Ashley Williams, Debbie Seaman, and Maureen Harrington. 2007. "Yes, I Use Botox." *People* (May 21): 81–84.

Adler, Jerry, and Karen Springen. 2006. "Can You Really Botox the Blues Away?" *Newsweek* (May 29): 8.

Adler, Patricia, and Peter Adler. 1978. "Tinydopers: A Case of Deviant Socialization." *Symbolic Interaction* 1, no. 2: 90–105.

Adler, Patricia A., and Peter Adler. 2011. *The Tender Cut: Inside the Hidden World of Self-Injury.* New York: NYU Press.

Akers, Ronald. 1969. *Deviant Behavior: A Social Learning Approach.* Belmont, CA: Wadsworth.

Akers, Ronald. 1992. *Drugs, Alcohol, and Society: Social Structure, Process, and Policy.* Belmont, CA: Wadsworth.

Aldrich, Robert. 2004. "Homosexuality and the City: An Historical Overview." *Urban Studies* 41, no. 9: 1719–1737.

Allergan Pharmaceuticals. 2012. "About Botox Cosmetic." http://www.botoxcosmetic.com. Accessed November 14, 2012.

American Academy of Anti-aging Medicine. 2011. "Anti-aging Medical News: 2011 Media Kit." http://mpamedia.com. Accessed November 14, 2012.

American Academy of Dermatology. 2012. "Position Statement on Medical Spa Standards of Practice (Approved by the Board of Directors: May 7, 2011; Amended by the Board of Directors August 18, 2012)." https://www.aad.org. Accessed May 10, 2016.

American Medical Association. 2014. *Physician Characteristics and Distribution in the U.S., 2014.* Chicago: American Medical Association.

American Med Spa Association. "AmSpa's Laws and Regulations Resource Page Helps AmSpa Members Comply with the Rules That Govern Medical Spas across America." http://www.americanmedspa.org. Accessed March 24, 2014.

American Med Spa Association. "What Is a Med Spa?" http://www.americanmedspa.org. Accessed March 7, 2014.

American Society for Aesthetic Plastic Surgery. 2012. "Almost Half of Americans Approve of Cosmetic Plastic Surgery Regardless of Income." http://www.surgery.org. Accessed September 10, 2012.

American Society for Aesthetic Plastic Surgery. 2013. "Statistics, 2013." http://www.
    surgery.org. Accessed May 28, 2014.
American Society for Aesthetic Plastic Surgery. 2014. "Statistics, 2014." http://www.
    surgery.org. Accessed June 9, 2015.
American Society for Dermatologic Surgery Association. "Putting the 'Med' Back in
    Medspa." https://www.asds.net. Accessed March 24, 2014.
American Society of Plastic Surgeons. "2014 Plastic Surgery Statistics Report." www.
    plasticsurgery.org. Accessed May 11, 2016.
Ameringer, Carl F. 2000. "Organized Medicine on Trial: The Federal Trade Commission
    vs. the American Medical Association." *Journal of Policy History* 12, no. 4: 445–472.
Anderson, Leon. 2006. "Analytic Autoethnography." *Journal of Contemporary Ethnog-
    raphy* 35: 373–395.
Andrews, Molly. 1999. "The Seductiveness of Agelessness." *Ageing and Society* 19, no. 3:
    301–318.
Atkinson, Jim. 2003. "The Next Great Drug." *Esquire* 140, no. 1 (July): 50–52.
Atkinson, Michael. 2002. "Pretty in Ink: Conformity, Resistance, and Negotiation in
    Women's Tattooing." *Sex Roles* 47, nos. 5–6: 219–235.
Atkinson, Michael. 2008. "Exploring Male Femininity in the 'Crisis': Men and Cos-
    metic Surgery." *Body and Society* 14, no. 1: 67–87.
Bailly, Jenny. 2007. "Skin Innovation." *Allure* (December): 138.
Bailly, Jenny. 2007. "The Truth about Medi-Spas." *Marie Claire* 14, no. 12 (November 1):
    76–80.
Baker, Joanne. 2008. "The Ideology of Choice. Overstating Progress and Hiding Injus-
    tice in the Lives of Young Women: Findings from a Study in North Queensland,
    Australia." *Women's Studies International Forum* 31, no. 1: 53–64.
Balsamo, Anne. 1995. "Forms of Technological Embodiment: Reading the Body in
    Contemporary Culture." In *Cyberspace/Cyberbodies/Cyberpunk: Cultures of Tech-
    nological Embodiment*, edited by Mike Featherstone and Richard Burrows, 215–237.
    London: Sage.
Balsamo, Anne M. 1996. *Technologies of the Gendered Body: Reading Cyborg Women.*
    Durham, NC: Duke University Press.
Banet-Weiser, Sarah, and Laura Portwood-Stacer. 2006. "'I Just Want to Be Me Again!'
    Beauty Pageants, Reality Television and Post-feminism." *Feminist Theory* 7, no. 2
    (August): 255–272.
Barnett, Rosalind. 2005. "Ageism and Sexism in the Workplace." *Generations* 29, no. 3:
    25–30.
Barret, Jennifer. 2004. "No Time for Wrinkles." *Newsweek* 143, no. 19 (May 10): 82–85.
Bartky, Sandra L. 1990. *Femininity and Domination: Studies in the Phenomenology of
    Oppression.* New York: Routledge.
Bauer, Martin. 1998. "The Medicalization of Science News: From 'Rocket Scalpel' to the
    'Gene-Mcteorite' Complex." *Social Science Information* 37, no. 4: 731–751.

Bauman, Zygmunt. 1998. *Globalization: The Human Consequences*. New York: Columbia University Press.

Baumgardner, Jennifer, and Amy Richards. 2000. *Manifesta: Young Women, Feminism, and the Future*. New York: Farrar, Straus & Giroux.

Bayer, Kathryn. 2005. "Cosmetic Surgery and Cosmetics: Redefining the Appearance of Age." *Generations* 29, no. 3: 13–18.

Bazzini, Doris G., William D. McIntosh, Stephen M. Smith, Sabrina Cook, and Caleigh Harris. 1997. "The Aging Woman in Popular Film: Underrepresented, Unattractive, Unfriendly, and Unintelligent." *Sex Roles* 36, nos. 7–8: 531–543.

Beck, Melinda. 2013. "Medical Spas Get a Checkup." *Wall Street Journal* (June 4). http://online.wsj.com. Accessed March 17, 2014.

Becker, Cinda. 2004. "Subatomic Turf Wars." *Modern Healthcare* 34, no. 48: 6–12.

Becker, H. Saul. 1953. "Becoming a Marijuana User." *American Journal of Sociology* 59, no. 3 (1953): 235–242.

Bennett, Jessica. 2015. "I'm Not Mad, That's Just My RBF." *New York Times* (August 1). www.nytimes.com. Accessed May 11, 2016.

Berkowitz, Dana, and Linda Liska Belgrave. 2010. "'She Works Hard for the Money': Drag Queens and the Management of Their Contradictory Status of Celebrity and Marginality." *Journal of Contemporary Ethnography* 39, no. 2: 159–186.

Berkowitz, Dana, Linda Belgrave, and Robert Halberstein. 2007. "The Interaction of Drag Queens and Gay Men in Public and Private Spaces." *Journal of Homosexuality* 52, nos. 3–4: 11–32.

Blum, Linda, and Nena Stracuzzi. 2004. "Gender in the Prozac Nation: Popular Discourse and Productive Femininity." *Gender and Society* 18, no. 3: 269–286.

Blum, Virginia L. 2003. *Flesh Wounds: The Culture of Cosmetic Surgery*. Berkeley and Los Angeles: University of California Press.

Bordo, Susan. 1989. "The Body and the Reproduction of Femininity: A Feminist Appropriation of Foucault." In *Gender/Body/Knowledge*, edited by A. Jaggar and S. Bordo, 13–33. New Brunswick, NJ: Rutgers University Press.

Bordo, Susan. 1990. "Material Girl: The Effacements of Postmodern Culture." *Michigan Quarterly Review* 29: 653–677.

Bordo, Susan. 2003. *Unbearable Weight: Feminism, Western Culture and the Body*. Berkeley: University of California Press.

Bourdieu, Pierre. 1984. *Distinction: A Social Critique of the Judgment of Taste*. New York: Routledge, Kegan, & Paul.

Bourdieu, Pierre. 1986. "The Forms of Capital." In *Handbook of Theory and Research for the Sociology of Education*, edited by J. Richardson, 241–258. New York: Greenwood.

Brand, Pamela A., Esther D. Rothblum, and Laura J. Solomon. 1992. "A Comparison of Lesbians, Gay Men, and Heterosexuals on Weight and Restrained Eating." *International Journal of Eating Disorders* 11, no. 3: 253–259.

Braun, Virginia. 2009. "The Women Are Doing It for Themselves: The Rhetoric of Choice and Agency around Female Genital 'Cosmetic Surgery.'" *Australian Feminist Studies* 24, no. 60 (June): 233–249.

Brooks, Abigail. 2004. "'Under the Knife and Proud of It': An Analysis of the Normalization of Cosmetic Surgery." *Critical Sociology* 30, no. 2: 207–239.

Brooks, Abigail. 2010. "Aesthetic Anti-aging Surgery and Technology: Women's Friend or Foe?" *Sociology of Health and Illness* 32, no. 2: 238–257.

Brown, Sarah. 2008. "Beyond Botox." *Vogue* 198 (October 1): 240, 243–244.

Brubaker, Sarah. 2007. "Denied, Embracing, and Resisting Medicalization: African American Teen Mothers' Perceptions of Formal Pregnancy and Childbirth Care." *Gender and Society* 21, no. 4: 528–552.

Brumberg, Joan J. 1997. *The Body Project: An Intimate History of American Girls.* New York: Random House.

Butler, Robert N. 1969. "Ageism: Another Form of Bigotry." *Gerontologist* 9, no. 4: 243–246.

Cacchioni, Thea. 2007. "Heterosexuality and 'the Labour of Love': A Contribution to Recent Debates on Female Sexual Dysfunction." *Sexualities* 10, no. 3: 299–320.

Caine, Maureen. 1993. "Foucault, Feminism, and Feeling: What Foucault Can and Cannot Contribute to Feminist Epistemology." In *Up against Foucault: Explorations of Some Tensions between Foucault and Feminism,* edited by Caroline Ramazanoglu, 73–86. London and New York: Routledge.

Calasanti, Toni M. 2005. "Ageism, Gravity, and Gender: Experiences of Aging Bodies." *Generations* 29, no. 3: 8–12.

Calasanti, Toni M. 2007. "Bodacious Berry, Potency Wood and the Aging Monster: Gender and Age Relations in Anti-aging Ads." *Social Forces* 86, no. 1: 335–355.

Calasanti, Toni M., and Kathleen F. Slevin. 2001. *Gender, Social Inequalities, and Aging.* Walnut Creek, CA: AltaMira Press.

Carpenter, Laura, and Monica Casper. 2009. "A Tale of Two Technologies: HPV Vaccination, Male Circumcision, and Sexual Health." *Gender and Society* 23, no. 6: 790–816.

Carruthers, Jean D. A., and J. Alistair Carruthers. 1992. "Treatment of Glabellar Frown Lines with C. botulinum-A Exotoxin." *Journal of Dermatologic Surgery and Oncology* 18, no. 1: 17–21.

Cash, Thomas, Julie R. Ancis, and Melissa D. Strachan. 1997. "Gender Attitudes, Feminist Identity, and Body Images among College Women." *Sex Roles* 36, nos.7–8: 433–447.

Cashmore, Ellis. 2014. *Celebrity Culture.* New York: Routledge.

Chao, Ning. 2008. "Beginners Botox." *Marie Claire* 15, no. 10 (October): 200–202.

Chapkis, Wendy. 1986. *Beauty Secrets: Women and the Politics of Appearance.* Boston: South End Press.

Charles, Alfred, and Jovita Moore. 2005. "Botched Botox Victims Speak Out." *WSB-TV Atlanta.* February 4. http://www.wsbtv.com. Accessed March 17, 2014.

Charmaz, Kathy. 2006. *Constructing Ground Theory: A Practical Guide through Qualitative Research*. London: Sage.

Chin Evans, Peggy, and Allen R. McConnell. 2003. "Do Racial Minorities Respond in the Same Way to Mainstream Beauty Standards? Social Comparison Processes in Asian, Black and White Women." *Self and Identity* 2, no. 2: 153–167.

Clarke, Adele. 2005. *Situational Analysis: Grounded Theory after the Postmodern Turn*. Thousand Oaks, CA: Sage.

Clarke, Adele, and Virginia L. Olesen. 1999. *Revisioning Women, Health, and Healing: Feminist, Cultural, and Technoscience Perspectives*. New York: Routledge.

Clarke, Adele, Janet K. Shim, Laura Mamo, Jennifer Ruth Fosket, and Jennifer R. Fishman. 2003. "Biomedicalization: Techoscientific Transformations of Health, Illness, and U.S. Biomedicine." *American Sociological Review* 68, no. 2: 161–194.

Cogan, Jeanine C. 1999. "Lesbians Walk the Tightrope of Beauty: Thin Is in but Femme Is Out." *Journal of Lesbian Studies* 3, no. 4: 77–90.

Cohen, Jay S. 2001. *Overdose. The Case against the Drug Companies: Prescription Drugs, Side Effects, and Your Health*. New York: Jeremy P. Tarcher/Putnam.

Connell, R. W., and James W. Messerschmidt. 2005. "Hegemonic Masculinity: Rethinking the Concept." *Gender and Society* 19, no. 6: 829–859.

Conrad, Peter. 1992. "Medicalization and Social Control." *Annual Review of Sociology* 18: 209–232.

Conrad, Peter, and Deborah Potter. 2000. "From Hyperactive Children to ADHD Adults: Observations on the Expansion of Medical Categories." *Social Problems* 47, no. 4: 559–582.

Conrad, Peter, and Joseph W. Schneider. 1992. *Deviance and Medicalization from Badness to Sickness*. Philadelphia: Temple University Press.

Cook, Peta, and Angela E. Dwyer. 2009. "'Small Pricks' at Lunchtime: Some Notes on Botox." In *TASA Refereed Conference Proceedings, 2009*, edited by Stewart Lockie. Canberra: Australian National University.

Cooke, Grayson. 2008. "Effacing the Face: Botox and the Anarchivic Archive." *Body and Society* 14, no. 2: 23–38.

Corliss, Richard. 2002. "Smile—You're on Botox!" *Time* 159, no. 7 (February 18): 59.

Coye, M. Joel. 2008. "Turf Wars: New Technologies Are Bound to Heighten Tensions among Your Physicians." *Hospitals and Health Networks* 82, no. 9 (September): 26.

Craig, Maxine L. 2013. "Beauty: A Funny Sort of Capital." Paper presented at the annual meeting of the American Sociological Association, New York, August 10–13.

Crapanzano, Aleksandra. 2012. "Frozen in Time." *Marie Claire* 19, no. 12 (December): 150–156.

Crawley, Sara L., Lara J. Foley, and Constance L. Shehan. 2007. *Gendering Bodies*. Lanham, MD: Rowman & Littlefield.

Curcurito, David. 2011. "The Third Most Insane Way I've Tried to Hold on to My Youth." *Esquire* 155, no. 7 (August): 62–63.

Danahay, Martin A. 1994. "Mirrors of Masculine Desire: Narcissus and Pygmalion in Victorian Representation." *Victorian Poetry* 32, no. 1: 35–54.

Darwin, Charles. 1872. *The Expression of Emotions in Man and Animals.* London: John Murray.

Davies, Bronwyn, Jenny Browne, Susanne Gannon, Lekkie Hopkins, Helen McCann, and Monne Wihlborg. 2006. "Constituting the Feminist Subject in Poststructuralist Discourse." *Feminism and Psychology* 16, no. 1: 87–103.

Davis, Caris. 2008. "Simon Cowell Admits to Using Botox." *People* (March 3). http://www.people.com. Accessed June 9, 2016.

Davis, Kathy. 1995. *Reshaping the Female Body: The Dilemma of Cosmetic Surgery.* New York: Routledge.

Davis, Kathy. 2003. *Dubious Equalities and Embodied Differences: Cultural Studies on Cosmetic Surgery.* Lanham, MD: Rowman & Littlefield.

Davison, Rebecca. 2014. "What HAS Renee Zellweger Done to Her Face?" *Daily Mail. com.* October 21. http://www.dailymail.co.uk. Accessed February 2, 2016.

DeMello, Margo. 1995. "'Not Just for Bikers Anymore': Popular Representations of American Tattooing." *Journal of Popular Culture* 29, no. 3: 37–52.

Demetriou, Demetrakis Z. 2001. "Connell's Concept of Hegemonic Masculinity: A Critique." *Theory and Society* 30, no. 3: 337–361.

Denzin, Norman K., and Yvonna S. Lincoln. 2002. *The Qualitative Inquiry Reader.* Thousand Oaks, CA: Sage.

Devriese, Pieter. 1999. "On the Discovery of *Clostridium botulinum.*" *Journal of the History of Neuroscience* 8, no. 1: 43–50.

Dickson, Lynda, Richard Dukes, Hilary Smith, and Noel Strapko. 2014. "Stigma of Ink: Tattoo Attitudes among College Students." *Social Science Journal* 51, no. 2 (June): 268–276.

Dimberg, Ulf. 1982. "Facial Reactions to Facial Expressions." *Psychophysiology* 19: 643–647.

Dull, Diana, and Candace West. 1991. "Accounting for Cosmetic Surgery: The Accomplishment of Gender." *Social Problems* 38, no. 1 (February): 54–70.

Dumas, Alex, Suzanne Laberge, and Silvia M. Straka. 2005. "Older Women's Relations to Bodily Appearance: The Embodiment of Social and Biological Conditions of Existence." *Ageing and Society* 25, no. 6: 883–902.

Dumit, Joseph. 2012. *Drugs for Life: How Pharmaceutical Companies Define Our Health.* Durham, NC: Duke University Press.

Duncan, Colin, and Wendy Loretto. 2004. "Never the Right Age? Gender and Age-Based Discrimination in Employment." *Gender, Work and Organization* 11, no. 1: 95–115.

Dunlop, Courtney. 2011. "What Would Your Derm Do?" *Marie Claire* 18, no. 2 (February): 174–176.

Dworkin, Sari H. 1989. "Not in Man's Image: Lesbians and the Cultural Oppression of Body Image." *Women and Therapy* 8, nos. 1–2: 27–39.

Dworkin, Shari L., and Faye L. Wachs. 2009. *Body Panic: Gender, Health, and the Selling of Fitness*. New York: New York University Press.

Ehrenreich, Barbara, and Deirdre English. 1974. *Witches, Midwives and Nurses: A History of Women Healers*. London: Compendium.

Ehrenreich, Barbara, and Deirdre English. 2005. *For Her Own Good: Two Centuries of the Experts' Advice to Women*. New York: Anchor Books.

Elliott, Anthony. 2008. *Making the Cut: How Cosmetic Surgery Is Transforming Our Lives*. London: Reaktion.

Elliott, Carl. 2010. *White Coat, Black Hat: Adventures on the Dark Side of Medicine*. Boston: Beacon.

Ellis, Carolyn, and Michael G. Flaherty. 1992. *Investigating Subjectivity: Research on Lived Experience*. Newbury Park, CA: Sage.

Erbguth, Frank J. 2004. "Historical Notes on Botulism, *Clostridium botulinum*, Botulinum Toxin, and the Idea of the Therapeutic Use of the Toxin." *Movement Disorders* 19, no. S8: S2–S6.

Esterberg, Kristin. 2002. *Qualitative Methods in Social Research*. Boston: McGraw-Hill.

Etcoff, Nancy. 1999. *Survival of the Prettiest: The Science of Beauty*. New York: Anchor Books.

Evans, Rory. 2009. "Skin Truths." *Allure* 19, no. 9 (September): 129–138.

Fahs, Breanne. 2011. "Dreaded 'Otherness': Heteronormative Patrolling in Women's Body Hair Rebellions." *Gender and Society* 25, no. 4: 451–472.

Faupel, Charles E. 1991. *Shooting Dope: Career Patterns of Hard-Core Heroin Users*. Gainesville: University of Florida Press.

Featherstone, Mike, Mike Hepworth, and Bryan S. Turner. 1991. *The Body: Social Process and Cultural Theory*. Newbury Park, CA: Sage.

Figueroa, Ana. 2002. "Smile. Relax. Smile. Relax." *Newsweek* 139, no. 19 (May 13): 58.

Fikkan, Janna L, and Esther D. Rothblum. 2011. "Is Fat a Feminist Issue? Exploring the Gendered Nature of Weight Bias." *Sex Roles* 66, nos. 9–10: 575–592.

Finzi, Eric. 2013. "Antidepressant Effects of Botulinum Toxin A: Scientific Rationale." *Journal of Psychiatry and Neuroscience* 38, no. 5 (September): E29.

Finzi, Eric. 2013. *The Face of Emotion: How Botox Affects Our Moods and Relationships*. New York: Palgrave-Macmillan.

Finzi, Eric, and Norman E. Rosenthal. 2014. "Treatment of Depression with OnabotulinumtoxinA: A Randomized, Double-Blind, Placebo Controlled Trial." *Journal of Psychiatric Research* 52 (May): 1–6.

Finzi, Eric, and Erika Wasserman. 2006. "Treatment of Depression with Botulinum Toxin A: A Case Series." *Dermatologic Surgery* 32, no. 5 (May 2006): 645–649, discussion on 649–650.

Flaherty, Erin. 2011. "Forever Young?" *Marie Claire* 18, no. 9 (September): 302–306.

Forbes, Gordon, and David A. Frederick. 2008. "The UCLA Body Project II: Breast and Body Dissatisfaction among African, Asian European, and Hispanic American College Women." *Sex Roles* 58, nos. 7–8: 449–457.

Foucault, Michel. 1979. *Discipline and Punish: The Birth of the Prison*. New York: Vintage.

Foucault, Michel. 1980. *Power/Knowledge: Selected Interviews and Other Writings, 1972–1977*, edited by Colin Gordon. Brighton: Harvester Press.

Foucault, Michel. 1988. "Technologies of the Self." In *Technologies of the Self*, edited by Luther H. Martin, Patrick H. Hutton, and Huck Gutman, 16–49. Amherst: University of Massachusetts Press.

Franklin, Sarah, and Helena Ragoné. 1998. *Reproducing Reproduction: Kinship, Power, and Technological Innovation*. Philadelphia: University of Pennsylvania Press.

Fraser, Suzanne. 2003. "The Agent Within: Agency Repertoires in Medical Discourse on Cosmetic Surgery." *Australian Feminist Studies* 18, no. 40: 27–44.

Fraser, Suzanne. 2003. *Cosmetic Surgery, Gender and Culture*. New York: Palgrave Macmillan.

Fraser, Suzanne. 2009. "Agency Made Over? Cosmetic Surgery and Femininity in Women's Magazines and Makeover Television." In *Cosmetic Surgery: A Feminist Primer*, edited by Cressida J. Heyes and Meredith Jones, 99–116. Burlington, VT: Ashgate.

Future Aesthetic Service Training. n.d. "About FAST." http://www.futureaestheticservicetraining.com. Accessed May 18, 2014.

Gagne, Patricia, and Deanna McGaughey. 2002. "Designing Women: Cultural Hegemony and the Exercise of Power among Women Who Have Undergone Elective Mammoplasty." *Gender and Society* 16, no. 6: 814–838.

Gaines, Jane, and Charlotte Herzog. 1990. *Fabrications: Costume and the Female Body*. New York: Routledge.

Galvin, Rose. 2002. "Disturbing Notions of Chronic Illness and Individual Responsibility: Towards a Genealogy of Morals." *Health* 6, no. 2: 107–137.

Ganahl, Dennis J., Thomas J. Prinsen, and Sara Baker Netzley. 2003. "A Content Analysis of Prime Time Commercials: A Contextual Framework of Gender Representation." *Sex Roles* 49, nos. 9–10: 545–551.

Gardner, Ann Marie. 2002. "Beyond Botox." *Harper's Bazaar* 3485 (April): 78–79.

Gearon, Christopher J., and Helen Fields. 2005. "Medicine's Turf Wars." *U.S. News and World Report* 138, no. 4: 57–60.

Gellene, Denise. 2004. "'Mr. Botox' Case Raises Some Brows." *Los Angeles Times* (August 22): pt. C, 1.

Giddens, Anthony. 1991. *Modernity and Self-Identity: Self and Society in the Late Modern Age*. Stanford, CA: Stanford University Press.

Gill, Rosalind. 2007. *Gender and the Media*. Cambridge: Polity Press.

Gill, Rosalind. 2007. "Postfeminist Media Culture: Elements of a Sensibility." *European Journal of Cultural Studies* 10, no. 2: 147–166.

Gill, Rosalind. 2008. "Empowerment/Sexism: Figuring Female Sexual Agency in Contemporary Advertising." *Feminism and Psychology* 18, no. 1: 35–60.

Gilman, Sander L. 2000. *Making the Body Beautiful: A Cultural History of Aesthetic Surgery*. Princeton, NJ: Princeton University Press.

Gimlin, Debra L. 2001. "Accounting for Cosmetic Surgery in the USA and Great Britain: A Cross-Cultural Analysis of Women's Narratives." *Body and Society* 13, no. 1: 46–60.

Gimlin, Debra L. 2002. *Body Work: Beauty and Self-Image in American Culture.* Berkeley: University of California Press.

Gimlin, Debra L. 2013. "'Too Good to Be Real': The Obviously Augmented Breast in Women's Narratives of Cosmetic Surgery." *Gender and Society* 27, no. 6: 913–934.

Ginn, Jay, and Sara Arber. 1995. "Only Connect: Gender Relations and Ageing." In *Connecting Gender and Ageing: A Sociological Approach*, edited by Sara Arber and Jay Ginn, 1–14. Buckingham: Open University Press.

Ginn, Jay, and Sara Arber. 1996. "Gender, Age and Attitudes to Retirement in Mid-Life." *Ageing and Society* 16, no. 1: 27–55.

Ginsburg, Faye, and Rayna Rapp. 1991. "The Politics of Reproduction." *Annual Review of Anthropology* 20: 311–343.

Giulianotti, Richard. 2005. *Sport: A Critical Sociology.* Cambridge: Polity.

Goffman, Erving. 1963. *Stigma: Notes on the Management of Spoiled Identity.* Englewood Cliffs, NJ: Prentice-Hall.

Goffman, Erving. 1966. *Behavior in Public Places: Notes on the Social Organization of Gatherings.* New York: Free Press.

Goffman, Erving. 1967. *Interaction Ritual: Essays on Face-to-Face Behavior.* New York and Toronto: Random House.

Goldstein, Laurence, ed. 1994. *The Male Body: Features, Destinies, Exposures.* Ann Arbor: University of Michigan Press.

Gonzalez, Jennifer. 2000. "Envisioning Cyborg Bodies: Notes from Current Research." In *The Gendered Cyborg: A Reader*, edited by G. Kirkup, L. Janes, K. Woodward, and F. Hovenden, 58–73. London: Routledge.

Goode, Erich. 1970. *The Marijuana Smokers.* New York: Basic Books.

Goode, Erich. 1973. *The Drug Phenomenon: Social Aspects of Drug Taking.* Indianapolis: Bobbs-Merrill.

Gordon, Don. 2002. "It's a Botox Blast." *Men's Fitness* 18, no. 9 (September): 78.

Gorney, Mark. 1989. "Who Is Responsible?" *Plastic and Reconstructive Surgery* 84, no. 5: 800–801.

Gray, Bradford H. 1986. *For-Profit Enterprise in Health Care.* Washington, DC: National Academy Press.

Green, Michelle, Fannie Weinstein, Fail Shepherd, Lori Rozsa, Siobhan Morrissey, and Jeff Truesdell. 2004. "Black-Market Botox?" *People* 62, no. 25 (December 20): 99–100.

Grosz, Elizabeth. 1994. *Volatile Bodies: Toward a Corporeal Feminism.* Bloomington: Indiana University Press.

Gullette, Margaret M. 1994. "All Together Now: The New Sexual Politics of Midlife Bodies." In *The Male Body: Features, Destinies, Exposures*, edited by Laurence Goldstein, 221–247. Ann Arbor: University of Michigan Press.

Gullette, Margaret M. 2004. *Aged by Culture*. Chicago: University of Chicago Press.

Haiken, Elizabeth. 1997. *Venus Envy: A History of Cosmetic Surgery*. Baltimore: Johns Hopkins University Press.

Hamermesh, Daniel, and Jeff E. Biddle. 1994. "Beauty and the Labor Market." *American Economic Review* 84, no. 5 (December): 1174–1194.

Hamilton, Kendall, and Julie Weingarden. 1998. "Lifts, Lasers, and Liposuction: The Cosmetic Surgery Boom." *Newsweek* 131, no. 24 (June 15): 14.

Handley, Richard T. 2009. "The Medi-Spa: A Current Cosmetic Dermatology Public Safety Concern." *Internet Journal of Academic Physician Assistants* 7, no. 1. *Internet Scientific Publications*. https://ispub.com. Accessed April 22, 2016.

Haraway, Donna. 1990. *Simians, Cyborgs, and Women: The Reinvention of Women*. New York: Routledge.

Harding, Jennifer. 1997. "Bodies at Risk: Sex, Surveillance and Hormone Replacement Therapy." In *Foucault, Health and Medicine*, edited by Alan Peterson and Robin Bunton. New York: Routledge.

Hartgraves, Tiffany. 2002. "DTC Prescription Drug Advertising: The History and Impact of FDA Regulation." Paper. Cambridge, MA: Harvard Law School. *Digital Access to Scholarship at Harvard*. https://dash.harvard.edu. Accessed April 22, 2016.

Harvey, David. 2005. *A Brief History of Neoliberalism*. New York: Oxford University Press.

Hatfield, Elaine, John T. Cacioppo, Richard L. Rapson. 1994. *Emotional Contagion*. Cambridge: Cambridge University Press.

Hennenlotter, Andreas, Christian Dresel, Florian Castrop, Andres O. Ceballos-Baumann, Afra M. Wohlschlager, and Bernhard Haslinger. 2008. "The Link between Facial Feedback and Neural Activity within Central Circuitries of Emotion—New Insights from Botulinum Toxin–Induced Denervation of Frown Muscles." *Cerebral Cortex* 19, no. 3 (June 17): 537–542.

Hesse-Biber, Sharlene N. 2007. "The Practice of Feminist In-Depth Interviewing." In *Feminist Research Practice: A Primer*, edited by Sharlene Nagy Hesse-Biber and Patricia Leavy. Thousand Oaks, CA: Sage.

Hesse-Biber, Sharlene N., Stephanie A. Howling, Patricia Leavy, and Meg Lovejoy. 2004. "Racial Identity and the Development of Body Image Issues among African American Adolescent Girls." *Qualitative Report* 9, no. 1: 49–79.

Heyes, Cressida. 2007. "Cosmetic Surgery and the Televisual Makeover: A Foucauldian Feminist Reading." *Feminist Media Studies* 7, no. 1: 17–32.

Heyes, Cressida. 2007. "Normalisation and the Psychic Life of Cosmetic Surgery." *Australian Feminist Studies* 22, no. 52: 55–71.

Heyes, Cressida J., and Meredith Jones. 2009. *Cosmetic Surgery: A Feminist Primer*. Burlington, VT: Ashgate Publishing.

Hilton, Lisette. 2007. "The Consumer-Patient." *Cosmetic Surgery Times* 10, no. 1: 15–16.

Hilts, Philip J. 2003. *Protecting America's Health: The FDA, Business, and One Hundred Years of Regulation*. New York: Alfred A. Knopf.

Hochschild, Arlie. 1983. *The Managed Heart: Commercialization of Human Feeling.* Berkeley: University of California Press.

Holliday, Ruth, and Allie Cairnie. 2007. "Man Made Plastic: Investigating Men's Consumption of Aesthetic Surgery." *Journal of Consumer Culture* 7: 7–78.

Holstein, Martha B. 2006. "On Being an Aging Woman." In *Age Matters: Realigning Feminist Thinking*, edited by Toni M. Calasanti and Kathleen F. Slevin, 313–334. New York: Routledge.

Hosoda, M., Eugene F. Stone-Romero, and Gwen Coats. 2003. "The Effects of Physical Attractiveness on Job-Related Outcomes: A Meta-analysis of Experimental Studies." *Personnel Psychology* 56, no. 2: 431–462.

Hurd Clarke, Laura. 2005. "Remarriage in Later Life: Older Women's Negotiation of Power, Resources and Domestic Labor." *Journal of Women and Aging* 17, no. 4: 21–41.

Hurd Clarke, Laura. 2010. *Facing Age: Women Growing Older in Anti-aging Culture.* Lanham, MD: Rowman & Littlefield.

Hurd Clarke, Laura, and Meridith Griffin. 2007. "The Body Natural and the Body Unnatural: Beauty Work and Aging." *Journal of Aging Studies* 21, no. 3: 187–201.

Hurd Clarke, Laura, and Meridith Griffin. 2008. "Visible and Invisible Ageing: Beauty Work as a Response to Ageism." *Ageing and Society* 28: 653–674.

Itzin, Catherine, and Chris Phillipson. 1993. *Age Barriers at Work: Maximizing the Potential of Mature and Older People.* London: Metropolitan Authorities Recruitment Agency.

Jaggar, Alison, and Susan Bordo. 1989. *Gender/Body/Knowledge: Feminist Reconstructions of Being and Knowing.* New Brunswick, NJ: Rutgers University Press.

Jagger, Carol. 2000. "Compression or Expansion of Morbidity: What Does the Future Hold?" *Age and Ageing* 29, no. 2: 93–94.

James, William. 1890. *The Principles of Psychology.* New York: Holt.

Janes, Beth. 2012. "Don't Worry, Be Pretty." *Self* 34, no. 1 (January 1): 90.

Jeffreys, Sheila. 2005. *Beauty and Misogyny: Harmful Cultural Practices in the West.* London and New York: Routledge.

Jeffries, Alexis. 2010. "Is Plastic Surgery the New Black for Black Women?" *Essence* (October 26). http://www.essence.com. Accessed December 18, 2015.

Jones, James W., Laurence B. McCullough, and Bruce W. Richman. 2005. "Turf Wars: The Ethics of Professional Territorialism." *Journal of Vascular Surgery* 42, no. 3: 587–589.

Jones, Julie, and Steve Pugh. 2005. "Aging Gay Men: Lessons from the Sociology of Embodiment." *Men and Masculinities* 7, no. 3 (January): 248–260.

Jones, Meredith. 2008. *Skintight: An Anatomy of Cosmetic Surgery.* New York: Berg.

Kalb, Claudia. 1999. "Our Quest to Be Perfect." *Newsweek* 134, no. 6: 52–59.

Kalfus, Marilyn, and Colin Stewart. 2012. "Does Botox Look Its Age? It's 10 Years Old." *Orange County Register* (April 10). http://www.ocregister.com. Accessed February 2, 2016.

Kaminski, Patricia L., Benjamin P. Chapman, Sandra D. Haynes, and Lawrence Own. 2005. "Body Image, Eating Behaviors, and Attitudes toward Exercise among Gay and Straight Men." *Eating Behaviors* 6, no. 3 (June): 179–187.

Kandel, Denise B. 2002. *Stages and Pathways of Drug Involvement: Examining the Gateway Hypothesis.* Cambridge: Cambridge University Press.

Kantrowitz, Barbara. 2006. "Brush with Perfection." *Newsweek* 148, no. 18: 54–55.

Kaplan, Eric Scott. 2007. *Dying to Be Young: From Botox to Botulism—a True Story of Survival.* Mequon, WI: Nightengale Press.

Katz, Molly E., and Brian S. Biesman. 2013. "Becoming an Injector: How One Practice Did It Successfully: Physician Approach, Nurse Perspective." *Journal of the Dermatological Nurses' Association* 5, no. 5: 257–260.

Katz, Stephen, and Barbara Marshall. 2004. "Is the Functional 'Normal'? Aging, Sexuality, and the Bio-marketing of Successful Living." *History of the Human Sciences* 17 (February): 53–75.

Kaufert, Patricia. 1982. "Myth and the Menopause." *Sociology of Health and Illness* 4, no. 2: 141–166.

Kaye, Cheryl Kramer. 2010. "Oh, Just Fake It! Secret Beauty Maneuvers Even Naturally Gorgeous Girls (Like Yourself!) Will Love." *Redbook* 215, no. 5 (November): 187–190.

Kazanjian, Dodie. 2006. "The Wrinkles We Keep." *Vogue* 196, no. 8 (August): 196.

Kimmel, Michael. 2011. *Manhood in America: A Cultural History.* New York: Oxford University Press.

Kleck, R. E., R. C. Vaughan, J. Cartwright-Smith, K. B. Vaughan, C. Z. Colby, and J. T. Lanzetta. 1976. "Effects of Being Observed on Expressive, Subjective, and Physiological Responses to Painful Stimuli." *Journal of Personality and Social Psychology* 34: 1211–1218.

Kron, Joan. 2005. "Nip/Talk." *Allure* (July). Posted at *Joan Kron Writes About . . .* http://www.facelift.com. Accessed June 19, 2016.

Kuczynski, Alex. 2006. *Beauty Junkies: Inside Our $15 Billion Obsession with Cosmetic Surgery.* New York: Doubleday.

Laws, Glenda. 1995. "Understanding Ageism: Lessons from Feminism and Postmodernism." *Gerontologist* 35, no. 1 (February): 112–118.

Leavitt, Judith W. 1983. "'Science' Enters the Birthing Room: Obstetrics in America since the Eighteenth Century." *Journal of American History* 70, no. 2 : 281–304.

Leve, Michelle, Lisa Rubin, and Andrea Pusic. 2012. "Cosmetic Surgery and Neoliberalisms: Managing Risk and Responsibility." *Feminism and Psychology* 22, no. 1: 122–141.

Levin, David C., and Vijay M. Rao. 2004. "Turf Wars in Radiology: The Overutilization of Imaging Resulting from Self-Referral." *Journal of the American College of Radiology* 1, no. 3: 169–172.

Levin, Roger P. 2006. "Increase Profits through Cosmetics." *Dental Economics* 96, no. 1: 20–25. http://www.dentaleconomics.com. Accessed April 22, 2016.

Lindesmith, Alfred. 1938. "A Sociological Theory of Drug Addiction." *American Journal of Sociology* 43, no. 4: 593–613.

Lipham, William J. 2004. *Cosmetic and Clinical Applications of Botulinum Toxin.* Thorofare, NJ: Slack Incorporated.

Lippman, Abby. 1999. "Choice as a Risk to Women's Health." *Health, Risk and Society* 1, no. 3: 281–291.

Lock, Margaret. 1993. "Cultivating the Body Anthropology and Epistemologies of Bodily Practice and Knowledge." *Annual Review of Anthropology* 22: 133–155.

Lock, Margaret, and Patricia Kaufert. 2004. *Pragmatic Women and Body Politics.* Cambridge: Cambridge University Press.

Loe, Meika. 2004. *The Rise of Viagra: How the Little Blue Pill Changed Sex in America.* New York: NYU Press.

Lupton, Deborah, and John Tulloch. 2002. "'Life Would Be Pretty Dull without Risk': Voluntary Risk-Taking and Its Pleasures." *Health, Risk and Society* 4, no. 2: 113–124.

Martin, Emily. 1987. *The Woman in the Body: A Cultural Analysis of Reproduction.* Boston: Beacon Press.

Masters, Maria. 2012. "The Most Vain Cities in America." *Men's Health* (June 13 2012). http://www.menshealth.com. Accessed June 13, 2012.

McKinney, Maureen. 2010. "Medical Spas Face New Scrutiny: New Regulations Sought for Some Common Cosmetic Procedures." *Modern Healthcare* 40, no. 51: 26–27.

McLaren, Lindsay, and Diana Kuh. 2004. "Women's Body Dissatisfaction, Social Class, and Social Mobility." *Social Science and Medicine* 58, no. 9: 1575–1584.

McRobbie, Angela. 2004. "Post-feminism and Popular Culture." *Feminist Media Studies* 4, no. 3: 255–264.

McRobbie, Angela. 2008. *The Aftermath of Feminism: Gender, Culture and Social Change.* London: Sage.

Mears, Ashley. 2011. *Pricing Beauty: The Making of a Fashion Model.* Berkeley: University of California Press.

Molloy, Beth L., and Sharon D. Herzberger. 1998. "Body Image and Self-Esteem: A Comparison of African-American and Caucasian Women." *Sex Roles* 38, nos. 7–8: 631–643.

National Center for Emerging and Zoonotic Infectious Diseases. 2014. "Botulism." April 25. http://www.cdc.gov. Accessed June 10, 2014.

Newman, Judith. 2007. "Breakfast and Botox?" *Marie Claire* 14, no. 10 (October 1): 22b–23b.

Newman, Judith. 2009. "The Career Lift." *Marie Claire* (March 1): 196–197.

Noonan, David, and Jerry Adler. 2002. "The Botox Boom." *Newsweek* 139, no. 19 (May 13): 50–53.

Nordqvist, Christian. 2012. "Fake Botox Warning by FDA to 350 Medical Practices." *Medical News Today* (December 27). http://www.medicalnewstoday.com. Accessed February 2, 2016.

O'Rourke, Theresa. 2012. "A Shot at Youth: The Truth about Injectables." *Redbook* 219, no. 4 (October): 162–165.

Owton, Helen, and Jacqueline Allen-Collinson. 2014. "Close but Not Too Close: Friendship as Method(ology) in Ethnographic Research Encounters." *Journal of Contemporary Ethnography* 43, no. 3: 283–305.

Park, Jane Shin. 2006. "Hot Shots." *Vogue* 196, no. 7 (July): 90.

Parker, Rhian. 2010. *Women, Doctors, and Cosmetic Surgery: Negotiating the Normal Body*. Basingstoke: Palgrave Macmillan.

Patton, Michael Q. 2002. *Qualitative Research and Evaluation Methods*. Thousand Oaks, CA: Sage.

Peplau, Letitia Anne, David A. Frederick, Curtis Yee, Natalya Maisel, Janet Lever, and Negin Ghavami. 2009. "Body Image Satisfaction in Heterosexual, Gay, and Lesbian Adults." *Archives of Sexual Behavior* 38, no. 5 (October): 713–725.

Peraino, Kevin. 2002. "Beware the Back-Alley 'Botox' Scam." *Newsweek* 140, no. 6 (August 5): 47.

Peterson, Alan. 1997. "Risk, Governance, and the New Public Health." In *Foucault, Health, and Medicine*, edited by Alan Peterson and Robin Bunton, 189–200. New York: Routledge.

PhRMA [Pharmaceutical Research and Manufacturers of America]. n.d. "Code on Interactions with Health Care Professionals." http://www.phrma.org. Accessed December 18, 2015.

Piccalo, Gina. 2003. "Taking Aim at Botox." *Los Angeles Times* (September 22): pt. F, 1.

Pierce, Todd. 1999. "Gen-X Junkie: Ethnographic Research with Young White Heroin Users in Washington, DC." *Substance Use and Misuse* 34, no. 14: 2095–2114.

Pitts, Victoria. 1999. "Body Modifications, Self-Mutilation and Agency in Media Accounts of a Subculture." *Body and Society* 5, nos. 2–3: 291–303.

Pitts-Taylor, Victoria. 2007. *Surgery Junkies: Wellness and Pathology in Cosmetic Culture*. New Brunswick, NJ: Rutgers University Press.

Pitts-Taylor, Victoria. 2009. "Becoming/Being a Cosmetic Surgery Patient: Semantic Instability and the Intersubjective Self." *Studies in Gender and Sexuality* 10, no. 3 (July–September): 119–128.

PR Newswire. 2013. "Orthopedics This Week Story Highlights Quickening Turf War of Minimally Invasive Spine Procedures." April 30. http://www.prnewswire.com. Accessed February 1, 2016.

ProPublica. n.d. "Dollars for Docs: Allergan Inc." https://www.propublica.org. Accessed December 18, 2015.

Raisborough, Jayne. 2007. "Contexts of Choice: The Risky Business of Elective Cosmetic Surgery." In *Risk, Identities, and the Everyday*, edited by J. Jones and J. Raisborough, 19–35. Aldershot: Ashgate.

Rapp, Rayna. 1999. *Testing Women, Testing the Fetus: The Social Impact of Amniocentesis in America*. New York: Routledge.

Rawlings, A.V. 2006. "Ethnic Skin Types: Are There Differences in Skin Structure and Function?" *International Journal of Cosmetic Science* 28: 79–93.

RealSelf. 2010. "How Does a Practitioner Correct That Awful 'Spock' Look after Botox?" https//www.realself.com. Accessed February 8, 2014.

Reed, Julia. 2008. "Without a Trace." *Vogue* (August 1): 224–225.

Relman, Arnold S. 1980. "The Medical-Industrial Complex." *New England Journal of Medicine* 303, no. 17 (October 23): 963–970.

Rhode, Deborah L. 2010. *The Beauty Bias: The Injustice of Appearance in Life and Law.* New York: Oxford University Press.

Riessman, Catherine. 1983. "Women and Medicalization: A New Perspective." *Social Policy* 14, no. 1: 3–18.

Robinson, Elisabeth. 2005. "Youth Crusade." *Vogue* (August 1): 246–247.

Rochelle, Anne R., and Peter Kaufman. 2004. "Fitting In and Fighting Back: Stigma Management Strategies among Homeless Kids." *Symbolic Interaction* 27, no. 1: 23–46.

Ronai, Carol Rambo. 1992. "The Reflexive Self through Narrative: A Night in the Life of an Exotic Dancer/Researcher." In *Investigating Subjectivity: Research on Lived Experience*, edited by Carolyn Ellis and Michael Flaherty. Newbury Park, CA: Sage.

Rose, Nikolas. 1996. *Inventing Our Selves: Psychology, Power, and Personhood.* Cambridge: Cambridge University Press.

Rothman, Barbara. 2000. *Recreating Motherhood.* New Brunswick, NJ: Rutgers University Press.

Rowe, John W., and Robert L. Kahn. 1998. *Successful Aging.* New York: Random House.

Ruiz, Rebecca. 2007. "In Pictures: America's Vainest Cities." *Forbes* (November 29). http://www.forbes.com. Accessed November 29, 2007.

Rust, Marina. 2009. "Cost and Effect." *Vogue* 202 (February 1): 122–128.

Salzman, Marian, Ira Matathia, and Ann O'Reilly. 2005. *The Future of Men.* New York: Palgrave Macmillan.

Schlimme, Jann E. 2010. "Addiction and Self-Determination: A Phenomenological Approach." *Theoretical Medical Bioethics* 31, no. 1: 49–62.

Schmid, Wendy. 2006. "Are You Risking Your Health for Beauty?" *Harper's Bazaar* (September 1): 339.

Schneider, Karen S. 2004. "Facing Off over Plastic Surgery." *People* 62, no. 16 (October 18): 60–66. http://www.people.com. Accessed April 23, 2016.

Schuler, Charli. 2015. "U.S. Cities with the Most Plastic Surgery." *Totalbeauty.com.* http://www.totalbeauty.com. Accessed January 17, 2015.

Scirrotto, Julia. 2007. "Botox Makes You Look Older? One Doctor Swears It Does." *Marie Claire* (August 23). http://www.marieclaire.com. Accessed June 19, 2016.

Scott, Marvin B., and Stanford M. Lyman. 1968. "Accounts." *American Sociological Review* 33, no. 1: 46–62.

Shilling, Chris. 1991. "Educating the Body: Physical Capital and the Production of Social Inequalities." *Sociology* 25, no. 4: 653–672.

Shilling, Chris. 1993. *The Body and Social Theory.* Thousand Oaks, CA: Sage.

Shugart, Helene. 2008. "Managing Masculinities: The Metrosexual Moment." *Communication and Critical/Cultural Studies* 5, no. 3: 280–300.

Silverman, Debora. 1986. *Selling Culture: Bloomingdale's, Diana Vreeland, and the New Aristocracy of Taste in Reagan's America*. New York: Pantheon Books.

Singer, Natasha. 2007. "And Thanks to My Agent, My Skin Doctor." *New York Times* (February 18). http://www.nytimes.com. Accessed February 18, 2007.

Singer, Natasha. 2009. "So Botox Isn't Just Skin Deep." *New York Times* (April 12). http://www.nytimes.com. Accessed February 1, 2016.

Skin Inc. 2014. "AmSpa Launches First Ever State-by-State Summary of Med Spa Laws." http://www.skininc.com. Accessed March 24, 2014.

Slevin, Kathleen F. 2006. "The Embodied Experiences of Old Lesbians." In *Age Matters: Realigning Feminist Thinking*, edited by Toni M. Calasanti and Kathleen F. Slevin. New York: Routledge.

Slevin, Kathleen, and Thomas Linneman. 2010. "Old Gay Men's Bodies and Masculinities." *Men and Masculinities* 12, no. 4: 483–507.

Smith, Alisa. 2002. "The Botox Diaries." *Vancouver* (June). http://www.vanmag.com. Accessed May 2005.

Sontag, Susan. 1972. "The Double Standard of Aging." *Saturday Review* (September 23): 29–38.

Stein, Joel. 2009. "Boytox: Botox for Men." *Time* 173, no. 3 (January 26): 53–54.

Stein, Joel. 2015. "Nip. Tuck. Or Else." *Time* (June 29): 41–48.

Stuart, Avelie, and Ngaire Donaghue. 2012. "Choosing to Conform: The Discursive Complexities of Choices in Relation to Feminine Beauty Practices." *Feminism and Psychology* 22, no. 1: 98–121.

Sullivan, Deborah A. 2001. *Cosmetic Surgery: The Cutting Edge of Commercial Medicine in America*. New Brunswick, NJ: Rutgers University Press.

Sullivan, Kate. 2011. "Kate Winslet Says No to Plastic Surgery, Gwyneth Paltrow Says 'Why Not?' to a Boob Job." *Allure* (August 18). http://www.allure.com. Accessed February 1, 2016.

Synott, Anthony. 1989. "Truth and Goodness, Mirrors and Masks—Part 1: A Sociology of Beauty and the Face." *British Journal of Sociology* 40, no. 4: 607–636.

Tait, Sue. 2007. "Television and the Domestication of Cosmetic Surgery." *Feminist Media Studies* 7, no. 2: 119–135.

Talley, Heather. 2014. *Saving Face: Disfigurement and the Politics of Appearance*. New York: NYU Press.

Tanner, Claire, JaneMaree Maher, and Suzanne Fraser. 2013. *Vanity: 21st Century Selves*. Basingstoke: Palgrave Macmillan.

Tarule, Jill M. 1996. "Voices in Dialogue." In *Knowledge, Difference and Power: Essays Inspired by Women's Ways of Knowing*, edited by Nancy R. Goldberger. New York: Basic Books.

Taylor, Jodie. 2011. "The Intimate Insider: Negotiating the Ethics of Friendship When Doing Insider Research." *Qualitative Research* 11, no. 1: 3–22.

Tillman-Healy, Lisa M. 2003. "Friendship as Method." *Qualitative Inquiry* 9, no. 5: 729–749.

Ting, Patricia T., and Anatoli Freiman. 2004. "The Story of *Clostridium botulinum*: From Food Poisoning to Botox." *Clinical Medicine* 4, no. 3 (May/June): 258–261.

Torrens, James. 1998. "*Clostridium botulinum* was Named Because of Association with 'Sausage Poisoning.'" *British Medical Journal* 316, no. 7125 (January 10): 151.

Triggs, Charlotte, and Maureen Harrington. 2008. "Botox Confessions." *People* 70, no. 21 (November 24): 64–68.

Tucker, Reed. 2006. "This Is Your Destiny." *Esquire* 145, no. 1 (January): 41.

Turner, Ralph. 1976. "The Real Self: From Institution to Impulse." *American Journal of Sociology* 81: 989–1016.

Urban Dictionary. n.d. "Bitchy Resting Face." http://www.urban dictionary.com. Accessed February 8, 2014.

U.S. Food and Drug Administration. 2003. "Warning Letter to Mr. Peter A. Kresel of Allergan, Inc." June 23. http://www.fda.gov. Accessed December 18, 2015.

Van Meter, Jonathan. 2008. "About-Face." *New York* (August 3). http://nymag.com. Accessed January 24, 2016.

Vaughan, Katherine Burns, and John T. Lanzetta. 1981. "The Effect of Modification of Expressive Displays on Vicarious Emotional Arousal." *Journal of Experimental Social Psychology* 17, no. 1: 16–30.

Voss, Gretchen. 2009. "Doctors without Borders." *Marie Claire* 16, no. 10 (October): 110–119. http://www.marieclaire.com. Accessed January 26, 2016.

Waskul, Dennis D., and Phillip Vannini. 2012. *Body/Embodiment: Symbolic Interaction and the Sociology of the Body*. Aldershot: Ashgate.

Weil, Andrew, and Winifred Rosen. 2004. *From Chocolate to Morphine*. Boston: Houghton Mifflin.

Williams, Christine, and Catherine Connell. 2010. "Looking Good and Sounding Right: Aesthetic Labor and Social Inequality in the Retail Industry." *Work and Occupation* 37, no. 3: 349–377.

Wilson, Gail. 2000. *Understanding Old Age: Critical and Global Perspectives*. Thousand Oaks, CA: Sage.

Wolf, Naomi. 1991. *The Beauty Myth: How Images of Beauty Are Used against Women*. New York: William Morrow.

Zeman, Ned. 2003. "The Botoxed and the Boldfaced." *Vanity Fair* (May):194.

Zetka, James R. 2001. "Occupational Divisions of Labor and Their Technology Politics: The Case of Surgical Scopes and Gastrointestinal Medicine." *Social Forces* 79, no. 4: 1495–1520.

Zola, Irving Kenneth. 1972. "Medicine as an Institution of Social Control." *Sociological Review* 20, no. 4: 487–504.

Zola, Irving Kenneth. 1991. "The Medicalization of Aging and Disability." *Advances in Medical Sociology* 2: 299–315.

INDEX

accounts: of anti-aging technologies as desirable opportunities, 135–136; by Botox users of logic of individualism and autonomy in their choice, 134, 169–171; construction of the self as autonomous and self-governing in, 135; of cosmetic procedures as similar to drug use, 152; cosmetic surgery presented in media, 50, 61; of cosmetic wellness taking precedence over caring for health, 124–125; modern norms and, 134–135; redemptive, 148

"actress Botox," 61

advertising. *See* marketing of Botox

aesthetic labor: complexities of decision making about, 121; constructed as sign of morality and responsibility, 157, 172; cultural scripts of, 157; defined, 132; gendered norms around, 30, 168; job market and expectation of engaging in, 132–133; kept invisible, 126, 165; modern norms condemning, 135; moral violation in not participating in, 50; normalizing the pain and discomfort, 148; women's commitment to continued, 161

African American women: body satisfaction in, 20–21, 191n64; Botox use by, 62

ageism, 14–15, 47, 122; in gay communities, 111; in history, 190n27; in the job market, 15, 131–132; notion of growing old gracefully and, 158–161

ageless bodies, Botox promoting, 156–161, 163. *See also* natural bodies

agency, 19, 20; Botox users communicating, 133–138, 169–171

aging: anxiety and fear about, 21, 99, 152; Botox as transformative innovation in battling, 2, 5, 37, 156–158; cultural capital and, 168–169; dating market and, 130–131; desire to control, 51, 53–54; as enemy of beauty ideal, 13; expectations about, 6; gender inequalities surrounding, 14–15, 66, 166; gracefully, 122, 158–161; perceptions of, 108–112; racial differences in, 62; societal view of, 10, 13–14, 69, 125; visible signs of, 9, 10, 140

Allergan, 3, 4, 6, 24, 69, 182; accused of minimizing Botox side effects, 38; competitors, 203n1; distribution of Botox by, 96; marketing Botox as responsible self-care, 51; payments to doctors promoting, 41; product placement strategies, 36; purchase of Oculinum, 35; success of marketing by, 45; sued for product liability, 39; training seminars, 96–97, 197n4

American Academy of Anti-Aging Medicine, 9

American Academy of Dermatology, 25, 37, 82, 95, 151, 182, 184

American Academy of Facial and Plastic Reconstructive Surgery, 94, 184–185

American Academy of Facial Esthetics, 70

American Medical Association, 35, 74

American Medical Spa Association, 93, 96, 185

family influences on use of cosmetic
procedures, 115–116
Federal Trade Commission (FTC), 35–36,
74, 75
feminism: beauty culture and, 15–17, 122–
123, 171–172; on cosmetic medicine as
"technology of gender," 99; empowerment and, 137–138; frameworks of
bodies and gender, 15–20, 122–123, 126,
171–172; interviewing strategies, 179;
and women's drive to invest in body
projects, 112–115
Finzi, Eric, 37
first experiences with Botox, 101–108; as
bonding rituals, 104–105; getting a
good deal and 1, 102–104; as happenstance, 105–108; how the face feels
after, 140–142; perceptions of aging
bodies leading to, 108–112. *See also*
users, Botox
Forbes, 23
Foucault, Michel, 17, 147, 182
Fraser, Suzanne, 18, 55, 61, 67

gateway drug, Botox as, 154–156,
202n29
gender: approval of cosmetic surgery
by, 44–45; body satisfaction and,
21–22; Botox use and, 4, 22, 24, 45,
64–69, 125, 180; embodied selves
and, 7–8, 166–169; feminist frameworks of body and, 15–20, 122–123,
126; and gendered lens, 13–15. *See
also* men
gendered lens, 13–15
geographic distribution of Botox users,
24, 200n19
Giddens, Anthony, 11–12
Gill, Rosalind, 17
Goffman, Erving, 131, 143, 157–158,
200n3
Goldfarb v. Virginia State Bar, 74

graceful aging, 158–161
Groupon, 3, 102, 105, 108, 165

habitus, 61–62
Haiken, Elizabeth, 49
hair: coloring, 103, 114, 118, 122, 129; cutting and styling, 84, 114, 118–119, 168;
loss treatments, 98; maintenance as
bodywork, 112; metrosexuals and, 68; removal, 83, 93, 113, 114, 121; thickeners, 67
happenstance, Botox experiences as,
105–108
Hasselhoff, David, 46
health concerns over Botox, 124–125
healthism, 5, 9, 51, 121
Heaton, Patricia, 47
Hennenlotter, Andreas, 145
Heyes, Cressida, 19–20
Hochschild, Arlie Russell, 144
human growth hormone, 9, 163

identity: empowerment and, 137–138,
167, 172; self and, 7–8, 166–169; sexual
orientation and, 111–112
individualism, 10–11, 134, 137
injections, 6, 9, 26, 38, 39, 187; certifications, 71; complications, 70–71; correc-
tive, 149; cost of, 42, 55, 64; frequency
of, 54, 64; lower dose, 61; in men, 65;
offered for free, 48, 70; performed
outside clinical settings, 47; as regular
body upkeep, 45; risks of, 71; skill and
talent required for, 89; techniques for
men *vs.* women, 71
Instagram, 77
International Medical Spa Association,
93, 96
interpretive process, 8, 112
investing, body projects, 112–115, 118

Jackson, Michael, 38
Jagger, Mick, 15

Givewell - 2015 "most effective" charities
TOP 3

(AMF) 1. Against malaria foundation → brings mosquito nets to Sub-saharan Africa

2. Give directly organization
   ↳ distributes cash to people in need

3. Schistosomiasis control Initiative
   ↳ provides tx for infected ppl.

more high profile charities

- United Way
- Salvation army
- make a wish foundation

★ "effective altruism" approach to charity

AMF - save a life for $3500

Donating
Time vs. money
pro-bono ~~work~~ work

Top Recipients = religious groups + educational institutions

Elephant in the brain Ch. 14

Book by Brian Kaplan
The case against education

Dana Berkowitz is Associate Professor of Sociology and Women's and Gender Studies at Louisiana State University.

I'm a llama

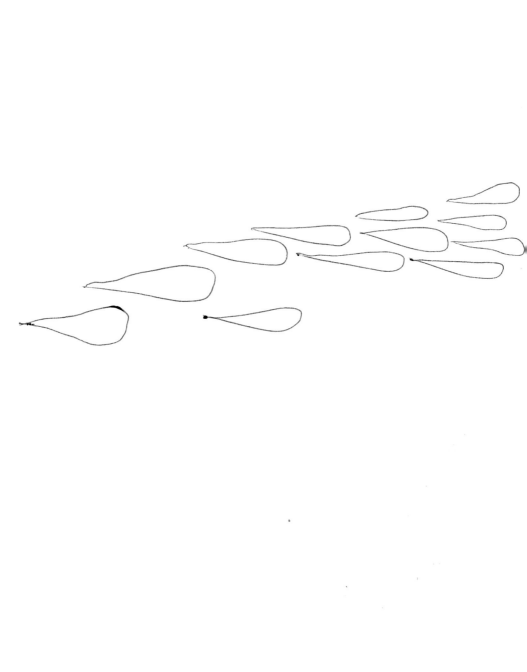

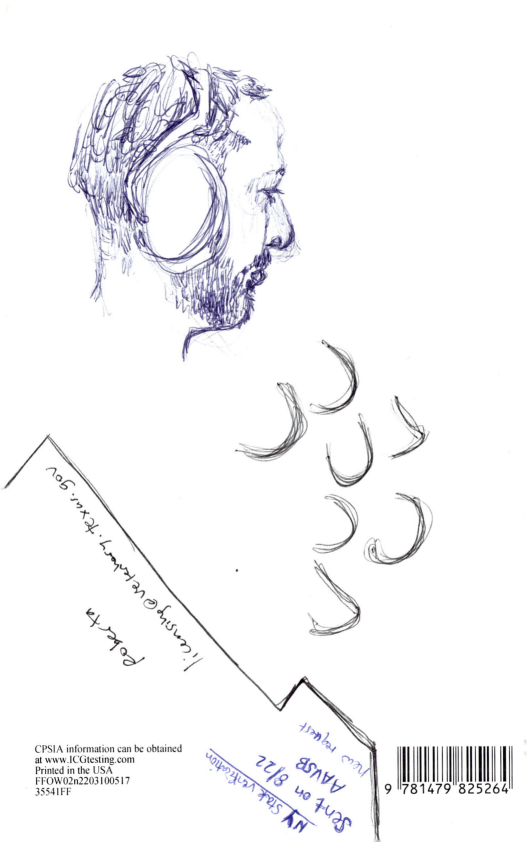

Roberto

licensing@verkfenn.texas.gov

Sent on 8/22
AAVSB
NY State verification
new request

9 781479 825264